RICHARD OVERY

Why War?

A PELICAN BOOK

PELICAN
an imprint of
PENGUIN BOOKS

PELICAN BOOKS

UK | USA | Canada | Ireland | Australia
India | New Zealand | South Africa

Pelican Books is part of the Penguin Random
House group of companies whose addresses can
be found at global.penguinrandomhouse.com

Penguin
Random House
UK

First published in the USA by W. W. Norton
and Co. 2024
First published in Great Britain in Pelican
Books 2024
005

Book design by Matthew Young
Set in 11/16.13pt FreightText Pro
Typeset by Jouve (UK), Milton Keynes
Printed and bound in Great Britain by
Clays Ltd, Elcograf S.p.A.

The authorized representative in the EEA is
Penguin Random House Ireland, Morrison
Chambers, 32 Nassau Street, Dublin D02 YH68

A CIP catalogue record for this book is available
from the British Library

ISBN: 978–0–241–56760–9

MIX
Paper | Supporting
responsible forestry
FSC® C018179

Contents

Preface

This book is an impertinence for several reasons. First, I am a historian of the world's wars waged during the 1930s and the 1940s, almost at the end of the very long history of human violence, yet the tens of thousands of years covered here are clearly not my professional field. Second, most of the writing that seeks to explain the story of human warlike violence from the early hominins onwards has been the preserve of the scientific humanities: anthropology, ethnology, ecology, psychology, human biology, archaeology. Historians have been conspicuously absent when it comes to answering the larger question of why humans make war, partly from an understandable diffidence, as historians lack the scientific training evident in what many non-historians write. Where contributing disciplines are listed in the literature that explains warfare, history is almost always absent. This is an odd phenomenon, because explanation of warfare in the past is uniquely a historical exercise.

My excuse, if one is needed, derives from my work over many decades on the largest and deadliest conflict in global history. Peace would no doubt have been preferred by most of those caught up in its coils, but, regardless of any restraint, warfare was pursued by states that all considered themselves part of an advanced civilization. How human beings reached that grim end point of modernity begs much larger questions about why warfare was an active choice not just for 'civilized' states in the mid-twentieth century but as far back into the historical record as it is possible to go, and even further back into prehistory. These are questions that I have been curious to explore, beginning, in my case, at the end of the story rather than with its distant origins. My other excuse stems from the historical nature of the discussion on the persistence of warfare throughout the human past. The discourse on war has its own history from Darwin and Freud to Pinker and Keeley, and it is useful to chart the way these ideas have been shaped by wider contexts during the past hundred years before presenting the point at which ideas about warfare have now arrived. This is something historians can do.

The book is aimed at a broad audience that might want to learn something more about the way modern scholarship has endeavoured to answer the question 'Why War?' I have tried to avoid too much technical complexity or specialized vocabulary except where it proves to be necessary. This is intended as an introduction to what has become a highly contested set of assumptions and arguments about past and present warfare. Indeed, on the origins of warfare, there exists a regular academic battleground; negotiating the minefields that surround the conflict is an exercise in itself. It is difficult not to take sides, and I make no pretence that I have always avoided partisanship where it seems sensible not to. I am very grateful for those with real expertise who have read some of what I have written with the critical eye it deserves, above all Anthony Lopez, Staffan Müller-Wille, and

Paul Roscoe. I would also like to thank Sarah Barker, Stacey Hynde, and Philip Parker for helpful advice. I am grateful as ever to the wise criticism of my two editors, Simon Winder in London and Steve Forman in New York, and for the help from my agent, Cara Jones. At Norton I'd also like to thank Don Rifkin, Jason Heuer, Lauren Abbate, Elizabeth Riley, and Steve Colca for their work in transforming manuscript into finished book and then positioning it for the public. Any remaining faults, mistakes, or misrepresentations are more than ever in this case my responsibility.

Richard Overy

BRESCIA AND EXETER, 2023

Why War?

Why War?

The question posed here is one of the fundamental questions concerning the human past and the human future. No surprise, then, that two of the intellectual giants of the twentieth century, the physicist Albert Einstein and the psychologist Sigmund Freud, engaged in a correspondence in 1932 in search of an answer. Einstein was invited late in 1931 by the League of Nations' International Institute of Intellectual Co-operation to select a correspondent on a subject of his choice. Already engaged in addressing antiwar organizations, Einstein decided to invite Freud as his correspondent to answer the question 'Is there a way of delivering mankind from the menace of war?' Freud, he assumed, would understand better 'the dark places of human will and feeling'.[1] The result was a short pamphlet, published in German, French, Dutch, and English, with the title *Why War?* Einstein was disappointed with the answer. Freud insisted that violence was characteristic of the entire animal kingdom, mankind included, and could see no effective way of inhibiting the urge to fight and destroy, which derived from what he called the 'death drive', a psychological impulse to destruction in every living being.[2]

Freud's morbid conclusion has been explored often since

in the attempt to understand the biological, psychological, cultural, and environmental mechanisms that make war an unavoidable part of the human story. The results of this attempt include at least five books with the title 'Why War?' and a great many more on its causes.[3] Yet the answer to the question remains contested, fractured, and frustratingly elusive after almost a century of further argument, both scientific and historical. Indeed, given the human propensity for organized, 'coalitional' warfare over much of the long human past, the question might be posed the other way round: 'Why not?' Humans have proved to be a belligerent species. As the psychologist John Bowlby put it in 1939 in a study of the urge to fight and kill: 'No group of animals could be more aggressive or more ruthless in their aggression than the adult members of the human race.'[4] Of course, humans do not wage war all the time or everywhere, otherwise *Homo sapiens* might well have become extinct. Warfare is a part of human evolution, one of the tools in what Azar Gat has called man's toolkit for survival, but only one of them.[5] War and peace are often presented as the only options, but they are part of a more complex set of survival strategies throughout human history. Understanding war also means explaining why periods of peace break down. The one constant has been the resort to collective, lethal violence between human groups when need, or fear, or ambition, or prejudice – even appeal to the supernatural – has prompted war, from the earliest evidence of violence to the wars and civil wars of the twenty-first century.

The purpose of this book is to examine the ways in which warfare has been explained by the major disciplines since

Freud and Einstein's inconclusive exchange and to assess the plausibility of these explanations. There are many distinct approaches, but they can be divided broadly into two kinds of explanation. The major human sciences – biology, psychology, anthropology, and ecology – have explained war in their own terms as evolutionarily adaptive, or culturally determined, or the product of ecological pressures. From these perspectives, human beings become the object of natural or cultural forces that can be understood to determine why warfare has occurred in the evolutionary past.[6] These form the subject matter of the first part of this book, and they are applied, unlike much of the research in these fields, to modern war as well as warfare over the past millennia. On the other hand, historians and social and political scientists (and many anthropologists and archaeologists) are more likely to explore warfare in terms of human cognition, with mankind as creator of the cultures that sustain warfare and human beings as conscious agents in the pursuit of objectives that can vary widely in time and place. What might be termed the 'proactive' explanations of warfare can be conveniently reduced to four broad motivational categories, which form the subject matter of the second part of this book: resources, belief, power, and security. Explanations that are based on this latter causal nexus are more consistent with warfare in the modern age as states developed the capacity to wage war between great powers, but belief, power, security, and the struggle for resources are evident drivers of early conflict, even among pre-state communities, in which war can be a product of all four. These are not irreconcilable approaches, as will be evident in what follows, but they are a convenient way of demarcating the many strands that have been explored when explaining war and warfare.

First, it should be made clear how war and warfare are defined here. The two terms are used interchangeably in much of the literature. A war is a particular event, even if its start and end can be less than clear-cut; warfare describes the many ways conflicts are planned, organized, and fought by societies and cultures where war is an anthropological feature. Nevertheless, what constitutes either war or warfare has been a strongly contested issue. It has led to prolonged argument over the past fifty years between those who see war as a product of relatively recent history once states were formed that were capable of mobilizing substantial forces, paying for war, and organizing its supply; and those who argue that all intergroup, lethal violence from the prehistoric or pre-state past is a form of warfare, however brief or sporadic it might be. The idea that war is something only civilized states can wage is a paradoxical one, though Freud assumed in *Civilization and Its Discontents*, published only shortly before the pamphlet *Why War?*, that the more civilized humans became, the more probable was a catastrophic descent into primitive violence (a view not out of step with the conflict that followed).

There is no gainsaying the historical evidence that wars became larger and more deadly in scale as states became consolidated, bureaucratized, and socially segmented, partly to be able to wage war more effectively. This obvious truth has allowed anthropologists and archaeologists for much of the past hundred years to argue for a more pacific narrative, in which archaic peoples (either from the remote past or still extant in remote regions of the world) resorted to lethal violence seldom if at all or did so in ritualized, usually nonlethal confrontations.[7] The anthropologist Bronisław Malinowski, writing in 1940, lauded the 'primeval pacifism' of primitive man as he deplored what he saw as the pointless, nihilistic violence of the modern age.[8] Many anthropologists writing today, while not ignoring the evidence of violence before the rise of the state, prefer to see it as local feuding, in-group homicides, or opportunistic raiding, which was neither endemic nor particularly deadly. On this reading, humans have evolved into successful cooperators for whom warfare is an aberration interrupting thousands of years of relatively peaceable coexistence.[9]

This is a view of war that seems scarcely tenable in the light of a wealth of new archaeological and ethnographic evidence. Lethal, intergroup violence is evident even before the first large-scale sedentary communities or the first states. A growing body of literature by those who study the remote past accepts the geographically wide and temporally long evidence of what can be called warfare defined as lethal, coalitional conflict between distinct groups of human beings, occurring even in a few cases in the long distant Pleistocene before *Homo sapiens* dominated the globe.[10] This is an argument that can be carried too far. The anthropologist Keith Otterbein, one of the earliest and most consistent advocates of a warlike past, hailed the discovery in a cave near Burgos in Spain of fossil hominin bones from 800,000 years ago that revealed eleven victims of cannibalism as 'the earliest known evidence of warfare'.[11] This remains a hopeful speculation that can be proved neither way, but there is overwhelming evidence from the more recent past that having a state was not the precondition for engaging in warlike violence. Neolithic remains in Europe show arrowheads lodged in vertebrae, crushed crania, and decapitated and disarticulated skeletons, clear signs of warlike violence.[12] The archaeologist Patricia Lambert has demonstrated that the evidence accumulated over decades of excavation and bone analysis in North America shows without doubt that in every major region of the continent there existed warlike violence, most famously at Crow Creek in South Dakota, where a mass burial of 415 identifiable skeletons from the mid-fourteenth century CE reveals that 89 percent had been scalped and 41 percent of a sample of 101 skulls had stone-axe injuries.[13] In the late period of the European *Linearbandkeramik* ('Linear Ceramic culture') 7,000 years ago, massacres have been unearthed at Talheim in the Rhine valley and at Asparn/Schletz near Vienna, the latter where sixty-six individuals killed mainly by axes were thrown into a rampart ditch; and so on.[14] The production of potential weapons from very early in human evolution, the iconography of combat on cave walls showing matchstick men armed and skirmishing, the near universal osteoarchaeological evidence of bones and skulls battered or pierced makes any idea of 'primeval pacifism' difficult to sustain.

In what follows, warfare is used in this broader sense of collective, purposive, lethal, intergroup violence, whether raids, or ambushes, or skirmishes, or ritual violence, or the more familiar pitched battles of the historic period. As a result, much of the discussion in this book, particularly in the earlier chapters on human sciences and war, deals with a past that stretches back well beyond the first organized states, for 20,000–30,000 years, sometimes much earlier when it comes to theories of biological and psychological evolution. The archaeological evidence for past violence can be used in tandem with the ethnographic evidence gathered about modern hunter-gatherer communities. Here, too, anthropologists have had to concede that lethal violence was and is more embedded in these societies than many have argued, whether among the aboriginal communities of Australia, the tribal hunters of New Guinea, or the tribal inhabitants of the American and Canadian far north.[15] Even arguments that proto-state polities used violence only to secure a number of captives for sacrifice have been shown in the case of the Maya and the Aztec Empires to be without foundation (and capturing sacrificial victims is in itself scarcely a peaceable occupation). Contemporary records show Aztec armies massacring entire populations; in the city of Cuetlaztlan, soldiers killed 'old people, women, young men, boys, girls, infants in the cradle'.[16] Maya culture was permeated by warfare and a warrior elite; one Maya record lists 107 war events between 512 and 808 CE at 28 different sites.[17] None of these revisions about the prevalence of war mean that the pattern or motives of warfare are invariable: they are clearly not. Different cultures pursue violence in distinct, sometimes unique ways. Early warfare is self-evidently not the same as warfare between large modern states, but the scale is relative and the proximate causes and aims can be strikingly similar. The end result is something that can be recognized as warfare whether it is what the anthropologist Nam Kim has usefully termed 'emergent warfare' among the very earliest communities or institutionalized warfare among modern nation-states.[18] Across the time span of the long evolution of human beings there has been collective, lethal, intergroup violence, and it is this phenomenon that has to be explained.

A few caveats need to be borne in mind for a book focusing on how the causes of warfare are understood. This is not a book intended to explain aggression in individuals, for which there is a rich specialist literature by neurologists, psychiatrists, and psychologists. Understanding about the function of the brain and the central nervous system is now so advanced that the pathology of aggressive behaviour in individuals that display it can be scientifically explained, even if the behaviour remains persistent.[19] Much of this research since the 1930s focuses on delinquent behaviour in modern adults and children, which cannot be easily compared with the violence exhibited in warfare. Aggression matters when it comes to collective or coalitional violence, such as the killing of lone chimpanzees ambushed by a group of neighbouring, marauding males, which early hominin violence probably mimicked. For a human group prepared to kill other humans, aggression plays a part, more obviously in earlier forms of warfare, which are face-to-face; in modern armies, where many individuals are not themselves aggressive, hand-to-hand combat forces aggression to the surface as a response to lethal threat. In these circumstances, collective rather than individual aggression is a surer guide to the way warfare has evolved. When tribal communities raided an 'enemy', they did so as a group, usually for collective purposes and all too often with a severe level of aggression.

Nor is this a book that addresses the question whether

mankind has become less violent over the past millennia. Steven Pinker's seminal study *The Better Angels of Our Nature*, published in 2011, has provoked wide discussion about whether violence in its many forms has actually declined, including warfare.[20] The absence of war between major states since 1945 (though there have been many very violent proxy wars) has prompted the argument that perhaps interstate war itself has become obsolete, even if civil war and transnational terror warfare clearly have not, though such an argument takes no account of the fact that thermonuclear war is still a possibility, however remote it might seem. The modern 'realist' view of international relations still has the option of war at its core, otherwise disarmament, nuclear and conventional, would be a worldwide reality.[21] None of this really relates to the question 'Why war?' Less violent statistically or not, the past century witnessed wars on an exceptional scale and of an exceptional aggregate lethality – both World Wars, the Russian Civil War, the Korean War, the Vietnam War, the Iran–Iraq War, and so on. If state-on-state warfare has declined, there are many other forms of modern conflict – civil wars, counterinsurgencies, terrorist campaigns, proxy wars, even 'hybrid wars' where irregular and regular warfare overlap. Indeed, there was not one year in the twentieth century without a war or civil war being fought somewhere. Now the twenty-first century has its first major interstate war, the conflict between Russia and Ukraine. Looking back over the millennia of the history of modern humans, an observer from another planet might sensibly conclude that war is anything but obsolete given the climactic warfare of just the past hundred years and the existence of weapons capable of extinguishing much of the human race. The issue of why wars happen is independent of the scale and intensity of human violence, and the two arguments should not be confused.

Finally, it needs to be said that this is not a history of wars, ancient or modern, neither of how they are waged nor with what consequences. Evidently, the sociocultural framework, the way that wars are conducted, the weapons technology available, and the consequences of warfare all play a part in any explanation for why wars have happened throughout history, but a particular war has its own historical explanation, placed in time and context. Warfare will be used in what follows in an exemplary way, not as part of a formal narrative of the bewildering number of human wars. The main concern here is to use that long violent history as a means of illustrating the principal avenues of explanation advanced ever since Einstein asked Freud to unravel 'the most typical, most cruel and extravagant form of conflict between man and man'.[22]

PART ONE

CHAPTER 1
Biology

> Nature keeps her human orchard healthy by pruning –
> war is her pruning hook.
> — Sir Arthur Keith, 1931[1]

> Biology does not condemn humanity to war . . . It is
> scientifically incorrect to say that war or any other
> violent behaviour is genetically programmed into our
> human nature.
> — Seville Statement on Violence, 1986[2]

Ever since the nineteenth-century father of evolutionary theory, the British biologist Charles Darwin, subscribed to the idea that all species engage in a 'struggle for survival', the relationship between biology and war has remained one of the most contested issues in attempts to explain why humans fight. The neo-Darwinian anatomist Arthur Keith, writing in the middle of the past century, endorsed the idea that warfare was biologically useful because human communities eliminated the weak and elevated the strong. This was, he assumed, a law of nature. At a 1986 meeting in the Spanish city of Seville, an international group of twenty prominent scientists from a range of human disciplines sought to overturn entirely the scientific effort to explain war as something dictated by biology, which they regarded as a pernicious distortion. In November 1989, UNESCO adopted the Seville statement to give it a formal status; it was widely disseminated and republished in 2002. The initiative did not end the argument. Though no scientist today would endorse Keith's crude metaphor, biology has remained, in one guise or another, a central reference point in discussion about war.

Biology, or more strictly evolutionary biology, has a solid claim to be the first science to engage with the question of why humans make war, but this was far from Darwin's intention. His argument that all species engaged in a struggle for survival was a piece of natural history, designed to explain how plants and animals adapted in evolutionary terms to the pressures of the environment or to competition within or between species.[3] 'Struggle' in this sense was a metaphor, not a synonym for warfare. He touched more directly on the possibility of ancestral human conflict in The Descent of Man, published in 1871, but again this was peripheral to his more significant ambition to explain how human beings evolved, particularly through sexual selection. By this time, Darwin was familiar with the idea of the 'survival of the fittest', first propounded by the social scientist Herbert Spencer in 1851, and Darwin's few remarks in The Descent of Man on how some ancestral tribes survived while others became extinct suggest that fitness was at least one, though certainly not the only, explanation. 'Extinction', he explained, 'follows chiefly from the competition of tribe with tribe . . . when of two adjoining tribes one becomes less numerous and less powerful than the other, the contest is soon settled by war, slaughter, cannibalism, slavery and absorption.' A decrease in numbers and a decline in fertility undermined the biological prospects for survival, but the final disappearance of a tribe was, he concluded, 'promptly decided by the inroads of conquering tribes'.[4]

Darwin said little else to suggest that warfare had a role of any significance in human evolution, but the idea that the fittest survived while the less fit perished was enlarged and distorted far beyond Darwin's original argument by several generations of 'Darwinists' who did argue that warfare had evolutionary utility. Among European and American writers, the survival of the fittest supported the argument that warfare and imperialism in the modern age reflected Western racial superiority in contrast to the savageness of the peoples that westerners conquered. Warfare was, as Arthur Keith was to argue, a phenomenon of nature, designed to ensure that the biologically best survived and expanded their number. The concept of race competition as an evolutionary fact was taken up with most enthusiasm in Germany, where the biologist Alfred Ploetz defined the *Vitalrasse* ('vital race') as one that inherited a collective fitness in strength, intelligence, and physical health. The racially maladapted were destined by nature to die out, and war was one of the instruments to ensure that it was the vital races who survived.[5] The German general Friedrich von Bernhardi summed up the argument in his bestselling *Germany and the Next War*, published in English two years before the crisis of war in 1914, in which he claimed that 'War is a biological necessity of the first importance, a regulative element in the life of mankind.' In the 'universal economy of Nature', the stronger prevailed by right, and the weaker collapsed.[6] The idea of the *Vitalrasse* strongly influenced the development of racial policy in the later Third Reich, where those alleged to be genetically 'maladapted' were sterilized or exterminated to avoid debasing the race and weakening it in what Hitler called 'this world of eternal struggle'.[7]

The First World War helped to cement the idea that the 'struggle for survival' was still a human reality. The idea that mankind had an instinct for pugnacity, rooted in man's evolutionary path, was easily reconciled with the reality of modern conflict. The surgeon Henry Campbell, writing on *The Biological Aspects of Warfare* in 1918 at the end of the war, defined man as the 'arch-slaughterer', instinctively engaging in violence.[8] Arthur Keith used his study of human fossil remains before 1914 to endorse the argument that humans had evolved 'by a series of zig-zags' in which more advanced species exterminated those less advanced in order to move humankind forward along the evolutionary path to the present conflict. Competition and enmity were human complexes that operated over time, from ancestral man to the modern day. In the foreword to a book on Darwinism by Alfred Machin, published in 1937, Keith praised the author for understanding that '"Natural Selection" is as potent in the world of today as it was when man was a mean inhabitant of the jungle.' Modern war, Keith argued at the end of the Second World War, 'is just the fierce war of ancient tribal days equipped by science and civilization'.[9] For Keith, war was the logical instrument of selection: 'Nature's scheme' was to produce a higher form of humanity through a necessary violence.[10] Although there was strong scientific hostility to the idea that pugnacity was innate and that war had evolutionary purpose, the view of man as the supreme exponent of violence – hunting, fighting, and killing his way up the evolutionary tree – could still be found in the 1950s and 1960s. The thesis of the 'killer ape' was popularized by the writer and amateur evolutionist Robert Ardrey, while the archaeologist Raymond Dart believed that the ancient *Australopithecus* fossils he had found showed clear evidence of deliberate violence – a view now rejected after later forensic investigation confirmed that the damage was postmortem and not the cause of death.

Opposition to the idea that war was somehow built into human beings biologically long predated the Seville statement. Indeed, Darwin's own writings focused not on ancestral conflict but on human sociality and cooperation as key elements in human evolution. He rejected the idea that human beings had an instinct for pugnacity and hoped that modern humans had put warfare behind them. It has proved easier to derive a 'peace biology' from reading Darwin than a biological selection for war.[11] The development of genetic science after 1900 exposed the difficulty in suggesting an inherited disposition for conflict, while the argument that war was useful as a way of ensuring the survival of the biologically fittest was ridiculed after the First World War because of the obvious dysgenic effects of a conflict that killed off millions of fit young men, leaving the less fit at home. Academic evolutionary biology after the war focused more on the nonhuman natural world and the prediction of species variation. War as a means of evolutionary selection for human populations remained a matter of belief rather than scientific certainty.

*

The crude Darwinism expressed by Keith and others, that war was caused by evolutionary competition and was thus a natural, biological phenomenon, was broadly rejected after the Second World War, alongside the marginalization of biological explanations for human nature. The 1951 UNESCO Statement on the Nature of Race and Race Differences rejected the idea that there was any innate difference between human groups to be explained biologically and gave the field to environmentalism and cultural anthropology as the only legitimate ways to understand human development.[12] One element of the argument, however, remained: how to understand collective aggression. Research on this question went back before the war. To show how early man must have behaved, Keith was one of the pioneers of the belief that understanding collective aggression among the higher primates would help towards understanding aggression in humans. Keith took detailed evidence about chimpanzees and gorillas from the zoologist Neville Sharp, who had undertaken scientific observation of the higher apes in West Africa. Sharp claimed that chimpanzees were capable of violent, even sadistic, behaviour, while gorillas were excessively aggressive in defence of territory against human trespassers. Research on howler monkeys and gibbons convinced Keith that primate territoriality and violence was the 'incipient stage of true war.'[13]

Similar conclusions were drawn from the study in the early 1930s of hamadryas baboons in London Zoo by the young anatomist Solly Zuckerman. During his observations, eight males and thirty females died in fights among the baboons, all the females as a result of male competition. Two

British psychologists, John Bowlby and Edward Durbin, used Zuckerman's research to argue that the naturalistic analogy between ape and human behaviour was robust enough to justify the conclusion that human warfare was a product 'of the most dangerous part of our animal inheritance'. Baboons fought over possessions, the intrusion of a stranger, and frustration, just as modern humans. The phylogenetic – or common – root of violence explained a shared pattern between primates and humans, which could be mobilized by what they called 'transformed aggression' to explain warfare between modern nations.[14] At the time they were writing, an Austrian zoologist, Konrad Lorenz, through his study of the instinctive responses of greylag geese, had begun to develop a new branch of biology devoted to understanding animal behaviour. It came to be known as ethology. Although Lorenz was not much interested in explaining warfare, his work on animals branched out to explore the instinct of aggression. Like Bowlby and Durbin, Lorenz could not resist the idea that human aggression might have a common root with the violence of the rats and doves he studied. In his popular study *On Aggression*, first published in 1963, he argued that warfare, and other 'stupid and undesirable' human activities, could be explained not by reason or cultural tradition alone but by 'phylogenetically adapted instinctive behaviour' from the deep evolutionary past.[15]

Ethology offered a potentially new biological approach to understanding human warfare, though the discipline was, like evolutionary biology, primarily concerned with understanding animals rather than humans. Although Lorenz's *On Aggression* is sometimes regarded as the founding statement on ethological understanding of human violence, his analysis was almost entirely devoted to explaining aggressive behaviour in animals and the mechanisms that generally inhibited its unrestrained use against members of the same species, or 'conspecific' killing. His few comments on human warfare were as peripheral and unsubstantiated as Darwin's. He assumed that for early human communities 'the counter-pressures of the hostile neighbouring hordes had become the chief selecting factor determining the next steps of human evolution.' Humans, he suggested, resembled chimpanzees when it came to defending the kinship group instinctively with 'unthinking single-mindedness', a response that must have had 'high survival value' for any tribe of developed humans and was still evident in the modern world.[16] But beyond regretting the sheer irrationalism of waging war, he had little else to contribute to understanding its origins. He shared the view that warfare was fundamentally dysgenic and was a firm supporter of Hitler's eugenic policies – eliminating the 'degenerate' element of the German population – so that the biological survival of the race could be ensured, views that he continued to hold well after 1945.[17]

If ethologists in the 1960s focused principally on explaining animal behaviour, the hints that human behaviour could be explained as homologous with that of animals, particularly the higher primates, sustained the search for a link between animal and human aggression begun in the 1930s. The connection between animal behaviour in the natural world and the world of humans was nevertheless a difficult one to show convincingly. Two pioneer ethologists, appropriately named Lionel Tiger and Robin Fox, argued that the primordial traces lingered on in the brains of human beings, in 'codes and messages' that were difficult to read but were still assumed to be manifest in modern man.[18] This was a slender inference at best. In practice, ethologists and zoologists devoted almost all their research to understanding the relationship between animal behaviour and the ecological niche each animal inhabited; the understanding of the many differing manifestations of aggression was only a part of that investigation, which covered a wide range of other behaviours that had little to do with violence.

The systematic scientific study of animals in the wild rather than under laboratory conditions became widespread only by the 1950s. When it came to aggression, certain species regularly cited in the ethological literature engaged in violence against their own kind and were thus potentially analogous with human societies and 'warfare'. They included fig wasps, whose males fought to the death over access to females, and the honeypot ant, which engaged in pitched battles and enslaved the defeated. Lorenz's colleague and pioneer of ethology Niko Tinbergen preferred as his example the stickleback fish, whose males fought off rivals for the female, a functional adaptation designed to secure survival, like the adaptations he thought human beings had developed in the evolutionary past.[19] These and many other examples could be found, but beyond demonstrating that the natural world hosted a wider range of intraspecific violence than previously believed, any comparison with the human world seemed tenuous at best.

To make the case more convincing, some biologists and zoologists used the example of social animals to demonstrate how certain social behaviours evolved, including group aggression, group altruism, or group nurturing practices. The study of group selection for the inheritance of particular traits that were evolutionarily successful came to be known as sociobiology, though it was closely allied to ethology, as most sociobiologists worked on nonhuman organisms. The leading theorist was the Harvard entomologist Edward Wilson, an expert on the study of the social behaviour of ants and other insects, but in his case as well the temptation was to look at human social behaviour through the same evolutionary lens. In 1975, Wilson published a highly controversial book titled *Sociobiology: The New Consensus*, when there was in truth anything but general agreement about the new discipline. Once again, almost all the book was devoted to understanding the evolution of social behaviour principally among social insects. He included a final chapter on humans, but his suggestion that humans also inherited traits that were adaptive to survival, including aggression, met with fierce resistance from social scientists and anthropologists who saw this as a form of biological determinism. Human social action, it was argued, was dictated by culture and environment.[20] Three years later, Wilson published a book titled *On Human Nature*, in which he enlarged the sociobiological argument on a range of human traits, including aggression, which he chose provocatively to describe as innate, even if its practice was conditioned by the environment and by social learning.[21]

The debate he provoked, loosely defined as the perennial debate between 'nurture' and 'nature', had a strong political core. Fellow biologists, and many academic nonbiologists, rejected what they saw as an argument in favour of genetic determinism, which could justify racial discrimination and eugenic policies such as those pursued in the Third Reich. To mobilize opposition to the idea, a Sociobiology Study Group was formed under the aegis of the left-wing Science for the People movement. Wilson briefly became a hate figure for American progressive opinion. At an academic conference in 1978, he was attacked on stage by members of the Committee Against Racism, who famously poured a jug of cold water over his head.[22] Wilson nevertheless won the Pulitzer Prize for *On Human Nature*, evidence that the argument, for all the vituperation poured metaphorically over his reputation, did not eliminate the sociobiological project. Indeed, one of the core elements in Darwin's own writing was to understand evolution in social biological terms. Modern behavioural genetics has to a considerable extent exonerated Wilson by showing that some traits have high heritability, including aggression. The important point made by sociobiologists (who soon came to term themselves behavioural ecologists to avoid sustaining the animus against the new discipline) was to focus on the group behaviour of individuals rather than on personal aggression.[23] Warfare, however defined, was carried out by coalitional groups, not by the individual acting alone, in insects as well as man. Over long evolutionary time, warfare was one way, so it was argued, for humans to adapt to behaviour that maximized survival potential.

Sociobiologists, like the early ethologists, found human coalitional aggression difficult to explain except as a surviving element of an evolutionary past that could not be recaptured. From the 1970s a different path was pursued. Like

Keith in the 1930s, ethologists who wanted to explain aggression in humans came to prefer the study of primates, which like early man lived in loose groups and foraged for their existence. For any comparison with man, the obvious species were the upper primates – gorillas, chimpanzees, orangutans, and bonobos, or 'pygmy chimpanzees' (only identified as a distinct species in the late 1920s) – which shared the same mammalian origin as hominins and about 98 percent of human DNA. The conventional zoological assumption about their behaviour had suggested that primates exhibited little aggression and lived in loose, ill-defined bands, but the first long-term observations of chimpanzees in the forests of central Africa, carried out from the 1960s until the 1990s by the British ethologist Jane Goodall and a small research team, overturned both assumptions. Chimpanzees lived in defined, if flexible, groups and did display extreme violence under certain conditions. Her conclusions were originally rejected by scientists who would not accept that chimpanzees shared with humans a set of similar emotions, gestures, and gender identities – to the point in one case of insisting that she write 'it' rather than 'he' or 'she' when writing about the individual inhabitants of her chimpanzee community.[24] But years of observation at Gombe National Park in Tanzania confirmed that chimpanzees were social animals, living in family groups dominated by older males. They had defined territories, which they defended against intruders; on occasion, groups of males and an occasional female would trespass into a rival territory with the object of finding a lone member of the neighbouring group to ambush and leave for dead after a battering with sticks and stones and a frenzy of ferocious biting. When Goodall's group divided, the weaker group was ravaged by the stronger group until it was wiped out, and the territory could be taken over by the victor, until the victor in turn became the victim of a stronger neighbour – a textbook version of natural selection.[25]

Goodall has been the single most important source in efforts to demonstrate that chimpanzee behaviour might be an analogue for the way early hominid foragers must have behaved, although she has not pioneered this claim. There have been other observations carried out among chimpanzee communities in East and West Africa: at Budongo and Kibale in Uganda, Mahale in Tanzania, and Taï in the Ivory Coast, where the violence has appeared more sporadically than at Gombe. At Kibale Forest in the late 1980s, the British zoologist Richard Wrangham, who had worked at Gombe with Goodall, began observation of a chimpanzee group that suffered a similar elimination at the hands of a stronger neighbour as observed in the community at Gombe. The number of dead was five, most unobserved. The total number of chimpanzees killed by members of their own species during the early decades of field research was no more than ten, a slender foundation on which to build any theory of primate violence.[26] Nevertheless, Wrangham has become the leading exponent of the argument that there are commonalities between the way chimpanzees behave in the wild and the way early man must have behaved as a hunter-gatherer, including occasional acts of coalitional violence. Chimpanzees live in groups, though population can be fluid as adolescent females gravitate to other groups or large groups fission into smaller ones; they exhibit a strong sense of sociality, inhibiting violence within the group; they are territorial, with ranges that are not marked with frontiers but which are understood by those on both sides of the line; when two groups of males of roughly equal strength confront each other, they engage in noisy rituals, screaming, gesturing, banging trees, or a brief charge and retreat, but no battle; real aggression is carried out against intruders into a territory or by a raiding party trespassing into neighbouring territory, but only where there is the advantage of numbers (usually a raiding group of five or six against one); finally, lethal aggression is meted out to the victim, while the attackers suffer no or only minor injury.[27]

These are all characteristics that can be found in anthropological observation of some modern human foraging communities. They inhabit fluid territories without fixed boundaries, in small kin groups whose populations can also be fluid, usually through exchange of members. The groups display bonds of cooperation and sociality, which limit the amount of violence. When violence occurs between groups, there can be ritual confrontations with noisy standoffs and little actual harm, but as with chimpanzees the raid is the most common form of attack. In addition, any strangers trespassing on territory will be met with collective resistance. Raids are conducted by groups of bonded males and are usually asymmetrical, against a neighbouring hunting party or a small forager camp, with low risk for the participating aggressors. In such cases, the violence can be exterminatory and frenzied.[28] There are examples often cited as possible comparators. Violence among clans on the Andaman Islands is a common one, where neighbouring communities engaged in surprise raids or ambushes, seeking to kill without suffering damage themselves and then retreating to home territory. In the far American north, Arctic tribes until recently regularly engaged in exterminatory raids on nearby villages, killing men, women, and children, a practice that archaeological evidence shows goes back several thousand years.[29] The anthropologist Napoleon Chagnon's study of the Yanomami of the Upper Amazon has often been used as an example precisely because the villages, which are based around kinship groups and prone to fission when numbers become too great, fight regularly with their neighbours, either in ritualized confrontations using axes or clubs between two fighters or in raids in which a small group of males, like the chimpanzees, seeks out one or two of the enemy to kill or a woman to abduct before hastening back to base. Although they are horticulturalists, not foragers, it is claimed that the Yanomami display at first glance similar behaviour to the raiding chimpanzees.[30]

The leap from natural observation of the behaviour of chimpanzees to the behaviour of humans has obvious limitations. Little is known about chimpanzees from the past or their evolved behaviour, so that it must be assumed that they behave as they do because of adaptive pressures that can only be guessed at. Little is known of the great variety of human foragers and hunter-gatherers of the past 2 million years either, but it is certain they were different from the foragers and hunter-gatherers of today. For collective aggression to be an adaptive function in both chimpanzees and humans, like sociality and cooperation, there ought to be some phylogenetic root for such behaviour, stemming back to the 'last common ancestor' of chimpanzees and hominins, usually dated to about 6 million years ago. Recent research on the phylogenetic roots of violence in mammals between members of the same species – or conspecific violence – looked at the record of 1,024 mammalian species. It was found that lethal violence was more prevalent in social and territorial animals and highest among primates, suggesting that humans too have inherited a propensity for violence from their position in the phylogenetic tree. The level of lethal violence increased with the emergence of settled communities, tribes, chiefdoms, and states, showing how the phylogenetic inheritance could be modified by changes in social and political organization. But violence, so it is claimed, is common to man's earliest ancestors at a level consistent with the behaviour of the mammalian clade to which humans belong; that is, six times higher than for other mammal groups.[31] It has even been suggested that both sociality and violence possibly date back to the early primate ancestors of chimpanzees and humans, particularly *Afropithecus*, alive some 18 million years ago, giving a phylogenetic root of exceptional ancestry.[32]

There are problems with this argument too. Chimpanzees are rarely lethally violent in the wild despite the observations recorded by Goodall and others. Aggressive behaviour does not appear to be generalized across the species, with some communities more aggressive than others. The bonobo, as closely related to humans as the chimpanzee, exhibits almost no violence either within or between communities, while the males play a more subordinate role to the females than is evident among humans. While limited violence among primates may have had a common and ancient root, humans from about 2 million years ago soon evolved in very different ways from other primates, not least in the development of a much larger and more complex brain, which allowed the development of unique cognitive abilities, including language, the mastery of early technologies, and a wide range of cultures.[33] The early prehumans had a brain capacity of about 400 cubic centimetres; early hominins had a brain capacity of about 600 cubic centimetres; *Homo sapiens* has a brain capacity of 1,370 cubic centimetres. The cerebral cortex may have evolved to enhance the human capacity to work out how to survive by selecting to use 'predatory aggression' against nonhuman predators or in competition with other humans. Those with larger brains may have been able to drive less adapted hominins to marginal environments, where their survival chances were greatly reduced.[34] Whether or to what extent these evolved physiological changes made coalitional violence possible or probable is open to speculation, but the violence is unlikely to be an exact replica of violence among chimpanzees or other primates. Indeed, it is precisely what differentiates human evolution from that of close primate relatives that makes the thesis of continuity between chimpanzee and human behaviour (and hence patterns of aggression) difficult to sustain. Chimpanzees over millions of years of development can still only use sticks and stones to forage for food or very occasionally to batter a neighbour to death; humans over the same period have moved from the use of sticks and stones to develop the thermonuclear bomb.

A more convincing case for the possibility that human intergroup violence had consequences for human evolution has been made by returning to classical Darwinism. Armed with current knowledge about human evolution and genetics unavailable to Darwin when he wrote, modern evolutionary science has developed the idea that humans adapted for survival in the face of significant ecological or environmental pressures. One of those possible adaptations was selection for coalitional violence for defence or attack against other humans. Rather than seeing this adaptation as a passport to species extinction, violence may have increased the possibility that the successful group protected kin and expanded its gene pool.

The key concept, as it was for Darwin, is fitness. This approach is complicated in the case of humans because most of the distinct hominid species now known to science are extinct, their fitness to survive evidently relative. The study of human evolutionary survival focuses on the capacity of *Homo sapiens* to adapt in ways that have so far avoided extinction. If hominid ancestors adapted over the time of their existence to pressures of climate, resource competition and ecological flux can only be guessed at, even for ancestors that lived over hundreds of thousands of years. If intergroup violence was one way of adapting to these pressures, it could as easily be regarded as maladaptive for small, vulnerable forager populations where lethal demographic losses could bring groups to the point of biological crisis. The puzzling thing about humans has been the emergence of widespread and deliberate killing of members of their own species, which challenges evolutionary theory because optimization of reproductive success is assumed to operate in all species, humans included. If there is any relationship between human intergroup violence and evolutionary survival, it must be demonstrated that adaptation for conflict really could contribute to ongoing reproductive success.

One way to confront the puzzle is the concept of 'inclusive fitness'. This idea was first developed by the young British biologist William Hamilton in two papers on the genetic evolution of social behaviour published in 1964. Hamilton has perhaps more of a claim than Wilson to be the originator of sociobiology (as Wilson himself acknowledged), and his conclusions have been used extensively in current discussion of human evolution, even though Hamilton's examples were ants, bees, and caterpillars, not modern humans.[35] In its simplest form, 'inclusive fitness' means that all those kin who are genetically related, even distantly, contribute to the genetic reproduction of the kin group. Hamilton stressed the role of the individual rather than group selection in maximizing genetic fitness for self and for close kin, though individual organisms can work together in a group. Applied to human evolution, inclusive fitness could explain both individual efforts to ensure survival and reproductive success and the reciprocity necessary to achieve them. For ancient human communities, the individuals making up the kin group cooperated on a reciprocal basis to maximize successful reproduction within a given environment. Social cooperation to help confront threats to the kin group increased benefits for the individuals involved and rooted inclusive fitness as the evolutionary design for survival.[36] Individuals accepted sociality because it enhanced their fitness benefits through access to shared resources, protection from predators and competitors, particularly for females, and the possibility of long-term nurturing of the young. Gene traits that maximized inclusive fitness were transmitted to the wider kin network through natural selection. Group living to enhance survival chances was almost certainly characteristic of human foragers (as with many other animals) from the onset of the human lineage as they confronted physical threats and environmental pressures, but why this should necessarily lead to heightened competition and conflict between individual kin groups requires a more elaborate explanation.

It seems likely that one of the consequences of group living was the development of a distinction between the kin network and those who did not belong. Rather like chimpanzees, early humans must have responded to others on the basis that they were not one of 'us'. Some biologists have even suggested that human groups saw others the way they saw different species, through a process of so-called pseudo-speciation, which legitimized competition and conflict.[37] More probably, competition over food resources that became concentrated and scarce encouraged what has been called 'competitive exclusion', when one kin group eliminated or reduced a neighbouring forager group in the ecological niche it occupied.[38] Where competition for resources or mates existed, conflict might bring fitness benefits, both for individuals who participated and for the group as a whole to which they belonged. In societies that were almost certainly based on polygyny (males mating with more than one female), conflict brought the possibility that additional mates could be secured and rival males eliminated. The objective was to increase inclusive fitness by spreading the genes of the group more widely, while at the same time reducing the inclusive fitness of a competitive group, an adaptation that increased possibilities for reproduction.[39] Evolutionary theory suggests that conflict should only occur where the benefits clearly exceed the costs (in death or injury). A larger or more efficient group would choose to attack outsiders when the balance of power was in its favour, enhancing the prospect of increased fitness through access to mates or resources. An evolutionary propensity for violence does not exclude the fact that human foragers and hunters could engage in social cooperation between groups or even exchange mates, as happens today between tribal societies. Humans seem to have reacted flexibly when it comes to adaptation for survival, which over long evolutionary time would be variable in response to the nature of the challenges they confronted. Violence and cooperation are not opposites but two elements of an evolutionary package hominins developed over hundreds of thousands of years to produce survival and reproductive benefits.[40]

There nevertheless must be a way of persuading individuals, almost invariably males, to participate in coalitional violence when their individual survival would be more likely if they did not. One way was to punish those who refused to take part; 'free riders' might face exile from the group or worse, and they would be denied a share of any captured resources. Otherwise, under conditions of group living, where self-protection was a function of group protection, it has been argued that males evolved a trait for altruism, which at times involved taking individual risks not only to assist immediate kin but also for the wider kin group, even for non-kin if they also belonged to the group.[41] The term commonly used to describe this kind of behaviour is 'parochial altruism'; that is, help for the kin group, not for outsiders. Conflict is possible where the net fitness benefits for the group exceed the costs incurred by individuals. If a group is victorious and seizes more resources or mates, those individuals who participated will also gain benefits, in particular the protection of immediate kin. As Darwin recognized, those communities with a greater number of 'sympathetic, courageous and faithful members', in other words a higher number of parochial altruists, were more likely to succeed by natural selection at the expense of those with few of them.[42] Altruism is, of course, a two-edged sword. Individuals taking part may gain a good deal, particularly in successful defence of the kin group, but they also run the risk of death, injury, or capture. Modern ethnographic studies of tribal communities confirm that intertribal violence often involves low-risk attacks, killing a few of the target group, capturing women, but taking low casualties. Among aboriginal Australians, regular lethal conflict over women was conducted through dawn raids, ambushes, or nighttime skirmishes, ways that limited the prospect of loss to the attacker. Coalitional violence by parochial altruists, either in defence or attack, should have been over long evolutionary time one means of ensuring survival and reproductive success.

Those who participated, which for early foragers and hunter-gatherers would probably have meant most able-bodied males, may also have increased their reproductive potential through securing additional mates from rival groups or becoming a more attractive mating prospect for the females of their own group. Warriors, particularly those with greatest success, may have enjoyed inclusive fitness benefits by siring more offspring, who would in turn carry their genes more widely. It has been suggested that the evolution of belligerence and bravery as male traits adapted to intergroup conflict could have had effects that enhanced reproduction of the group by increasing male access to mates and through providing more resources (territory, food supplies, and so forth) for females.[43] In aggressive raiding, most of the fighters would have been young men, not only fired up with testosterone at its peak but also most anxious to find a mate or mates by proving their fighting ability and securing additional individual fitness benefits.[44] Conflict would then have an adaptive value for males, confirming the biological advantage of aggression as a reproductively beneficial strategy.

For females, on the other hand, there were substantial fitness costs because they were often the target of violence or capture or suffered from the killing of male partners or kin, which reduced their protection and access to resources. To enhance fitness in the face of these selective pressures, it seems likely that women devised strategies for biological survival through flight from or submission to lethal aggression.[45] There is also archaeological evidence that suggests women participated in fighting to protect themselves and their kin or devised tactics to confound their attackers. At the 700-year-old Norris Farm cemetery in central Illinois, among the forty-three skeletons showing violent, traumatic death there were equal numbers of men and women; among those with healed injuries to the cranium there were nine men and six women. Female skeletal remains in this and other American sites show injury sustained while facing an attacker, which again suggests, though it cannot confirm, that women participated in fighting when necessary.[46] The early nineteenth-century account of life with an Australian aboriginal tribe by an escaped convict, William Buckley, tells of regular skirmishes and larger fights in which women also took part to protect the kin group, risking death in the process: of one battle he recalled, 'the women threw off their rugs, and each armed with a short club, flew to the assistance of their husbands and brothers ... Men and women were fighting furiously, and indiscriminately, covered with blood; two of the latter were killed.'[47]

It is possible that the females of early human groups encouraged the evolution of traits for belligerence because they assumed that more effective fighters would in turn defend them more effectively. A tribe or clan with a reputation for fierceness would offer better protection; a man successful in fighting (that is, one who survived) was a better guarantor of survival for female partners. A limited experiment carried out with sixty male and sixty female participants from Liverpool (60 percent were university students) tested the hypothesis that women were more likely to select brave altruists as partners than risk-averse males. The results of the survey showed that women indeed preferred brave altruists as long-term partners but that they also rated bravery above altruism as a trait. Risk-averse males were poorly rated. Male students corroborated the conclusion by similarly rating bravery above altruism and risk aversion. The outcome was no doubt predictable, as few women would volunteer to have a wimp as a long-term partner, while few males would want to identify with the risk-averse rather than the risk-prone.[48]

But if those choices reflected embedded ancestral sentiments rather than culturally defined responses, as the researchers suggested, it is plausible to argue that females in the extended kin group did prefer men who could defend and provision them, while men who were successful in combat may have sustained a polygynous culture that allowed numerous offspring. Whether success in fighting did make males more attractive as mates has some contemporary corroboration. One Yanomami warrior chief was said to have had forty-five children from eight wives, with the result that three-quarters of the people in the village cluster he ruled were his descendants.[49] Another survey of sixty-one elderly Yanomami men, all of them former fighters, found that four of the cohort had between them 191 grandchildren.[50] On the other hand, the legendary nineteenth-century African king, Shaka Zulu, had women made pregnant by his soldiers murdered so that the men could focus on their soldiering.

The evolution of conflict as one means (but by no means the only one) of securing inclusive fitness, if consistent with current evolutionary theory and scientific plausibility, must remain speculative in the absence of firm evidence from the long human past. Critics of the idea that simple hominid communities must have competed, sometimes violently, over access to mates or the use of resources prefer to see the long period of simple foraging and hunting as one in which conflict was largely within rather than between groups and was usually resolved through appeasement or migration, though this is an argument largely based on current ethnographic examples projected hopefully into the past, and equally speculative.[51] Such criticism is difficult to reconcile with the current view, now widely accepted, that early man pursued strategies for survival and inclusive fitness, which over time required flexible and variable responses including a resort to competitive violence to ensure biological success. As ethology has shown, such a biological outcome is consistent with the evidence for many other species.

The evolutionary argument must also take account of the development of warfare in the historic period, over the past 5,000 years, when soldiers fought alongside those who were not their kin and sacrificed themselves in what seems biologically pointless numbers. Most evolutionary biologists recognize that conflict in the recent past – recent in relation to the millions of years of hominid existence – also involved the evolution of cultures that sustained the initial commitment to adaptations for inclusive fitness. Indeed, a trait for the capacity to develop culture seems to have been inherited from deep in the human past as another means of securing survival and reproductive success. Success as a species has depended on what have been called 'genetically evolved cultural adaptations'.[52] The concept of biological-cultural co-evolution is clearly useful for the more recent historical era because the motives that underlie the pursuit of fitness and survival in biological terms are matched by cultures that sustain and normalize warfare as an instrument for survival.[53] The fitness-enhancing element in evolutionary theory can be applied to more developed chiefdoms and states as they fought for resources and power, even for women, who were likely to be seized as sexual booty. Indeed, amalgamation into tribal societies, then larger proto-state institutions and finally developed states, evidently resulted from increased and often violent competition that required a more organized and substantial military response. Changes in social organization were thus selected in both biological and cultural terms to favour warfare when necessary, which for much of human history was about the survival or extinction of a given community or polity.

Parochial altruism can also, without too much distortion, be applied to conflict between modern states and nations where ethnocentrism binds together a warring people, whose warriors sacrifice themselves for the wider survival of the community, even at the risk of high individual cost. It is striking that in Germany and Japan towards the end of the Second World War, fear of biological extinction through castration of the males and sexual conquest of the females became part of government propaganda, encouraging desperate defence when the rational choice was to surrender. Both countries also exhibited an exaggerated sense of racial purity and racial belonging, which mirrored on a larger scale the 'inclusive fitness' paradigm for early humans. Indeed, in the German case there was a self-conscious embrace of biological imperatives to fitness, encouraging increased fertility among German women, seizing children from conquered areas to fill the German racial pool, and classifying the 'included' in terms of biological criteria. It was also evident during the Second World War that soldiers were little influenced by the wider ideological goals of the national leadership. Instead, they displayed commitment to the small units they belonged to in the belief, among other reasons, that their role and sacrifice was to protect kin at home, exemplified by the photographs of family universally carried by soldiers in combat. Acts of exceptional heroism, involving self-sacrifice, were commonly undertaken to assist the immediate circle of comrades, which formed a surrogate kin group among men who were not linked by genetic connection.

The Seville statement on violence was revisited in a conference in the same city in 2017 organized by the group Warfare, Environment, Social Inequality and Peace Studies, among whose aims was to 'uncover effective solutions which promote peace' while rejecting still the idea that violence is genetically transmitted. However, in the more than thirty years since the statement was first issued, evolutionary theory advanced a good deal in trying to test the hypothesis that conflict lies deep in the human past for reasons to do with biological survival.[54] The idea that war is 'in our genes', like the older idea of an instinct for pugnacity, has been modified by a more sophisticated understanding of genetic transmission through evolutionary adaptation, but it now seems an unavoidable conclusion that for most of human existence the pursuit of inclusive fitness included not only sociality and cooperation but also conflict when the circumstances made it seem necessary. The persistent argument that it is nurture rather than nature that has produced war – social and cultural environment rather than biology – is an unhelpful dichotomy. Biological survival in the distant past depended on reproductive success, which in turn resulted from evolutionary adaptations that included sexual dimorphism, parochial altruism, kin selection, and male aggression to protect the inclusive group or to advance its survivability. Not all adapted traits guaranteed survival, which could depend on random effects, such as major climatic change or a decline in food sources. The extinction of most human species indicates that there were also evolutionary dead ends for hominins. Even *Homo sapiens* experienced periods when population levels were low enough for it to almost qualify as an endangered species. But those traits that evolved with *Homo sapiens* were sufficiently robust to secure competitive survival, even when the cost was to increase the killing of competitors on an ever greater scale.

Distrust of biological explanation as both too deterministic and too speculative remains embedded in many social science approaches to conflict and human evolution. 'Biobabble' was the dismissive epithet of one anthropologist surveying popular books on human aggression.[55] 'Human biology', wrote the sociologist Steve Bruce in 1999, 'does nothing to structure human society', an assertion clearly difficult to defend.[56] A year earlier, Edward Wilson, father of sociobiology, in response to widespread social science criticism, declared that the social sciences ought to be replaced by a biological approach to human behaviour.[57] Extreme though his stance might seem, it now seems unhelpful to deny the significance of evolutionary biology in offering a modified version of Darwin's 'struggle for survival' through which traits for conflict, as well as traits for sociality and cultural construction, had a part to play in explaining the human outcome.

CHAPTER 2

Psychology

> How many millions are spent by the League of Nations or at the instigation of the League on psychological research into the nature of war impulses? How many psychological institutions are working day and night in different countries to fathom the riddles of human conflict either individual or social? . . . not one country in the world spends a sou on investigating the psychological phenomena and motivation of war.
>
> — Dr Edward Glover, 1931[1]

Edward Glover, one of the leaders of the Freudian group at the British Institute of Psychoanalysis, was among a growing circle of Western psychologists in the 1930s who believed the cause of war was to be found in the human mind. Identification of the instincts that made for war would, it was hoped, make possible a new psychology of peace even if it meant, as one enthusiast suggested, psychoanalysing much of the adult population. The ambition to use developments in the relatively recent discipline of psychology to answer the riddle of persistent warfare was the reason Einstein invited Freud to speculate on the answer. If Freud's insistence on an immutable 'death drive' seemed a pessimistic conclusion, the search for more useful ways of linking conflict and aggression with the workings of the mind has continued ever since.

In many ways, Freud was the wrong person for Einstein to ask. Psychoanalysts were focused on medical practice and clinical results for individuals with psychotic conditions, not for whole societies or states. In the 1920s, it was broadly assumed by the profession that its work was on the inner life of its small body of patients, not on the wider issues of the external world, including the etiology of war. Nevertheless, psychologists did see the horrors of the First World War as the point at which they ought to have something to say about the origin of conflict. Writing shortly after the outbreak of war in August 1914, the American psychologist Daniel Phillips dismissed the unimportant surface explanations for the war in favour of the 'deeper and real causes' to be found in a perennial instinct for pugnacity. 'All history', he wrote, 'affords evidence of this smouldering war-volcano'.[2] Freud in 'Thoughts for the Times on War and Death', written in 1915, shared Phillips's view that there must be deep within men 'primal impulses' for violence.[3] He developed this idea after the First World War in 'Beyond the Pleasure Principle', in which he elaborated for the first time his view that all organic matter sought to return to its inorganic state, contrasting the pleasure principle with what he called the death drive. This bifurcation, he thought, explained how mankind could both love and hate, beginning with the relationship to the parents, which he termed the Oedipus complex – infant love for but also frustration towards the mother, love but also hostility towards the father. Aggression arising from this psychic tension was usually repressed by a sense of guilt but could be mobilized in certain circumstances, as it had been in the recent conflict. Freud was nonetheless wary of applying this insight to analysis of the group rather than the individual, because he understood that the problem for any attempt to move beyond the level of the individual was the absence of clinical evidence. In 1939, shortly before his death, Freud hinted at the 'archaic heritage of human beings . . . the subject-matter-memory traces of the experience of earlier generations' that could be applied to groups, even to nations, as they grappled with the 'death drive', but he did not develop any general psychological theory on the causes of war, which explains his half-hearted response to Einstein.[4]

The application of psychoanalysis to the wider issue of war was left to Freud's psychoanalytical successors, particularly in Britain, where, in the 1930s, theories of aggression came to dominate over any interest in the 'pleasure principle'. Because war was widely regarded as an act of collective insanity, psychology seemed an entirely appropriate discipline to explain it, and confronting the issue of war seemed an urgent responsibility for a science in its relative infancy. By the 1930s, in the face of a mounting international crisis, psychoanalysts endeavoured to exploit Freudian theory to explain the phenomena not only of human aggression in an individual but also of the collective aggression expressed in warfare. The result, as one later critic put it, seemed 'loose and indiscriminate', but Freud's successors saw an opportunity to expand the profile of their branch of psychology in areas otherwise dominated by the social and political sciences. They were generally unconvinced by Freud's 'death drive', which was open to wide misinterpretation (not least because it was usually translated in English as 'death instinct', which suggested a biological root, for which there was no evidence). The 'death drive' did not, as the psychologist Otto Fenichel pointed out in his 1935 book *War and Peace*, aim at war at all, but merely tried to make sense of man's divided self, caught between the unconscious drive for destruction and the positive capacity for love.[5] Instead, psychoanalysts focused on the Freudian interpretation of early childhood through the Oedipus complex as the source of future aggression. The mentality for war, claimed Glover, is 'built up during the nursery period'.[6]

Glover was by far the most important of the psychoanalysts trying to explain the origin of war and was invited to Geneva in 1931 to address the Federation of League of Nations Societies on his ideas about war and its cure. A Freudian focus on the early years of infancy, Glover claimed, was central to understanding the future adult. Each suckling child is capable of love for the mother but aggression when denied the breast; each child loves the father but hates his intrusion between infant and mother. This Oedipal reaction was manifested, Glover claimed, in a tension between love and hate, affection and sadism, only overcome in 'normal adults' by unconscious repression of the negative traits. Aggression could be provoked if the repressed guilt and sexuality were released and projected against a potential enemy in war, but warfare was only possible at all because the psychic situation was already well prepared in infancy.[7]

This view of the origin of aggression was reinforced by the clinical work of the Austro-Hungarian psychoanalyst Melanie Klein (recruited to Glover's institute in the 1930s) and the British developmental psychologist Susan Isaacs. Their observation of infants suggested, as Glover did, that the process of suckling provokes love for the mother, while denial of the breast is the primary source of anxiety and aggression. The tension generated by these two impulses creates in every infant a strong sense of aggressive frustration but also fear of the aggressor-mother. Klein insisted, against strong opposition from her peers, that the inner world of the very young infant was a web of terror, destructiveness, sadism, and persecution, a nightmare world of which aggression in later years was a key product.[8] The child analyst Joan Riviere, Klein's collaborator and supporter, gave a vivid image of the sheer violence at the heart of an infant's aggressive fantasies: 'Limbs shall trample, kick and hit; lips, fingers and hands shall suck, twist, pinch; teeth shall bite, gnaw mangle and cut; mouths shall devour, swallow and kill (annihilate).'[9] Klein and her followers did not set out, any more than Freud, to provide an analogue of war, though Klein was strongly influenced by the impact of war and postwar suffering when she began working in the early 1920s with children scarred emotionally by the conflict.[10] But the theory of infant aggression was taken by others as 'the prototype of war psychology'. The argument was appropriated to demonstrate that the psychic impulse for aggression and war was a product of the very earliest hours and days of a human being's life, a view for which there was not a shred of clinical evidence.[11]

After 1945 and the experience of a second vast and catastrophic conflict, psychologists turned more willingly to the idea that the causes of war and aggression had psychological roots more fundamental than material, ideological, or political rivalry. For psychoanalysts, the Freudian models developed in the 1930s continued to serve as the foundation for understanding war. The Oedipal impulse to hate the father could be projected onto the enemy, while love for the father figure could be reserved for national leaders or military commanders. On the other hand, violation of a country represented the attempted rape of the mother figure, to which a man will respond with furious anger. These destructive instincts, wrote the analyst Alix Strachey, one of the translators of Freud's works, 'are the greatest single cause of war'.[12] Because much of the son–father rivalry involved repressed sexuality, psychoanalysis posited the idea that in war, which released repressed aggression, the son wishes to castrate the father now personified by the enemy. At the same time, the fear of castration can generate its own violence. The French analyst Marie Bonaparte, in *Myths of War* published in 1947, suggested that Germans saw the Polish Corridor, which separated East Prussia off from the rest of Germany, as nothing less than the castration of the nation, while news in summer 1939 that Poles were castrating ethnic Germans living in Poland was exploited by Hitler to justify his war of aggression and perhaps to overcome his own fear of emasculation.[13]

The Italian psychoanalyst Franco Fornari, author in 1966 of *The Psychoanalysis of War*, still the only serious volume on the subject, pursued further the idea that infantile experience coloured behaviour in the Second World War. When the atomic bomb was successfully tested at Alamogordo Bombing Range in New Mexico in July 1945, the project director, General Leslie Groves, cabled to President Truman 'baby is born', which Fornari saw as a significant choice of words. Even more telling, claimed Fornari, was the decision by Paul Tibbets, the pilot of the B-29 bomber that dropped the bomb on Hiroshima, to name the aircraft *Enola Gay*, after his mother.[14] Fornari went further in suggesting that warfare itself was a way of overcoming the profound anxieties generated by the death drive and its associated aggression ('outward deflection of the death instinct [*sic*]'). This outward projection of an inner psychic turmoil turns war itself into a form of therapy, because it removes the guilt associated with infantile aggression. Projection places guilt on the enemy, who can now be killed as the personification of the evil that lurks inside all men (and Fornari talks only of men). The slaughter of the enemy is equivalent to the destruction of the 'bad things' associated with the death drive, whether in 'primitive' warfare, where Fornari thought that projection is evident from recent ethnographic studies, or in modern war, where the unconscious motives are obscured but are real nonetheless. Fornari's so-called paranoic war is not a result of some innate aggressiveness in men but a form of 'innate madness, through which [man] establishes his earliest relationship to his environment, that is, to his mother', as Tibbets did with the *Enola Gay*.[15] Only nuclear war, Fornari concluded, changes the psychoanalytic picture because it would destroy not only the hated enemy of Oedipal fantasy but also the love object, the mother country and the mother.

The strong element of repressed sexual fear and aggression manifested in war became a psychoanalytical trope in discussing the nature of warfare from the 1930s onwards. War was the expression of unconscious stresses brought suddenly to the surface, and it generated symbolic acts associated with unconscious fears. According to the American psychiatrist Maurice Walsh, speaking at a major conference on the causes of war held in 1973 at the University of Notre Dame in Indiana, this explained the example in ancient Egypt of cutting off the foreskin of the defeated enemy rather than taking trophy heads. He might have added the practice among some Arctic warring tribes of severing the vulvas of massacred women and hanging them on a line for enemy males to view, for which Freudian psychology would certainly have had an explanation.[16] The Oedipal drive, Walsh considered, was strong enough to get older men to send their sons to war to be killed (also known as the Cronus complex after the Greek god who devoured his sons) and for the young men to kill the enemy as the hated image of the intruding father in infancy. Unable to kill or emasculate the father, the enemy is killed as a scapegoat. These psychological complexes could explain everything from the raids and head-hunting of 'primitive war' to modern organized warfare.[17]

The conference in Indiana might be viewed as a turning point in the application of psychoanalysis to the causality of war. Among the academic participants, there was a general reluctance to accept that psychology could really do what it claimed when it came to moving from the personal to the social or institutional. The biologist Irenäus Eibl-Eibesfeldt regarded the Oedipal complex as nothing more than a fiction, a view widely shared even among other psychologists, and it appeared even more fictive when applied to warfare. One of the participants, the psychiatry professor Robert Cancro, in an unguarded moment, confessed his personal view of the contribution of psychopathology to understanding the causes of war: 'I think it is bloody little.'[18] Summing up the contribution of psychoanalysis to understanding war twenty years after the conference, the psychotherapist Diana Birkett found that the discipline had returned to its roots in trying to heal the inner life of patients rather than the outer life of world affairs, a direction already taken by American psychoanalysis long before.[19] In the past twenty-five years, there has not been a single article on war or collective aggression in the *International Journal of Psychoanalysis*, the discipline's principal publication.

Freud's answer to Einstein has done little to further a psychological explanation for war. The death drive is regarded as little more than a metaphor of doubtful value. There is no way of demonstrating that the abstractions of the Oedipus complex were responsible for war and aggression or that Kleinian theories of violent infant fantasy proved the origin of 'war psychology'. Even though Freud and his followers understood that some external stimulus was necessary to call up the repressed inner self, the idea of infantile repression if it were valid was supposed to be universal, in both time and place and for both men and women, which was again beyond either proof or plausibility. Infantile aggression, as any parent will know, is real enough, but whether that translates into a later willingness to go to war must remain speculation rather than fact.

If psychoanalysis proved to be an explanatory dead end, the study of psychological traits necessary for warfare has remained a major area of argument over what the discipline can convincingly contribute. The result is a debate closely linked to the biological question of whether aggression, and hence war, is a product of evolutionary pressures. There is no disputing that aggressivity is a characteristic of some (chiefly male) human beings, but the psychological argument differs from the biological inasmuch as aggression is seen as a psychological reaction to situations that prompt frustration or fear and, thus, a learned psychology rather than the biological imperatives explored in chapter 1. The process of learning over many generations shapes the psychological adaptations necessary for evolutionary survival, one of which may be a predisposition for warfare, another the evidence for a kind of 'mental dimorphism' through which males are psychologically disposed to do the fighting, while females cope with reproduction. None of these propositions has produced consensus about what the relationship is between human psychology and the long history of warfare.

Since the 1980s, evolutionary psychology has been a major stepping-stone to understanding the long-term development of the human mind. As a discipline, it is still a work in progress, with much room for debate, but the evolution of warfare is one of the themes the discipline has engaged. For evolutionary psychologists, there are no general tools that the mind has developed but instead a series of modular mechanisms to deal with each specific problem of evolutionary adaptation.[20] The interaction among a number of these modules may have produced the capacity for warlike violence in human ancestral behaviour. This violence can only be the product of a group, or coalition, which needs to protect itself in the prehistoric landscape from predators and other humans. Among the key arguments from the perspective of evolution, the one that has generated the most debate is the so-called male warrior hypothesis, which suggests a psychological adaptation for conflict among the males of the group, an argument closely related to the biological pursuit of inclusive fitness for men. The chief issue here is to define the psychological mechanisms that allow men to form coalitions for conducting violence against another group. These mechanisms are distinct from the psychology of individual or personal aggression, because by definition it is the capacity to cooperate that makes collective violence possible. They operate within a range of distinct contexts, both cultural and environmental.[21] Over deep evolutionary time, the fears engendered by the need to defend the group or tribe against the threat of a rival may have produced learned psychological responses for coalitional warfare among men, including an altruistic willingness to run individual risks for the protection of the rest of the community and its reproductive success.[22] On this view of evolution, the male in-group learns over time the advantages of coalition in the face of threat and reacts accordingly against an outgroup when there are clear cost benefits for the collective. Over time, groups for which aggression proves successful are more likely to see future aggression (either in defence or offence) as psychologically acceptable, tending to establish norms for aggression that the warrior male can identify with.[23] Critics of the male warrior hypothesis see these processes as something transmitted culturally, through what is called cultural group selection, but the process of repetition and imitation over a long time suggests that the propensity for coalitional violence does become psychologically norma-tive for some males, so that the learned adaptation becomes an evolved one.

The problem for evolutionary psychology is the diffi-culty of establishing unambiguous evidence that might in-dicate a psychological predisposition for coalitional violence over the long time in which human males may (or may not) have engaged in conflict between groups. Two historic ex-amples may help to illustrate the extent to which warrior elites relied on a normative psychology to validate coali-tional warfare, though these examples are not about evo-lutionary adaptation, which occurs over very much longer timescales. The first is the example of the Greek city-state of Sparta in the first millennium BCE; the second, the warfare of Viking Scandinavia in the first millennium CE. The Spar-tans (or Spartiates as they called themselves) developed a famously militaristic culture in which the wealthy male citi-zens all had a responsibility to bear arms and fought regular-ly against other Greek city-states or, in the well-known case of the invasion by Xerxes's Persian armies, against foreign intrusion. The Spartan defence of the pass at Thermopylae by 300 men against the Persian host in 480 BCE, in which the king, Leonidas, and his soldiers were slaughtered to the last man, was an emblematic battle in which the Spartans knew that every man had to be prepared to sacrifice himself for the community and did so as the citizen oath required. If any Spartan broke ranks or fled the battlefield, he was known as a 'Trembler' and was supposed to shave off half his beard and wear a shabby cloak as a badge of disgrace. The young sons of Spartan citizens were brought up under a rigorous regime of initiation and preparation for the day they would become soldiers in turn. Flogged regularly for any infraction, encouraged to excel in sports, and separated from their families, they were exhorted to shed emotions of fear, shame, and pride and to be prepared psychologically for the severe demands of military discipline even when that meant their sacrifice in battle.[24] Spartan culture clearly reinforced these values, but the psychological acceptance of warfare as a male obligation, generation by generation, must have required more than the cultural context to become embedded so forcefully over hundreds of years.

The Scandinavian Vikings have also emerged, like the Spartans, with a reputation for militarized society dominated by the so-called hegemonic males, a warrior elite whose sacrifice in battle for the wider community was regarded as a glorious death. As in Sparta, cowardice turned a man into a social pariah, grounds in Viking culture for a wife to divorce the culprit. Young boys were provided with toy weapons to encourage preparation for combat when they reached adolescence, including knives, bows and arrows, spears, and axes. In *Egil's Saga*, the young Egil is praised by his mother for killing another boy in an argument because it showed that he had the makings of a fine warrior.[25] Viking war bands were characteristic in-groups, with a strong sense of identity, animated by traits necessary for combat, even to the point of sacrifice, as the Viking armies found in 1014 at the battle of Clontarf, outside Dublin, where they were slaughtered by the victorious Irish. It was possible for outsiders to join a Viking troop, as archaeological evidence has shown, but they did so by swearing oaths of fealty and adopting the symbols of the in-group, with common weapons, banners, and distinctive shield colours. Military values dominated Viking society, and a heroic reputation paved the way for wider influence and a fine marriage partner.[26] The psychology of military manliness, protection of the community, and a willingness to sacrifice the self in war seems to have been embedded in Viking society as it was in Sparta, perhaps reflecting the ancestral patterns of evolutionary theory.

The cult of manliness is easily recognized in modern warfare, where there are none of the challenges faced in trying to reconstruct the psychological disposition of humans in early history. The anthropologist Godfrey Maringira served fifteen years with the Zimbabwean army before entering a very different profession. He writes of his experience as a recruit and trainee in which the instructors made every effort to get them to see themselves as dominant males. 'We have entered into the house of men', they were told, 'and we had to leave behind the womanhood.' They quickly adapted to a milieu in which they were trained to understand and celebrate killing and to despise civilians as 'women'. Even after the end of their military service, they thought of themselves as set apart by their sense that they were both valorous and strong – male warriors in mind and body.[27] A psychological study of forty-three American men about to enter military service showed the same contempt for civilians and a desire to exploit their time in the service to construct a hegemonic masculinity with traits that would scarcely have separated them from the Vikings and Spartiates: willingness to engage in aggression and violence; physical fitness; self-discipline and self-reliance; emotional control; and risk-taking of a high order.

The modern military institution, whether in the United States, Zimbabwe, or elsewhere is uniquely positioned to create a masculine identity and a warrior psychology.[28]

The obvious objection to any analysis of the psychological element in warfare remains the uncertain nature of the evidence. The mind leaves few traces in the archaeological record that can be easily interpreted in psychological terms. Even for historic warfare, psychological explanation is difficult to disentangle from the influence of cultures and social structures, and as with ideas of masculinity and manliness, defining the dynamic relationship between psychology and culture is a classic chicken-and-egg exercise. The American evolutionary psychologist Anthony Lopez has argued that it is easier to work back from the present to understand how human psychology for warfare has evolved. 'Our adapted mind', he argues, 'is a window into the ancestral past.' Opening that window is nevertheless a challenge. Lopez was interested in the proposition that there were different but related psychological adaptations for defensive warfare and for offensive aggression, the first bringing survival benefits for the whole community, the second offering benefits chiefly to those who conduct the aggression. For much of human history, the quick raid was the typical form of warlike violence, carried out by what he calls 'small, unstable, fraternal coalitions', perhaps led by the more aggressive, dominant males. The evolved psychology provided the impulse for a variety of forms of warfare and could apply to ancient intertribal fighting or to wars of the present.[29]

To test this hypothesis, in 2007 Lopez conducted a social psychological experiment in which 195 college students

(83 female, 112 male) were presented with two imagined scenarios for a Pathan nomadic tribe in 1050 CE, one scenario based on defence and the other on offence: in the first, the tribe must decide whether to fight in defence against a probable attack from the Chinese province of Xinjiang; in the second, the tribe must decide whether to attack a Chinese city to secure its riches. The questions students were then asked derived from other current experiments on collective human action – whether they would participate, what benefits they expected for themselves or the group, how to punish free riders and reward those who did take part. It turned out that males were more willing to participate than females; males expected more benefits than females from offensive but not from defensive warfare; there was little difference between the sexes in perceived benefit for defensive warfare (because survival would clearly benefit all); free riders were expected to be punished in defence, while rewards for those participating in aggression were approved. Lopez concluded that the evidence did not show that 'humans are naturally war-prone', but that humans have evolved a specialized psychology that can respond to a specific contingency conditionally, as the students did when faced with war-making options in the same way that archaic tribesmen may have done.[30]

Modern analogues for past psychology have also been pursued through the study of child behaviour, though in ways very different from psychoanalysis. The American developmental psychologist Joyce Benenson spent years observing the behaviour of boys and girls at primary-school level and the fears they articulate. She found that boys tended to express fears about enemies and their responsibility to defeat them. Male language was replete with related metaphors – battle, combat, attack, defeat. Boys' play focused on fighting games, wrestling, and defeating enemies. One study showed that 70 percent of boys of primary-school age took part in games that involve attack, defence, chasing, escape, and capture, while girls did so hardly at all. Boys invent enemies to be destroyed and, as is well known, are fascinated by weapons, which they fashion out of any available object even in schools and nurseries where weapons are banned. In a survey organized by Benenson of 200 boys and girls aged between four and nine in the British port of Plymouth, the boys when asked what they did with their toys produced a majority of stories about attacking an enemy, but the girls told stories that had nothing to do with conflict. Boys, observed Benenson, are also more likely to form groups that cooperate together against out-groups defined in enemy terms. Her conclusion is that over a long time, evolutionary psychology created 'males who are efficient cooperative fighters'.[31]

The importance of play in creating in predominantly male children a familiarity with what Wendy Varney has called 'war fare' has a long history. Toy weapons and soldiers date back thousands of years. Small toy metal soldiers were minted in Europe from the thirteenth century and by the nineteenth had become a mass-market phenomenon; in Britain in the years just before the outbreak of the First World War, more than 10 million toy soldiers were produced each year. Commercial advertising suggested that play with war toys prepared boys for the real world of war to come. In the United States, war-related toys have become best sellers. The

modern child consumer is introduced to the dehumanization of the enemy by making the enemy a fantasy figure to be
destroyed and the hero a familiar approved model, whether GI Joe, best-selling holiday toy of 1982, or Desert Storm
Barbie produced at the time of the First Gulf War.[32] Across
the world, the consumerization of warfare for the young per-
petuates at some level the psychological acceptance of war as
a necessary, even essential part of the contemporary world, a
mechanism sustained into adulthood by the world of violent
video gaming, which sustains fascination with warfare and
military metaphors – *Battlefield 2042*, *Mortal Kombat*, *Command and Conquer*, *Call of Duty*. The Hollywood film industry
has also reinforced popular American militarism with regular tropes of heroic defence of American values, defeat of the
evil 'other', and warfare as an exhilarating spectacle. Militarism as an element in American culture is widespread and
widely endorsed, suggesting a deeply embedded psychology
that the culture both reflects and reinforces.[33]

There have been many kinds of objection to studies that
try to project back current psychology to an ancestral past or
find differential roles between male and female psychology
that explain the male propensity for belligerence. The study
of children's behaviour raises the obvious objection that they
live in social environments that reinforce male and female
stereotypes and bombard them with consumer advertising.
The capacity of females to participate in conflict, though
limited historically, shows that a psychology for belligerence
is not necessarily male-only. The objections to biological arguments for the emergence of early forms of warfare appear
to apply with equal force to evolutionary psychology – that

most men, most of the time in the prehistoric past, were not fighting and were capable instead of developing non-violent means of collaboration.[34] This argument does not preclude some form of psychological adaptation over evolutionary time to account for violence when it does occur, but the temptation is to see this as a secondary learned reaction rather than a primary one. Variations in the type and location of warfare over long historical time also suggest that a universal psychological predisposition to take part in violence is unlikely or unproveable, while cultural evolution and material pressures are more probable explanations for the willingness or otherwise of men to risk the costs of warfare.

These many objections nevertheless fail to explain why evolutionary psychology should work for some instances of evolved human nature such as sociability or empathy but not for one that is common across all cultures and all recorded time. It seems unlikely that the myriad cultures, great and small, that have flourished over the past millennia all arrived independently at the idea of using violence under certain circumstances or developed independently the institution of a warrior elite committed psychologically to belligerence. The evolution of a psychology for warfare is a universal, species-typical adaptation, even though it is manifested in different locations and times in a variety of ways.[35] Nor is the psychology of war a simple phenomenon. The psychology is linked more broadly to evolution, particularly to the defensive protection of the warrior's own kin, community, tribe, or nation, or in undertaking offence to reap benefits at low cost (if possible) for the aggressor, or through the development of a social order in which warfare, led by the warrior elite of hegemonic males, becomes normative over time. In this sense, evolutionary psychology provides a framework for understanding warfare not only millennia ago but also for the modern age of warfare in which these psychological assumptions operate still, but are seldom articulated. Hitler's *Blitzkrieg* against Poland has more in common with a sudden aggressive raid by one tribal village on another than is immediately obvious. Motives of revenge for alleged Polish violence against ethnic Germans in Poland, demonization of the Slavic enemy, and a covetous desire for Polish land and resources could be the psychology of tribal warfare writ large. Later, in what became the Second World War, the psychology that led German soldiers to fight to the very last in 1945, and to penalize those who refused, has analogues throughout the historic past, not least the defence of the pass at Thermopylae by Leonidas's suicidal 300.

What evolutionary psychology cannot explain is the outbreak of a particular war, for which conditional factors are necessary. Nor can it adequately explain the idea of an 'enemy', without which wars would not happen. Defining enemy from friend is a critical element in understanding how wars have arisen throughout history, and why they have so often been pursued in devastatingly violent and exterminatory terms. For understanding the concept 'enemy', social psychology has much more to contribute, not only for the current concern with coalitional violence but also for understanding the historic past, and by implication the deeper past of hominin existence.

In 1932, the German legal philosopher Carl Schmitt

proposed the radical idea that humankind divides its world into 'friend or foe' (*Freund oder Feind*). This was, he argued in his *Concept of the Political*, a characteristic of all state structures in which the community identified with the sovereign power and treated as an 'enemy' any group that could not be absorbed into the dominant collective. In his view, other nations were, by definition, the enemy. Although his chief concern was to define a state in terms of its capacity to organize a community bound by obedience and to fight against all those who did not belong (the anti-Semitic Schmitt included among them Jews), the concept 'friend or foe' focused more generally on issues of belonging and exclusion, as the Third Reich a year later exemplified. Overcoming the enemy within required a form of domestic warfare to protect the state; overcoming an external enemy required no other means save warfare.[36] 'Friend or foe' is perhaps the most lasting element of Schmitt's philosophy. It lies at the heart of much contemporary social psychological research that seeks to explain how an in-group is constructed and an out-group defined in terms of exclusion, even hostility. Defining a community as inclusive seems to require a definition of the 'other', or in Schmitt's lexicon the 'enemy'.

Social psychological experiments to test the way identity could be constructed through conformity of the group began seriously in the 1950s with the work of the Polish American Solomon Asch, who showed that a majority of an experimental group were willing to accept the group's judgment even when it seemed wrong because they preferred to share a sense of belonging to the group. Well-known experiments in the 1950s led by the Turkish social psychologist Muzafer

Sherif confirmed that when a set of twelve-year-old boys was divided experimentally into two competing groups (the Robbers' Cave Experiment), they formed close in-group bonds that led to conflict and hostility when the two groups were brought together. Philip Zimbardo's famous Stanford Prison Experiment in 1976, where students were divided into guards and prisoners, had to be suspended after six days instead of completing the two weeks allocated, because the guards were becoming increasingly brutal to their charges. These experiments have been cautiously used as evidence, as they were conducted under laboratory conditions in which the experimenter played an important part in defining the question to be addressed and the roles assigned to those taking part. Social psychology has spent much of the past fifty years refining the early theories explaining in-group identity and out-group denigration, with all it implies for conflict.

The key factor is the close identification between the members of a group, who establish a distinctiveness from other groups through shared values and symbols, including language. In-group attachment is psychologically rewarding, and the in-group sees itself as a moral unity superior to neighbouring groups for which there is no necessary fund of trust, sympathy, or admiration. The out-group can be denigrated or dehumanized to reinforce the sense of belonging, even the superiority of the in-group.[37] Experiments carried out to demonstrate that an in-group can typically regard itself as more 'human' in terms of key emotions found that on a range of human psychological traits, the experimental out-group was regarded in negative terms. While this need not necessarily lead to conflict, the construction of this kind of difference can fuel or justify prejudice, hatred, contempt, or fear of the 'other' and can, in certain circumstances of perceived threat, lead to violence. The dehumanization of the enemy makes such violence appear legitimate, reinforcing the sense of psychological identity of the in-group and removing any sense of guilt at inflicting harm. It is a short step from dehumanization to demonization, in which the enemy seems possessed of threatening powers to which a violent response seems the only remedy.[38]

There are many examples of this psychological device in the modern age, in which language plays an important part. In the Rwandan genocide, the Hutu labelled the victim Tutsis as 'cockroaches' to create an absolute difference between the two peoples and to justify exterminatory violence. In Hitler's war on the Jews, the repeated images of the Jew as leech, vermin, or bacillus defined the enemy as less than human and exalted the genocide to a form of pest control or medical intervention. Joseph Goebbels, Hitler's minister of propaganda and popular enlightenment, compared the flea with the Jew: 'since the flea is not a pleasant creature . . . our duty is rather to exterminate it. Likewise with the Jew.'[39] The metaphor was finally turned into reality by use of the insecticide Zyklon B, originally used to fumigate barracks to get rid of lice but later employed at the Auschwitz-Birkenau extermination camp to murder Jews. The war in the Pacific also saw the Japanese enemy presented as vermin or animalized as monkeys, rats, or spiders, a view that was reinforced by news of Japanese atrocities and wide belief that Japanese troops were 'subhuman'. The Japanese, wrote one American soldier back home, 'live like rats, squeal like pigs, and act like monkeys'.[40] The Japanese were routinely defined as less than human, and their treatment reflected the definition. In return, Japanese propaganda presented Allied servicemen as beasts of prey to be culled like any predatory animal, while the Chinese were simply regarded as 'pigs' to be slaughtered like animals in an abattoir.[41] In Vietnam, the American term 'gook' to describe the Vietnamese enemy turned them, as one veteran recalled, from humans into subhumans so that 'it makes it a little bit easier to kill 'em.' [42]

The social psychology of imputing value to the group and negative attributes to other groups is widely evident in conflict among pre-state communities of the recent past. Here again, the psychology is easier to define and to describe for smaller groups than it is for larger, segmented societies because small kin groups or tribes have a strong sense of shared identity and easy means of identifing friend or foe. Among such groups, the enemy was usually a near neighbour, even one with whom trade, exchange, and kinship links provided no guarantee of immunity. Warfare was endemic among the tribal communities in the Andaman Islands in the Indian Ocean, rooted in distrust of others, fear of retaliation, and ritual competition, even though they lived in close proximity. The Tiwi tribes of northern Australia killed all strangers on sight to prevent intrusion by the 'other' and to secure the tribe's own identity; in Australia's Murray-Darling Basin, the names for outside groups – Barapa Barapa, Wemba Wemba, Wadi Wadi – all translated as 'no-no', indicating their outsider status.[43] Even among the more pacific Semai people of central Malaya, the word *Hii'* defined all the members of a village, while *Mai* described all strangers who were beyond the circle of trust in the village in-group. For the Semai, nearby forests were inhabited by enemies both real and supernatural against whom the in-group had to be constantly vigilant.[44] The Greek term *bar-bar-bar*, origin of the modern word barbarian, similarly indicated outsiders whose language was in-comprehensible to the Greeks. It has become a term widely used from antiquity onwards to separate the in-group from the 'barbarous' other.

In the modern age, where there are commonly multiple sources of identity, the construction of the in-group and defamation of the out-group can take place where national sentiment or political manipulation is sufficiently developed. A psychological projection of negative attributes onto a rival nation can have the effect of cementing an otherwise potentially fractured in-group. The development of the idea of the *Volk* in Germany between the wars – the sense of a people ethnically and culturally united in a common endeavour – was used by the Hitler dictatorship to construct a vast in-group and to justify, in Carl Schmitt's terms, the identification and destruction of enemies of the *Volk* within, and then enemies without. First the Poles then the inhabitants of the Soviet Union were pilloried as barbarous peoples whose characteristics were entirely negative. The invading armies shared the image of the 'enemy' constructed by the German leadership. The willingness to accept the dehumanization of the enemy relied, as Alex Haslam and Steve Reicher have argued, not only on leaders but also on what they have called 'followership', without which the social psychological endorsement of friend versus foe would not be possible. The war between Russia and Ukraine has been a classic example of constructing a negative image of the enemy, this time as neo-Nazis, to ensure that the 'followership' in Russia will identify with the image of Russian virtue and Ukrainian vice.

These last examples highlight the most common form of identity difference in the modern age. Ethnic difference, whether measured by language, religion, race, or caste, has been a driver of many modern conflicts as the ethnic in-group measures its solidarity and inclusiveness through opposition to the ethnic out-group, forging psychological commitment to the one and xenophobic exclusion of the other.[45] The result can be an extreme case of psychological endorsement of violence, evident in the massacre of Armenians by Turks during the First World War in which exceptionally sadistic atrocities were committed or in the murder of Tutsis by their Hutu neighbours in Rwanda in 1994 in a spasm of ethnic savagery. Ethnic conflict is common in civil wars, less so in state-on-state wars, although the mobilization of emotions against an enemy people can quickly be achieved once war has started, as it was in both World Wars. In these cases, the concept of the 'other' had to be constructed in entirely negative terms to justify the killing of those not previously regarded as a specifically ethnic enemy. It is striking that most defined ethnic groups can live side-by-side without violence, even if there is a residue of hostility and suspicion between them, but when ethnic war does result, it is often directed at neighbours, not a distant threat. The mobilization of directed hatred of the defined out-group can happen remarkably quickly, creating the psychological ground not only for dehumanizing the enemy but also for justifying the extreme violence against neighbours, now seen as a threat to be exterminated. The civil war in Yugoslavia in the 1990s was fuelled by an extreme ethnonationalism that eroded any psychological barriers to perpetrating atrocities against people who only months before had been fellow citizens.[46]

The principle of inclusion and exclusion exerts a powerful social psychological effect. The consequences can explain the willingness to perpetrate extreme violence against the dehumanized other once the political or social triggers for conflict have materialized. Much of the recent research on the social psychology of exterminatory violence has been fuelled by the perpetration of genocide in the twentieth century, from the destruction of the European Jews during the Second World War to the genocides in Cambodia, Bosnia, and Rwanda. In these cases, the challenge is to explain how it is possible for killers to engage in mass murder, often in grotesque ways, without any sense that what they are doing is inhuman and illegitimate. For the longer history of warfare, these are questions that scarcely need to be asked. Victors routinely murdered entire communities, even the size of a city, including women and children. Whether Roman soldiers putting the inhabitants of Antipatrea in Macedonia to the sword, or the massacre of the urban population of Samarkand by the armies of Genghis Khan (now usually transcribed as Chinggis Khan), or the murder of Protestants by Catholics and vice versa during the sixteenth-century Wars of Religion, there was almost certainly no sense of guilt, but the opposite, what has been called the 'celebration' of a violence that seemed unquestionably justified.[47] In tribal warfare, the psychological commitment to the in-group was absolute, ensuring that violence directed at another tribe or community not only would be but should be conducted with remorseless brutality. Indeed, in many cases the failure to act with sufficient violence would have adverse social consequences for the warriors involved. In some Native American tribal communities, the initiation of young males to warfare required them to return with at least one scalp of an enemy – a 'coup' – to demonstrate that they had passed the threshold to adult warrior status. Failure might reduce social status and prompt ridicule. The scalped victim mattered not at all.

In all these cases, modern and ancestral alike, treatment of the group defined as the enemy betrayed a profound 'empathy deficit'. The enemy to be killed deserved no sympathy because that enemy had no place in the moral universe of the killers. Indeed, it becomes psychologically necessary to see the violence as a product of a virtuous society and the victims as not only lacking virtue but also in many cases the embodiment of evil.[48] Once again, this psychological feature is more easily evident in intertribal conflict where a neighbouring tribe is accused of witchcraft or harbouring evil spirits and must be cleansed violently to protect the threatened community or when the death of a tribal member is blamed on sorcery from outside the community and is to be punished with violence, even exterminatory violence, by the in-group. Among aboriginal Australians, suspicion that a neighbouring group used sorcery to inflict harm could provoke a retaliatory raid and the slaughter of an entire community.[49] The trait of vengeance plays a role in a great many different historical settings, justifying extreme violence while penalizing the out-group for the evil it perpetrates. In many cases, the result of victory is a spectacle of cruelty – cutting trophy heads from live victims, flaying captives alive, gory rituals of sacrifice – that allows the victors to celebrate both their physical and psychological triumph. The scenes of post-conflict violence inflicted on captives or sacrificial victims arouses in the spectators a heightened emotional state that may well derive, so it has been argued, from a deep psychological seam of human cruelty. The sociologist Norbert Elias, reflecting in the 1930s on the 'civilizing' of Western man, observed that warriors for millennia had found in war 'savage joys . . . in destroying and tormenting anything hostile or belonging to an enemy'. The emotional investment in savagery was possible only because the perpetrators were psychologically predisposed to inflict it on their dehumanized victims as their societies and cultural values dictated.[50]

There is geographically extensive evidence of the willingness of warriors to desecrate the bodies of those they have killed, though it has not been a universal response, and even less so in the modern age where in some cases formal agreements have governed respect for the enemy dead. Where it has happened, the treatment of the dead often derived from ritual norms of the group, which permitted or encouraged differing forms of mutilation and for differing purposes. But as a practice it is not necessarily culturally specific, suggesting a more general psychological root in the willingness to see the enemy as the 'other', outside and beyond the universe of the victor, to be treated as an enemy deserves. There are many examples. In intertribal warfare in North America, the practice of scalping, decapitation, and mutilation is widespread in the archaeological record, including the dismemberment of enemy bodies – ears, nose, forearms, feet, and hands. In central California, the twelve tribes inhabiting the region as close neighbours nevertheless engaged in chronic warfare; osteoarchaeology has revealed on seventy-nine skeletons evidence of scalping, skull removal, and the cutting of upper and lower limbs as trophies.[51] In the Cauca valley in northern Colombia, where forty-four chiefdoms fought one neighbour against another, the inhabitants of the raided village would be massacred, head and limbs cut off and mutilated, hearts cut out and eaten on the spot, washed down with the victims' blood. In the modern age, the Jívaro of the upper Amazon basin still engaged in raiding against neighbours who, they claimed, 'speak differently' or 'filled us with evil spirits'. Entire communities were massacred and beheaded; if some women were captured to be brought back, they were commonly beheaded and dismembered by the exultant warriors before they reached their village.[52] To show that these were practices not confined to the long distant past, in the American-Japanese war in the Pacific, American servicemen took trophies, including heads, teeth, ears, and forelimbs. *Time* magazine ran a cover with a girl gazing at the Japanese skull on her desk sent home by her soldier boyfriend. One Japanese bone from a forearm was modelled into a letter opener and sent by an American senator as a gift to President Roosevelt. In this case, too, mutilation was possible because the Japanese were regarded as 'less than human'.[53]

When Norbert Elias published *The Civilizing Process* in 1939, he could hardly have imagined the level of visceral, unrestrained violence released by the war to come, which in the most extreme cases had everything in common with the practices of earlier centuries. The most extreme example was the war Hitler waged against the Jews, when German security personnel and soldiers committed multiple acts of atrocity against defenseless communities defined as a menace to Germany's survival. Social psychologists have expended much effort over the past two decades trying to explain how German genocidal perpetrators could undertake in cold blood the mass murder of the Jews as if they really were waging a war against an opponent defined as a mortal danger to Germany's future. The existence of a powerful in-group identity with the conquering *Volk* and the calculated exclusion of the Jews as an element of decomposition in the healthy body of the Reich framed the eventual Holocaust, but the perpetration of violence depended on subordinate levels of identity and dehumanization in which ideology played a more limited part.

Social psychologists have generally abandoned the idea first prompted by Stanley Milgram's 1963 experiment on obedience to orders that the men doing the killing were automatons, doing what they were told. Instead, the killers (both German and non-German) consolidated themselves into their own small in-groups, dedicated to helping each other, and indifferent to the fate of victims whose humanity was eliminated from their view. In the German Federal Republic in the 1960s, pretrial depositions of some of the policemen who had taken part in the atrocities make it evident that the only moral qualm these individuals could recall was failure to participate and help their comrades, even if they found the genocidal tasks they carried out squalid and demoralizing. Even years after the event, the psychological distance established between perpetrator and victim eliminated any sense of shame or guilt. At the time, the murders were treated as essentially valuable to the future of the *Volk*. In the process of killing, each man was given a particular task and was expected to perform it well: some killers did their job with enthusiasm; for others the murders became, as one psychologist has put it, 'thoughtlessly routine'. Adolf Eichmann, head of the Gestapo office responsible for organizing the Jewish deportations to the killing centres, reflected in his South American exile on the outcome: 'My innermost being refuses to say that we did something wrong.' Eichmann claimed that if he had succeeded in killing all 10 million European Jews, he would have said, 'All right. We have exterminated an enemy.'[54] The Holocaust is an extreme case but one that exemplifies the capacity of social psychology to explain how in-group–out-group psychology can provide a fuller understanding of the perpetration of wartime violence.

Explaining warfare in psychological terms has gone through a variety of stages since the early days of the discipline, when the First World War prompted the search for some explanatory connection. Like the biological discourse on war, psychology cannot be made to explain any particular war. When Edward Glover suggested that infantile aggression had prompted Kaiser Wilhelm II to go to war in 1914, the chair of the British League of Nations Union, the Oxford classicist Gilbert Murray, told Glover that nothing would persuade him that 'unconscious sadism' explained the outbreak of war. Murray's view that 'the psycho-analytical approach is not the most promising' has been borne out by the subsequent history of the discipline.[55] Evolutionary psychology has produced a more convincing understanding of the possible roots of a psychology in which fighting when occasion demanded it came to be regarded as normative because it bestowed survival benefits. As human groups became larger, fighting was a learned adaptation for the defence of territory and resources or for the aggressive pursuit of those belonging to others. This does not amount to saying that humans are psychologically committed to warfare any more than it can be shown to be the case with biology, but the emergence everywhere of a warrior class, a clear gender division of labour, and coalitional forms of conflict must suggest a more universal psychological predisposition for warfare, rather than simply seeing warfare as a product of the cultural values or material ambitions of a particular society.

This capacity to pursue, elevate, and endorse warlike violence has a social psychological explanation in the theory of the in-group, with its powerful centripetal pressure to conform and belong, and the 'enemy' or out-group, which is valued not at all and can as a result become an object of justified aggression. The principle of inclusion and exclusion does not make war inevitable any more than does the Oedipus complex or an evolutionary selection for violence, but it provides a way of understanding how a shared identity can bind a warring society together. Exclusion can permit often extreme levels of violence against the 'other' when it is perceived as a threat to the existence of the group and is driven by shared hatreds and fears. Unlike other psychological approaches, social psychology can be applied both to the conflicts of small tribal communities and to the wars of the past century. In-group virtue and out-group wickedness can be demonstrated in laboratory experiments, but history is replete with examples of how social psychological certainties have justified aggressive warfare, just as they have justified a robust defence. The psychology of the coalitional group, whatever its size, is central to understanding how, under specific circumstances, those coalitions make war.

What none of these theories engage with is the evidence that for warriors in the past – and indeed the present – war was regarded as psychologically rewarding in terms of the honour, esteem, prestige, or glory that accompanied the successful survivor or from the sheer pleasure of fighting. The emotional attachment to fighting and its rewards clearly has a long pedigree, but the idea that men take pleasure in combat for its own sake is not a perspective usually explored in evolutionary or cultural accounts of the causes of war, even though there is plentiful evidence from the past few thousand years that warfare was perceived by many of those who engaged in it as psychologically stimulating and exhilarating, despite its risks. Risk-taking had an evolutionary function and provided a source of psychological satisfaction; when risks paid off, the result enhanced the warrior's status with females and contributed to the community's reputation for successful aggression. The emotional appeal of war might in many cases in the past have played a significant part in the cause of conflict as warrior leaders happily contemplated the next battle, and it is a psychological adaptation that has not disappeared in the modern age. It deserves a fuller treatment in any account of the psychological roots of war.

CHAPTER 3
Anthropology

> Warfare is just an invention known to the majority of
> human societies by which they permit their young men
> either to accumulate prestige or avenge their honor or
> acquire loot or wives or slaves or sago lands or cattle or
> appease the blood lust of their gods or the restless souls of
> the recently dead. It is just an invention, older and more
> widespread than the jury system, but none the less an
> invention.
>
> — Margaret Mead, 1940[1]

The American anthropologist Margaret Mead's claim that
war was just an invention was a rejection of the idea that
warfare was programmed in human beings by either biology or psychology. It was an invention, she claimed, like any
other means by which human lives were ordered: writing,
marriage, trial by jury, cooking food, or burial of the dead.
Her own anthropology made little of war or violence, and she
deplored an invention whose utility was clearly not beneficial. She supposed that mankind would invent a better way
to resolve conflict. Much anthropology, and the closely allied
disciplines of archaeology and ethnography, has until recently tried like Mead to talk about the development of human

societies in terms that broadly exclude or marginalize warfare and violence in favour of the cultural practices and social structures that defined and define the lives of their subjects.

Mead was wrong about war. If very unlucky, marriage or cooking may kill you, but warfare is lethal, destructive, and traumatic on a broad scale. The question that Mead dangled in front of fellow anthropologists nevertheless remains a pertinent one. If war was a cultural invention, when was it invented and for what reasons? Over the answer to this question there rages another debate between those anthropologists and archaeologists who see human societies in prehistory as fundamentally peaceable, with conflict rare and maladaptive until the rise of the state, and those who instead argue that violent conflict resembling warfare among clans, tribes, or chiefdoms long predates the establishment of states, perhaps far into the human past. The argument is not merely an academic squabble. Understanding when human warfare began and from what motives puts centre stage the study of ancestral human society and culture instead of the imperatives of biology or psychology.

The anthropological division rests on some major practical issues in assessing the nature of the evidence available, which remains in many cases frustratingly ambiguous. For almost all human history, from the early hominins onwards, the archaeological record is limited in the extreme, too insubstantial to make any secure claim about the existence or nature of intergroup violence or indeed of a peaceable past. For most of human history until the past 10,000 years, humans were hunter-gatherers or fishers, operating in groups of irregular size and using implements of stone, bone, and wood. Their mode of existence explains why a mobile, foraging species left remarkably few surviving fossil skeletons. Organic implements of wood and bone, whether tools or weapons, have decomposed long ago; stone implements have survived, sometimes in plentiful quantities, but whether they were dual-purpose tools and weapons is irrecoverable information. To define past communities as prehistoric does not mean that these were peoples without history, only that the history they had is unknowable. Archaeological anthropology must do the best it can with what evidence there is. For the rest, as archaeologist Elsa Redmond has put it, there are 'sites unseen' and 'things unfound'.[2]

There are four major types of evidence for conflict from the prehistoric past. The first, and most significant, is skeletal trauma; second is the evidence of iconography, symbolic renditions of violence; third, the evidence for fortified settlements; and finally, the existence of weapons, evidence that often relies on mortuary practice in cases where weaponry was interred with a warrior's body. In each case, there remain uncertainties about how the material evidence should be interpreted. Skeletal trauma – the deliberate damage shown on a skeleton – can be open to wide interpretation. Study of the extant skeletons of Neanderthal man has shown that 55 percent had injuries to head, neck, arm, and shoulder. While this might plausibly suggest a violent people, the injuries, it has been argued, are consistent with the close-range hunting of megafauna ungulates. On this reading of the evidence, Neanderthals seem to have been accident-prone rather than violent.[3] However, recent scientific analysis of fragments of Neanderthal crania and bones from the Krapina rock shelter in Croatia, the largest collection of surviving Neanderthal remains, dated to 130,000 years ago, suggests that the wide number of injuries evident and their skeletal incidence is consistent with interpersonal violence, not accident. Bone damage has also been interpreted as evidence for cannibalism. The debate continues.[4]

Osteoarchaeology in many other contexts is open to the same range of interpretations. A broken skull can be the result of an argument between two people, an accident, or deliberate group violence. Some skeletal trauma comes from animal scavengers or secondary damage during reinterment and must be distinguished from blunt-force or sharp-force injury. The best evidence is projectile points embedded in surviving bones, of which there are a substantial number, although most projectile injuries would have left no sign on the skeleton. Wounds to soft tissue and organs have left no trace. The use of javelins, atlatls (spear throwers), swords, and daggers from at least 5,000 years ago would have reduced the evidence of cranial trauma and damaged bone but not the reality of lethal injury. Research by the US Army in the nineteenth century on the effect of arrow wounds showed that two-thirds left no sign on the bones of the victim, and 61 percent of fatal shots hit the abdomen.[5] As a result, a significant proportion of fatal injuries in the past are now invisible, as are the great majority of skeletal remains of those who perished.

Iconography, fortification, and weaponry are similarly problematic. There is visual evidence in cave drawings of what looks decidedly like a skirmish or a battle between rival groups, but an anthropological explanation might see this as symbolic representation, not proof of real violence, or a hunting scene mistakenly conceived as warfare. Fortifications have now been shown by archaeology worldwide to be a common feature of Neolithic and Bronze Age settlements, but their significance remains contested. These, too, can be viewed as symbolic structures, perhaps protecting a tribe's sacred spaces; in some cases, the fortifications are deemed to be enclosures for livestock; in others, they are expressions of power or distinction for a chief or his clan, intended for display rather than defence; or they are gathering spaces for tribal or chiefly rituals.[6] The absence of arrowheads or skeletons with perimortem injury at fortified sites can be added to the list of caveats about how they should be interpreted. With weaponry, the ambiguity ought to be less marked, but weapons are not necessarily all they seem to be. Bronze Age swords in Europe have been one of the many sources of contention. It has been argued that elaborate and costly swords were symbols of authority for chiefs or kings, a mark of status rather than belligerence. However, careful forensic examination of a wide range of swords by the Danish archaeologist Kristian Kristiansen has shown that they were regularly resharpened because of damage or wear from combat or had missing tips and hilt shoulders, conclusive proof that the swords were wielded on the battlefield, whatever their ceremonial function.[7]

Anthropologists are further divided in interpreting when and why warfare emerged by arguments over what constitutes warfare. Here there are problems of both scale and intention. For those who argue that warfare is a recent invention, made possible only by the development of organized states having the administrative, economic, and social capacity to raise and provision armies – a view with which many historians would agree – the evidence of pre-state violence is defined as vendetta, feuding, ambush, or raiding by groups that might number just a few to musters of perhaps a few hundred. These are what the anthropologist Raymond Kelly calls 'warless societies', which certainly display violence through homicide or bullying or punishment but do not make war.[8] For others, the existence of coalitional conflict between defined groups is warlike whether it is a lethal ambush of rival tribesmen, or the annihilation of an enemy village and the massacre of its inhabitants, or a skirmish between rival warriors intent on killing, or the violent seizure of slaves and sacrificial victims. The example of the massacre illustrates the semantic problem, as numerous massacres have been unearthed in the recent archaeology of prehistoric Europe, China, and the Americas. On one interpretation, massacres must indicate warlike violence against the victim community. On the other hand, massacres can be seen as products of cultural and social processes in which massacre of the enemy 'other' enhances social cohesion and ritual norms, filling the massacre with symbolic meaning distinct from merely waging war.[9]

In truth, more separates the two anthropological approaches to warfare than just debates over evidence and definition. The differences are as much ideological as practical, and they can be traced back to the early days of scientific anthropology well before the Second World War. For example, the early fieldwork of William Perry and Elliot Smith among tribal communities in Africa and the Pacific was used to demonstrate that the behaviour of hunter-gatherer communities gave no ground for assuming any predisposition to aggression; warfare was, wrote Perry in 1924, 'an accidental excrescence' of early civilization that owed its origins to ancient Egypt. The two iconic figures of early anthropology, Ruth Benedict and Margaret Mead, both writing in the 1930s, took a similar approach in playing down any evidence of warfare among the peoples they studied. Writing about the Mountain Arapesh of New Guinea, Mead claimed that 'Warfare is practically unknown' among the men and women, who were 'naturally maternal, gentle, responsive, and unaggressive'.[10] Ruth Benedict's 1934 study of the tribes of the southwestern United States applauded the 'peaceful Pueblos', a judgment that survived on into the 1970s. In 1939, she described the conflicts of 'primitive' peoples as the 'non-lethal species of warfare' in contrast to the modern 'lethal variety' about to break out.[11] Like Mead, the influential Polish anthropologist Bronisław Malinowski, holder of Britain's first chair in anthropology at the London School of Economics, studied tribal society in the Pacific. He concluded in 1929 that aside from some ritualized violence, the Trobriand islanders did not engage in warfare, and he used his findings to support a broader view that warfare was neither a necessary nor a permanent feature of the human condition. 'The anthropological argument is this', he wrote, 'human development about 600,000 years. About 400 [000] of this no war.'[12] For Malinowski, like Benedict, modern war was the problem: it seemed to serve no evolutionary or cultural purpose that an anthropologist could understand.

The view of prehistoric societies as pacific was widely

endorsed and warfare as a social process or cultural reality was marginalized in mainstream anthropology until the 1960s. From then on, and on an increasing scale, warfare and other forms of violence were incorporated more fully into mainstream branches of anthropology, not as a distinct anthropology of violence but as an element in understanding human social and cultural processes past and present. Nevertheless, the notion of a 'pacified past' has survived. Modelled from ritual fights among existing tribes, some anthropologists have argued that pre-state fighting was also ritualized, with noisy battle lines but no real combat, more game than war. Violence among simple peoples, wrote William Newcomb in 1960, is 'crude, sportive, brief, generally unorganized'.[13] Even among more developed societies – republican Rome in the first millennium BCE or the Maya civilization in Central America – the fashion was to cast them as unwarlike. In recent years, two American anthropologists, Brian Ferguson and Douglas Fry, have revived the argument that warfare only arrived with civilization and that 'simple nomadic hunter-gatherers', as Fry put it, 'are non-warring'; that is, for 98 percent of human history. Neither denies the existence of violence, but they see it as limited, relatively nonlethal, and sporadic – not an essential element in past human societies, in which aversion to conspecific killing seems more likely to have been the norm. Ferguson has made much of an alleged 10,000-year period in the Middle East that occurred across the period of transition to farming and which appears from limited archaeological evidence to have been entirely peaceful. He has also developed the theory of the 'tribal zone' to show that only contact with European empires encouraged violence between tribal peoples over access to European prestige goods, or trade routes, or the supply of slaves, shifting the motives for war onto the malign influence of imperialism. The so-called musket wars among the Maori in the nineteenth century and the brutal tribal warfare in the eastern United States from the seventeenth century onwards could be seen as possible test cases. Warfare in these cases and among developed chiefdoms and states was about access to material goods, when, it is argued, there was something worth fighting for.

The presentation of a largely peaceful past has its own agenda, as it had for the eighteenth-century French philosopher Jean Jacques Rousseau, who contrasted the 'noble savage' with the degenerate world of states and unequal classes that followed. In the years from the 1920s to the 1960s, the prevailing view of ancestral communities was evolutionary. Anthropologists chose to contrast a past world with the extreme violence of war, revolution, and civil war all around them. Modern, warring man must have evolved from simpler, more egalitarian, and less violent communities, which had to be understood in their own terms, not as an analogue for the current disordered and violent present. Malinowski's pioneering work in New Guinea during the First World War led him to the conclusion that pre-state societies had to be studied from the inside out to grasp very different value systems, cultural norms, and social practices. For anthropologists, the 'cultural relativism' pursued by Malinowski, Mead, and Benedict was a humanistic endeavour to rescue simple peoples from conventional denigration: they had to be 'gentle and benign', as the anthropologist Keith Otterbein put it, not 'savage and brutal'. In many cases of field research, evidence of warlike violence was ignored, overlooked, or reinterpreted to fit the paradigm of warless communities. Even the famous prehistoric 'Iceman', Ötzi, discovered preserved in an Alpine glacier in 1991, had to wait ten years before it was learned that he had an arrowhead lodged in his back and the blood traces of at least three other humans on his knife blade. That Malinowski, among many others, was a convinced and active pacifist made the view of a peaceful past psychologically appealing. More recently, anthropology has had to avoid accusations that interest in war sustains present-day militarism and that ascribing war to tribal peoples, both contemporary and in the past, sustains a racist, postcolonial, Western view of exotic and barbarous peoples. If the 'peaceful savage' cannot easily be sustained into the twenty-first century, the belief that for most of the human past there has been no war suggests, as Mead had done, that human societies have the potential to embrace a pacified future. It is hoped that the study of peaceful societies (there have not been many) may provide clues as to how that future might be achieved.[14]

The wave of anthropological and archaeological research on present and past warfare among nonstate peoples that has washed over the discipline in the past fifty years now makes it difficult to sustain the image of a 'pacified past'. As early as 1915, the pioneer social scientists Leonard Hobhouse, Morris Ginsberg, and Gerald Wheeler in a study of 'simpler peoples' found that only 4 percent of 298 societies studied were without war.[15] Since the 1950s, ethnographic study of existing tribal societies has combined with detailed forensic archaeology to present a very different anthropological case. Two popular and polemical studies, the first by Law-rence Keeley, *War Before Civilization*, published in 1996, the second by Steven LeBlanc, *Constant Battles: Why We Fight*, published seven years later, have argued that warfare of some kind existed long before states and organized conflict. By then there was already a substantial body of fresh research that incorporated warlike violence into the study of past and present small-scale societies. For apparently peaceable con-temporary communities, it was possible to show that state intervention had restricted or abolished traditional forms of conflict among peoples who had been extremely warlike until the recent past, including Mead's Mountain Arapesh, whose violent behaviour was exposed by her anthropologist ex-husband a few years after she made her original claim.[16] For archaic and classical communities, the integration of the archaeology of violence into interpretation of the social and cultural environment has added in many cases a missing di-mension to the way these societies operated and with what purposes. Indeed, the cultural imperative is now regarded as one of the most significant explanations for why most soci-eties small and large make or have made war, an argument more consistent with Mead's cultural determinism than she would have wished.

One example may show how the study of past intergroup violence, whether defined as warlike or not, is essential to understanding the broader social and cultural milieu that endorsed it. Ruth Benedict's view of the Pueblo culture as essentially calm and peaceful, as indeed it was when she researched the descendants of ancient tribes, has not sur-vived close interrogation, even at the time she was writing.

Osteoarchaeology in the past decades has instead unearthed widespread evidence of past violence, whether ambushes, skirmishes, raids, witch executions, or intergroup aggression, including massacres of whole communities going back at least 2,000 years. In the Anasazi region, thirty-two sites dating before 900 CE have been identified for violence, including Wetherill's Cave in southern Utah, where the skeletons of ninety-two individuals were found, mostly male, that showed evidence of bludgeoning to death, scalping, and decapitation. At the Sacred Ridge site in Colorado, the massacre of a minimum of thirty-three men, women, and children took place about 700 CE; the ritual killing by blunt blows to the head followed torture to feet and ankles, disembowelling, removal of the ears and lips, and scalping, all evident in the skeletal remains. The bodies were dismembered and the bones smashed into small pieces. The detailed attention given to the killing and dismemberment suggests that the massacre was a ritual killing, what is now called 'performative' violence, filled with symbolic meaning for the tribe that carried it out, almost certainly for motives related to the tribe's cosmology (discussed in more detail in chapter 6). A massacre from 1100 CE uncovered at the Mancos site in Colorado demonstrated identical ritual practices, suggesting that the performance of a massacre was understood in the cultural lexicon of the tribes and transmitted from generation to generation.[17] While the massacres do not represent conventional battle, it is difficult not to see them as an expression of warlike conflict. The massacred were evidently not volunteers.

It would be wrong to see the division between the two

approaches to the anthropological and archaeological evidence as polar opposites, as they often appear, 'hawks' versus 'doves' as Otterbein put it. The distinction has become less relevant today. There are areas of convergence, and no anthropologist from either side denies the evidence of warfare once chiefdoms and states became the characteristic form of social organization, even if their behaviour was not universally the same. There is also general acceptance that warlike violence displays great variability and flexibility over time and between cultures. No one would dispute that, where war does occur, it is essential to interpret the cultural meaning and social purposes of warfare for different societies rather than simply list all wars and casualties as if they had the same root. Nor is there any disagreement that humans were and are capable of cooperative and sociable interaction, and indeed that this is what holds human societies together, even in the act of fighting. The principal difference remains the willingness or otherwise to accept that warfare is common, not rare; that it is integral to those societies that wage it, not an aberration; and that it has occurred worldwide in time and space, for which the evidence is now overwhelming.

The issue of when and why warfare emerged as a cultural and social reality can be answered with greater certainty now than was possible fifty years ago, but only for the Holocene and perhaps the last 10,000 years of the Pleistocene; in total, the past 20,000 years. That still leaves the great majority of human existence, and most of the 200,000 years of the existence of *Homo sapiens*, as something of a blank slate. The existing archaeology that hints at possible violence during almost the whole Pleistocene can be listed on a single page of typescript.

The conditions that might make conflict a possibility go back several million years – to the first stone tools worked by early hominins, the use of fire, the shift to eating meat, the development of language, and the use of symbols. Early humans seem almost certainly to have been coalitional foragers; then with the development of hunting tools, the typical human community would be a mobile group of omnivorous hunter-gatherers. The first hand-axes go back to almost 2 million years ago; the first spears have been identified to about 500,000 years ago; the first wooden weapons/tools to about 400,000–300,000 years ago; the first projectile points as early as 200,000 years ago; the first bows and arrows to about 60,000 years ago.[18] But because these were hunting communities, it is possible that these were instruments for the hunt rather than weapons for intraspecies killing. The discovery of intact wooden spears and a lance dating back 300,000 years at a site in Schöningen in Germany reveals a relatively sophisticated level of understanding about the weight, length, and lethality of the artifacts but no conclusion over whether these were dual purpose, for hunting but also, when required, for fighting.[19] Evidence from skeletal remains is slight because very few intact or partial skeletons have been discovered. The first identified stone-tool damage to crania dates from about 600,000 years ago in an Ethiopian human fossil. Eleven disarticulated, cannibalized skeletons discovered at the Gran Dolina site near the Spanish city of Burgos have been dated to approximately 800,000 years ago, but whether this reveals conflict is unverifiable, and its cultural meaning is guesswork.[20] In Europe, only twenty burials have been excavated from the Middle Paleolithic and one hundred from the Upper Paleolithic (approximately 100,000–15,000 BCE). Among the twenty-one injuries identified for the first period, only two appeared to be fatal; among sixteen in the second period, the number was three.[21]

This represents almost all the evidence currently available, and it is open to speculation whether such a slender list suggests that hominins were capable of coalitional violence or not. One way of testing hunter-gatherer propensity for violence between groups is to work by analogy using evidence from hunter-gatherers in the modern world, though this is far from problem-free given the modern social and cultural environment that surrounds them. There are many examples of symbolic thought and cultural practices establishing important parameters for the conduct of intergroup violence. The Jívaro of the upper Amazon basin have until recently raided regularly against enemies who filled their land with evil spirits; a leader is found, usually a renowned warrior (*kakáram*), who calls the warriors to a celebration house where they consume manioc beer together with the hallucinogenic *natéma* and summon up ancestors to predict whether the raid will succeed. Black paint is worn for camouflage and courage. After a raid, and the careful decapitation of the corpses, victory feasts are held. The successful warriors are said to have a new power granted to them from their ancestors; those who have killed the most can become *ti kakáram*, the most powerful warrior.[22] Among the hunter-gatherers of Australia, violence was a regular occurrence and it took many forms. There was ritual battle, in which perhaps only one person might be killed or wounded, but there was also revenge killing, or ambush or a lethal raid leading to the massacre of a whole group. Ritualized warfare and real, lethal violence were not incompatible among pre-state cultures. With intentional violence to outsiders, symbolic ritual played an important part, from pre-raid painting of the body, the use of special 'Death Spears' for war not for hunting, and the extraction of the kidney fat of slaughtered enemies for its magical properties. A major motive for intertribal violence was violation of the sacred 'Dreamtime' sites of a tribe, allocated by spirit ancestors at the start of time.[23]

There are obvious caveats about reading back from the behaviour of hunter-gatherers in the recent past to the Paleolithic, but it is at least plausible to suggest that human groups behaved in ways not entirely dissimilar. Among modern hunter-gatherers, 61 percent engage in war, and 27 percent fight continually and often.[24] Among archaic hunter-gatherers, warlike violence was no doubt neither universal nor continual, as the statistics for their modern descendants suggest. But it must surely have occurred, even if the motives and cultures that prompted it have vanished. To argue that absence of evidence means evidence of absence when it comes to speculating about the level of coalitional violence is unconvincing, at least in the many millennia of *Homo sapiens'* existence. It seems inherently unlikely that the regular violence evident in the Mesolithic and Neolithic from about 10,000 years ago, for which there is much more plentiful evidence, began from a standing start rather than drawing on a lineage of violent practices and behaviour among late Paleolithic humans and the clans, villages, and tribes in which they were organized.

On the existence of warlike violence in the Neolithic and beyond, from at least 10,000 years ago, there is little room for argument, though few scholars would go as far as the French anthropologist Pierre Clastres, who claimed in the 1970s that 'primitive society could not subsist without war . . . primitive society is a *society for war*, it is in its essence warlike.'[25] The changeover to horticulture and settled communities, then to more broad-based agriculture and larger polities, well before the establishment of civilizations, states, and cities, is integrated with the evidence of warlike conflict, some of it generated by the new frontiers between sedentary societies and the large range of surviving hunter-gatherers. This evidence is closely associated with the transition to defined political structures, whether egalitarian tribes or chiefdoms in which a warring culture developed. The evolution of these societies was not a linear one, and their development and timing varied from region to region, but in every part of the world where the archaeology has been undertaken, tribal and chiefly warfare has been identified: in Europe and Eurasia, the Middle East, China and Japan, Polynesia and Australia, the Americas, and in all cases well before contact with European colonizers. It has even proved to be the case for Brian Ferguson's 10,000 years of Near East peace, where the evidence, though still scarce, suggests some level of small-scale conflict or ritual violence throughout the Neolithic with evidence of cranial injury, parry fractures, and decapitation.[26] The one exception is the archaeology of sub-Saharan Africa, where humans originated; there are still too few clues

to the way African societies developed in the African equivalent of the Neolithic to be able to identify warring cultures.
It is widely agreed that tribal and chiefly societies were the
transmission belt between the archaic past and the development of larger state polities or federations (indeed that is
why many anthropologists have chosen to work among contemporary tribal societies). Where enough of the past can be
reconstructed, warfare appears to have been endemic among
communities whose militarization rendered them unstable
or ephemeral, characterized by brief, insecure alliances and
an absence of trust. Persistent warfare at the social level of
the tribe or chiefdom opened the way to the emergence of
states and warfare as an institution in Europe, Asia, and the
Americas.

At this point, the cultures that sustained warfare in the
age of tribes and chiefdoms can be understood more readily
by returning to the wealth of archaeological material on fortification, weaponry, iconography, and skeletal trauma that
provide the material fabric for reconstructing past conflict.
Putting the archaeology into social context then makes it
possible to understand not only why warfare seems to have
been so embedded in small-scale societies but also what purposes it was supposed to serve. Fortified settlements associated with the transition to settled horticulture or farming
can be found in Europe from about 5500 BCE. Here as elsewhere there was great variability in the timing and nature of
fortification: it was more common in areas where there was
a frontier between farmers and hunter-gatherers or where
there exists evidence of large-scale migrations that placed
pressure on existing settlements. In many cases, natural

protection was exploited by situating settlements on prom-
ontories, hillsides, or outcrops of rock or on sites protected
by river and marsh on two or three sides. The natural protection could then be supplemented by construction of palisades, baffle gates, bastions, and causeways, all of which
feature widely in the archaeological record.[27] In between settled areas there were sometimes buffer zones, without settlements, a no-man's land to offer some protection by distance.

As population in Europe expanded and competition for
resources and land increased, fortification became more
common and the need for defence more pressing. At the
Spanish site of Los Millares in Almería in the third millennium BCE, elaborate defences were constructed: built on a
promontory and defended on three sides by steep escarp-
ments, the site had three lines of walls, bastions, and towers
protected by a ditch, with small forts built at a distance to
guard the approach. The elaborate level of protection made
no sense except for use as a defence against some perceived
threat.[28] Here as elsewhere, evidence that portions of the
defences had been burned down suggests violence; where
fortifications remained intact, it was a testament to their effi-
cacy. In cases where multiple arrowheads have been found or
where bodies were heaped unceremoniously in a surrounding ditch, siege and battle seems the most convincing explanation. At the British site of Carn Brae in Cornwall, protected
by a ditch, a stone rampart, six complex gateways, and an
inner wall two metres high, excavation revealed 800 flint arrowheads and destruction by fire, clear evidence of conflict.[29]
At another British site – the fortified site at Danebury of the
first millennium BCE, which had a ditch and a rampart that

was a remarkable sixteen metres high – occupation ended when one of the gated entrances was burned down, and the bodies of almost one hundred men, women, and children were thrown into pits by the raiders.[30] In central and eastern Europe, ditches, ramparts, and palisades are common features. Along the fault line between the Neolithic *Linearbandkeramik* and Mesolithic foragers, defensive fortification seems to have been common, as evidenced by large ditches some 2.8 metres wide and 1.6 metres deep, some with palisades and complex entry gates. The site at Zāmaček in Slovakia had a remarkable ditch 4.5 metres deep and 10 metres wide. One defended Neolithic settlement at Dölauer Heide in western Germany had no fewer than six ditches in front of a wooden fence, again a level of commitment by the community that made sense only in defensive terms.[31] Although some defended sites seem not to have been inhabited, they were possibly refuges for local farmers if conflict threatened or protection for a sacred or ritual site from outsiders, once again a response to threat.

Beyond Europe, fortification coincided again with the transition to settlement and increasing population density. In China, fortification appeared around 4000 BCE as farmers and hunter-gatherers clashed. By the third millennium BCE, villages were surrounded by stone walls or stamped-earth defences as warfare became more widespread. In the Ural steppe, fortified settlements appear at the same time and possess walls and towers, deep V-shaped ditches, and embankments to protect concentrated communities.[32] Fortification occurred later in the Americas as population density increased and settled horticultural communities were established, although the earliest evidence of defensive construction has been dated as far back as 4000 BCE. The evidence is widespread by the end of the first millennium CE. Conflict between hunter-gatherers and farmers or between rival farming tribes encouraged the development of fortified sites from the tenth century onwards across the central United States – first simple palisades, and ditches, then firmer defences with walls, bastions, and lookout towers. The cluster of villages that combined into the chiefly centre of Cahokia, near present-day St Louis, was defended by a three-kilometre barrier made of heavy logs.[33] In the Mississippi and Tennessee valleys, warfare between rival chiefdoms and tribes became endemic for 600 years beginning about 900 CE. The thirteenth-century Etowah chiefdom in Alabama had fortified spaces with buffer zones against hostile groups; the central site had a giant palisade 3.7 metres high and a vast ditch 9.5 metres wide. Even this proved insufficient. The palisade was burned down and the settlement abandoned by the fifteenth century.[34] The archaeology of North American fortification shows that the building of defences fluctuated with the degree of threat or the dispersal of populations, but defence when it was needed meant fortification.

By comparison with the millennia of the Paleolithic and the Mesolithic, the evidence for skeletal trauma is widespread for the Neolithic (and later for the Copper and Bronze Ages) and more obviously related to fighting of some kind. The injuries sustained from combat are chiefly blunt or sharp blows to the head, parry fractures to the arm in warding off blows, and projectile points embedded in bone or associated with the skeleton. Some of the injuries were not lethal, and nonlethal injuries sometimes represent the majority of injuries among a group of skeletons. While this might suggest ritualized combat, healed injuries can simply indicate survival from a skirmish or battle, as in modern war, when more are generally wounded than killed. Disarticulation, decapitation, scalping, and trophy taking are widely present, the outcome of violent conflict or raiding for captives and sacrificial victims. Much emphasis for the origin of warfare has been laid on the discovery of massacres, which have attracted perhaps a disproportionate amount of attention because of their spectacular nature. Though they may represent in anthropological terms, as already observed, forms of ritual killing, they may also be the gruesome conclusion of intertribal competition for resources or a savage vengeance for motives now unknown. They certainly reflect a sudden eruption of violent conflict between killers and victims. The Neolithic site at Herxheim in Germany from about 5000 BCE is one of the best known, with 173 skulls and skull parts, and the disarticulated and probably cannibalized remains of 334 men, women, and children, seized to fulfill some cultic purpose from areas a long way from the ceremonial centre. At the site of Asparn/Schletz, near Vienna, the skeletons of sixty-six people found in a ditch (there are probably well over one hundred) were almost all killed by axes; at Talheim in the Rhine valley, about 5700 BCE, sixteen children and infants, nine men, and seven women were killed with axes, clubs, and arrows in a raid on a small settlement.[35] In the Americas, massacres occur in the archaeological record from north to south. At a site on Paracas Bay, on the coast of Peru, a pile of fifty-six disarticulated adult bodies were thrown into an ossuary some 7,000 years ago in an early example of Paleoamerican violence.[36]

More significant than massacres for the evidence of combat as an ever-present reality for tribes and chiefdoms is the detail of regular if small-scale skeletal trauma inflicted by weapons of stone, bone, and finally early metals. Embedded projectile points and cranial injury are the key indicators, and if not abundant, there are enough to indicate that war-like violence was neither limited nor random. Among Paleo-american skeletons from 8000 to 7000 BCE, 58 percent met a violent death. In the Mississippi valley area, violence dates to at least 6,800 years ago; embedded projectile points, skel-etal trauma, and trophy taking are all evident from the fourth millennium onwards. The violence continued into the first millennium CE. In the Late Woodland culture (500–1000 CE), one-quarter of skeletons show parry fractures and em-bedded projectile points; trophy taking included heads and hands.[37] In coastal British Columbia, for the tribal period between 3500 and 1500 BCE, 21 percent of fifty-seven skele-tons showed trauma effects, but along the coastal north from 1500 BCE to 500 CE, one-third of excavated skeletons had damage from violence.[38]

In Neolithic, Bronze Age, and Iron Age Europe, embed-ded points and cranial trauma indicate violence across the continent, although there has been less systematic effort to catalogue skeletal damage. A survey of the Spanish late Neolithic showed that forty skeletons from thirteen differ-ent sites revealed death from projectile weapons, while some also displayed healed fractures from earlier violence. Recent excavation of a Spanish Iron Age village at La Hoya has revealed a violent raid by a neighbouring tribe that burned the village down and murdered the villagers in the street as they tried to flee; the thirteen skeletons so far excavated include one decapitation and two amputated arms.[39] Research at the Neolithic settlement of Jelšovce in Slovakia found 27 percent of the skeletons had injuries to the cranium, most of them resulting in death.[40] Among the Neolithic funerary pits at Bergheim in France from about 6,000 years ago, one was found that contained disarticulated skeletons, arms, and hands, piled together at the same time, almost certainly victims of armed violence rather than funeral rites.[41] The list is a long one, but it points to a clear conclusion that violence on various scales, between or within tribal communities, in circumstances that can now only be surmised, was a regular feature of the thousands of years before the evolution of larger proto-state or state entities.

The evolution of weaponry available to tribal and chiefly communities shows steady development from stone, wood, or bone implements that could double as weapons or tools to a dedicated arsenal of specialized instruments that were designed chiefly for combat. The early weaponry was divided between long-range projectiles, whether javelin, spear, atlatl, or the bow and arrow, and close-combat weapons for clubbing an opponent to death, such as the stone axe, a modified antler, or a mace fashioned from hardwood. The bow and arrow, first developed in Africa perhaps as long ago as 80,000 BCE, was of singular significance worldwide when it spread into Eurasia and into the Americas many thousands of years later. It could be used for hunting game or killing humans, and flint points were in some cases modified to distinguish between the two; points with barbs or a triangular leaf shape were designed to break off in the wound and cause death. Most bows have disappeared with time, but those that survive show a relatively sophisticated understanding of how to maximize their impact by choosing the right wood (yew or elm were preferred in Europe) or by creating composite bows of horn, wood, and sinew, a model that became the hallmark of the horse archers of the Eurasian steppes. The bow and arrow took time to cross the Americas from its first arrival in the Arctic north from northeastern Asia at some point after 9000 BCE. The technology remained in the far north until the second half of the first millennium CE, when the bow and arrow spread across North America, replacing the spear-thrower used in hunting. The archaeological evidence suggests that the new weapon was used in warfare to the advantage of the tribes that exploited it.[42]

The development of metal technology from the third millennium BCE in Europe and Asia made it possible to develop close-combat weapons of increased lethality. Daggers, swords, halberds, rapiers, metal arrowheads, thrusting spears, and metal lances populate the burial grounds of Copper Age and Bronze Age Europe; helmets, body armour, and shields made of wood, leather, heavy fabric, or metal developed side-by-side with the new weaponry. In north-central Asia, metalworking produced heavy spears and javelins and the first war chariots, large enough to carry a driver and javelin thrower. Farther south in China, jade and bronze weapons, bronze helmets, leather armor, and war chariots were widespread by the second millennium BCE. Across the Mediterranean and into Eurasia there developed the early equivalent of the arms trade as specialized manufactories appeared for everything from flint points, daggers, and axes to bronze swords and knives. Access to the trade or the ores and stone that made production possible became a motive for early warfare. Even where metalwork did not develop, the range of weapons could be elaborated to cope with increased warfare. When the Spaniards landed on the Yucatán Peninsula in 1519, they were met by a Maya array armed with slings, spears, bows and arrows, fire-hardened darts, and two-handed wooden swords edged with obsidian. First contact in New Zealand/Aotearoa found the Maori armed with elaborate and deadly warclubs made of whalebone, wood, or stone. South American tribes were armed with slings, spears, bows and arrows, poison darts, axes, and maces long before contact with Europe.[43] These were all tribal or chiefly societies where warfare was already embedded. It was not invented only to oppose the new colonizers.

The question of who wielded the new weaponry raises more difficult issues in identifying what kind of social structure or hierarchies might have operated in early tribal and chiefly societies. Some tribes were no doubt egalitarian, as some modern tribal communities, in which all the adult males might take part in raids or revenge attacks, but in others there may well have evolved early hierarchies in which a warrior elite emerged among the most daring or resourceful of the men. The evidence from graves of the period in Europe and Asia suggests that, over time, some males were interred with their weapons as a mark of respect for their social and martial status. In an early example, dating from the fourth millennium BCE on the Danish peninsula of Jutland, warriors were buried with arrowheads, hatchets, flint daggers, and an occasional halberd (traded from a source in Italy).[44] In northern and eastern Europe, graves from the late Neolithic containing weaponry, and presumably a warrior's skeleton, make up 37 percent of those excavated.[45] Late Neolithic and Bronze Age burial sites regularly show the apparatus of warfare interred with the warrior who bore it. In the so-called Single Grave culture from the mid-third millennium BCE, warriors have been easily identified for a thousand-year period by the axes, daggers, wrist guards, and arrow points buried with them.[46] The iconography of the period also begins to show more clearly the status and image of the warrior. There are numerous examples across the world: the 500 bronze statuettes found in Sardinia dating from the early first millennium BCE bearing daggers, helmets, bows and arrows, and armour, or the South American goldwork illustrating warriors with clubs, lances, atlatls, and trophy heads, or the Andean monolithic sculptures of warriors with weapons and disarticulated enemy corpses dating from around 900 BCE. In Australia's Arnhem Land, rock drawings of warlike violence date back to about 10,000 years ago, with matchstick figures pierced by spears and dodging boomerangs; by 6,000 years ago, there are scenes of what appear to be real battles, in one case with sixty-eight drawn figures with weapons. Although critics suggest that the images are metaphors whose meaning cannot now be understood, the tribes of Arnhem Land in the modern age did engage in regular lethal conflict that replicated the patterns on the rock.[47]

Exactly when and how a warrior class emerged clearly varied from culture to culture, but it was a common experience except in those cases where the norm was for all males to participate, as it was among the tribal communities of the Americas or many of the warring societies of Scandinavia and Eurasia. Even here, some warriors distinguished themselves in combat, killing more of the enemy perhaps or assuming regularly the role of chosen leader for a raid or ambush. These were the men whose military prowess perhaps opened the way to becoming a tribal chieftain. Anthropology of modern tribal communities has many examples like the Jívaro men who strive to become a *kakáram* or the Yanomami of Venezuela constantly at war because men want a reputation to be fierce (*waiteri*) or to be a distinctive killer (*unokai*).[48] Warfare in Polynesia was designed to allow the warrior (*toa*) to kill the enemy and consume his power, or *mana*, and make the warrior stronger. It is not difficult to imagine that similar symbolic worlds operated with tribal and chiefly communities over the past thousands of years to give the warrior an exalted role and to legitimize the conduct of warfare against enemies, imagined or real.

The archaeological and anthropological building blocks for understanding the evolution of warfare are now more nearly in place than they were a generation ago. The problem is to use these blocks to build an image of the warring cultures that they represent. If warfare is to be understood as something driven by cultural evolution, as many anthropologists now argue, it is still necessary to show how this process worked over time. The anthropology of tribal and chiefly societies in the modern age, including a wide range of cultures, is a starting point, even if a small minority are not typically warring. These cultures can endure over a long time – the values, norms, beliefs, meanings, expectations, and cosmologies transmitted generation by generation in what the anthropologist Clayton Robarchek has called 'culturally constructed experience'.[49] Evidence for cultural adaptation for warfare suggests that violence is not only advantageous in material terms (seizing goods, food, captives, wives) but also embedded in social practices that privilege warfare, such as initiation rites for young men, revenge for accusations of sorcery or witchcraft, or the insatiable demand of local deities for captives to sacrifice or mutilate.

The chiefly warfare of the Cauca River valley in northern Colombia, recorded by the Spaniards when they arrived in the sixteenth century, gives some sense of how violence is perpetuated and performed in the context of a specific culture. Warfare was prepared at village councils during which blood sacrifices were offered to summon a fierce feline figure to support the warriors. Weapons and provisions were stored in advance. Their own settlement was commonly protected by palisades, towers, and ramparts, because warfare was an endemic threat. Before the raid, warriors feasted and painted their bodies before departing for an attack at dawn, announced by drums, conch-shell trumpets, and instruments made of human bone. The inhabitants of the raided settlement were massacred and dismembered for eating, while a few captives were taken back to the chief's compound for use as slaves or sacrifices. In one war waged by the Carrapa and Picara against the chiefdom of Pozo, 300 victims were sacrificed and 200 loads of flesh sent back to be consumed by the victors. Trophy heads, limbs, and stuffed skins were hung by the chief's enclosure to reinforce the ranking of the community's warriors. The ritual cannibalism that followed victory was supposed to increase the power of those warriors who took part. In this case, the warring cultures reflected practices that had a long pedigree. Modern trophy heads were often cut with the first three spinal vertebrae attached, but an example of a similar skull and vertebrae was discovered at the Asia District archaeological site in Peru dating back to 1400 BCE.[50]

Similar embedded violence existed in the tribal cultures of North America. Among the Yukpa people, warfare was a means of respecting the existing social order and had been practiced for generations. The young men were all expected to take part. Initiation involved eating live wasps to test them. 'I am a man. I am brave', they chanted, 'and I will fight.' Apache cosmology suggested a world of strangers and danger outside the tribe. The Monster Slayer kept enemies away and gave the young warriors of the tribe strength and cunning when engaged in fighting. The need for warfare was culturally determined, and it required strict rules of preparation and conduct in which all males from the tribe participated.[51] Indeed, in many known cases the rituals were essential to prepare men to accept the killing of other humans, whether dancing, drinking, the use of hallucinogenic drugs, or the summoning of ancestral spirits. War in this sense appears as a phenomenon programmed into the culture, a product of domestic social organization as much as a response to external circumstances.

It is possible to apply this cultural anthropology to the evidence from more ancient cultures, even if the function and meaning of warfare is still open to interpretation. The head trophies at Herxheim suggest comparison with the headhunters of the Cauca valley; the early iconography that displays trophy taking, dismemberment, and sacrifice records practices that lasted for thousands of years. There are glimpses of this kind of 'performative' violence in the archaeology of Iron Age Britain in the first millennium BCE, which shows regular raiding, desecration of hill forts, and ritual deaths. Captives and slaves were taken for sacrifice or sale. Iron fetters and neck chains have been found to indicate captive labour or victims for ritual killing; skeletal evidence shows ritualized sacrificial violence and disarticulation of adults and children. The practice of head-hunting may have been carried out to promote the prosperity of the village and the prestige and reputation of the hunters, as anthropology has argued for the headhunters of the recent past.[52]

The record is fuller with the gradual transition from tribal societies and chiefdoms to larger polities that regularly made war just as their tribal and chiefly predecessors had done. Indeed, the evolution of warring cultures is closely tied to the emergence of larger social and political structures that elided the practices, meaning, and conduct of tribal and chiefly warfare with their own. By this stage, warfare was already an irreversible element in the organization and conduct of human societies and has remained so ever since. Two examples demonstrate the way warring cultures were articulated and then transmitted over time, and both are examples that were originally believed to demonstrate the opposite. The first is early Rome from its tribal origins; the second is the Maya culture of Central America in the first millennium CE. During the period from approximately 600 to 300 BCE, Rome moved from a loose tribal federation to an urban-centred proto-state. Earlier interpretation of Rome as reluctantly drawn into war in the first centuries of Roman expansion has been overturned in favour of seeing Rome as a highly militarized society. Indeed, the well-known myth of Rome's foundation was based on war: Romulus and Remus, the twin sons of Mars, the god of war, were supposed to have formed a raiding party to found the city. The foundation myth became linked to the concept of warrior heroism, which became a permanent motif in a culture dedicated to waging war.[53]

The myth served its own cultural purpose. In truth, Rome emerged when a number of tribal villages came together astride the Tiber and key trading routes to create a larger urban aggregate at some point between the eighth and sixth centuries BCE. The tribal federation engaged in raiding and cattle rustling against neighbouring clans. Raiding bands were commanded by distinguished warriors representing the twenty tribal clans from the countryside and the town, led by a tribal warlord or 'king'. Much early warfare was confined to the area immediately around the tribal centre; even as late as the fourth century BCE, the city of Veii captured in 396 BCE (immortalized in Shakespeare's *Coriolanus*) was only fifteen kilometres from Rome.[54] The wars were sustained by a citizen militia in which all men were expected to serve – indeed the Latin word *populus* originally meant 'army' rather than 'people'. The later emergence of the office of consul was closely linked to warfare, as consuls were expected to make war regularly and to lead the Roman armies in person. The office of quaestor was established to ensure that the spoils of warfare were distributed fairly among those who fought. This was a culture dominated by military values.[55]

Warfare involved complex rituals to confer success; before combat, divine approval was sought by the *fetiales*, priests who stood at the enemy frontier to throw spears onto enemy soil as a challenge. At the end and beginning of each campaigning season, elaborate ceremonies to the god Mars were conducted. The doors of the Temple of Janus in the centre of Rome were by custom closed only when Rome was not at war. Ancient authors confirm that they were closed only once in a pause at the end of the First Punic War in the mid-third century BCE. A century and a half later, there was a gap of twelve years without war, which prompted the Senate to declare war on the Dalmatians because, in the words of the Greek historian Polybius, 'They did not want the men of Italy to become weak and womanly in any way because of a long period of peace.'[56] The goddess of peace, Pax, was little respected when she entered the Roman pantheon late in the republican period; war was celebrated much more, exemplified in the regular triumphs granted to particularly successful commanders when captives and booty were paraded through the city, on an average, so it has been calculated, once every one-and-a-half years.[57] Defeats, which were rarer, were routinely blamed on the failure to observe the auguries or to conduct the prewar rituals scrupulously enough. Warfare was built into Roman culture, from its tribal beginnings to the onset of imperial expansion in the third century BCE.

The second example of a culture in which warfare was once thought to be largely absent can be found in the Maya societies of the Yucatán Peninsula (which includes parts of present-day Mexico, Belize, and Guatemala). Echoing Margaret Mead, Thomas Gann and Eric Thompson claimed in a

1937 account that 'the Maya . . . were one of the least warlike nations who ever existed.'[58] This view has been overturned by archaeological evidence discovered in the past five decades, which has transformed not only understanding about the scale and regularity of different forms of Maya warfare but also the place that warfare enjoyed in Maya society and culture. As in the Roman example, Maya warfare expanded with the transition from local tribal chiefdoms, characteristic of the Pre-Classic period before 250 CE, into the small, urban-centred polities that marked the Classic and Late Classic periods of the next eight hundred years. The Maya towns fought against each other, often over relatively modest distances, in some cases perhaps to protect or capture trade routes (particularly access to salt and the minerals obsidian and chert used for weapons), but more certainly to secure captives for sacrifice, to exact tribute, or to enlarge the power of local warrior-lords. Conflicts in some regions can be dated back with less certainty to the first millennium BCE from evidence of fortification, weaponry, and iconography, but the nature of conflict and the culture surrounding it is better understood for the Classic centuries from approximately 250 to 1000 CE, for which there are hieroglyphic records whose complex meaning is finally being deciphered.[59] During the first millennium CE, warfare seems to have been an integral part of Maya experience across the Yucatán, endorsed by a range of warring cultures whose existence is no longer in doubt, even if the scope and meaning of the violence is still open to interpretation.

Maya warfare was sustained by a warrior elite, including the lord/king and the scribes and artists who populated his court. The lords were served by a military caste, the *nacoms*, from among whom war leaders could be elected, and a core military force, the *holcans*, for battle. Images of lords on murals and stellae show them in elaborate military costume, bearing weapons, sometimes with bound captives or their decapitated and mutilated corpses. Iconography, particularly the murals discovered at Bonampak, are a rich source for all the stages of conflict: battle between rival groups, capture of prisoners, procession with priests leading victims for sacrifice, and the ritual execution of the victims.[60] The discovery of further mural evidence has demonstrated the extent to which warfare was embedded in the public narratives of the Maya centres. In the hilly Puuk region of northwestern Yucatán, once thought to have been less warlike than the lowlands to north and south, similar murals show warrior-lords accompanied by warriors with plain and decorated spears, shields, and banners. The close attention to elaborate costume and dedicated weaponry indicates societies in which military display and performance, as well as a military 'economy', were central elements.[61] In the hieroglyphic texts and carvings, glyphs have now been identified that denote conflict and its aftermath, and they appear regularly. The axe, *ch'ak*, symbolized victory; it appears in verb forms, *ch'akah* ('to axe or decapitate') and the more elaborate *ch'akah kun*, thought to signal the destruction of a rival seat of power. One list of war events uses glyphs for chop, fall, or capture, listing 107 events in twenty-eight centres from the sixth to the ninth centuries CE.[62]

In these communities, warfare was closely related to supernatural practices and beliefs, which had to be observed even if the principal motive for conflict was material gain. Lords were closely identified with deities, adopting their names and personifying them in religiously sanctioned rituals. Before a raid or battle, oracles were consulted to seek divine guidance and support, often sited in or near caves. The oracle *Hobol* ('hollow belly') had a cavity for sacrificial victims; another called *Ah Hulneb* ('archer') was represented with an arrow painted across the image. Banners and images of supernatural figures were carried into battle to be consulted as the conflict unfolded.[63] One object of warfare was to capture and destroy the sacred places of the enemy while protecting the sacred places and spiritual forces of the attacker. Loss of the sacred space signalled the collapse of community; a victorious army ritually desecrated the enemy city and performed rites of termination to deny the enemy any spiritual power. Termination was commonly used when a new building or temple was to replace an old one, but in warfare termination was grimly literal. In a concealed tomb in the northern Maya town of Yaxuná, dating from about 400 CE, archaeologists discovered the murdered bodies of eleven men, women, and children, including the local lord, all decapitated. The tomb contained an image of the Great Goddess of Aztec cosmology and an image of a warrior dressed for the Thaloc-Venus war cult, deliberately left to mark the demise of the conquered dynasty of Yaxuná and the probable triumph of the nearby city of Oxkintok, ally of the Aztecs.[64] At the town of Colha, a centre of chert production of tools and weapons, a sudden attack in the eighth century CE resulted in the ritual termination of the elite and the destruction of the buildings. A pit containing thirty skulls of decapitated men, women, and children, their faces flayed, revealed the role of ritual following victory or defeat. A second pit found more skeletons ritually desecrated, mutilated, and broken up. The city was not reoccupied.[65]

In both these cases, Rome and the Maya, society revolved around the prospect or practice of violence in the name of gods. Ritual endorsing warfare and the warriors who fought it was built into the longer-term evolution of the community, passed on to generations for whom warfare was an essential part of the cultural lexicon. It is here at the point where cultures of war became embedded in the social reality and prevailing cosmology of tribal, chiefly, and proto-state polities that anthropology has something to demonstrate about the origin and evolution of war. Once the genie was out of the bottle, it proved impossible to force it back in. Perhaps that explains why anthropology has had less to say about the historic warfare of the past 2,000 years, in contrast to the close attention paid to the ethnography of contemporary small-scale societies and the growing anthropological interest in explaining how similar societies in the past did or did not make something recognizable as a form of warfare. Where modern anthropology addresses modern warfare, it is more often to understand the anthropological effects on the victims of war than to reflect on why modern humans have continued to fight and kill on an ever greater scale.

Does culture cause war? Any more than genes or the workings of the mind? Mead's view of war as an invention that might one day be uninvented still acknowledged that the prevailing culture was shaped very much by war: 'Warfare is here, as part of our thought; the deeds of warriors are immortalized in the words of our poets, the toys of our children are modelled upon the weapons of the soldier, the frame of reference within which our statesmen and diplomats work always contains war.'[66] The many examples from the present and the past worked on by anthropologists today focus on the way culture shapes the beliefs, expectations, and practices that make warfare possible, desirable, or in some cases more or less inevitable in societies rooted in warfare. The archaeological evidence for warfare deep into the past cannot any longer be gainsaid. There is some argument that culture works like nature: successful warlike cultures secure the survival of the community at the expense of less warlike or capable competitors. This idea of cultural Darwinism is deterministic in much the same way as the theory of natural selection, and it is open to the obvious criticism that many cultures with an apparent selection for aggression fail to survive at all. Cultures are created by the people who live in them, and there is ample evidence now that a persistent strand in human cultural development over the past 10,000 years, whether through imitation or diffusion, has been a preference for some form of warfare – whether raid, or feud, or open battle, or in many cases all three – that shapes and is shaped by the prevailing culture. Cultural variability dictates how warfare might be regarded in different times and contexts, while material or immaterial motives for war are still necessary for warfare to happen. But cultures of war are universal, which suggests that biology and psychology might still have something to contribute alongside culture in explaining a phenomenon that is more than just another invention.

CHAPTER 4
Ecology

> Climate change acts as a threat multiplier for instability in
> some of the most volatile regions of the world . . . Unlike
> most conventional security threats that involve a single
> entity acting in specific ways and points in time, climate
> change has the potential to result in multiple chronic
> conditions, occurring globally within the same time
> frame . . . Projected climate change will add to tensions
> even in stable regions of the world.
> — Center for Naval Analyses Report, 2007[1]

The possibility that ecological disaster might lead to conflict,
either within or between states, has become a twenty-first-
century obsession. In 2007, eleven retired US generals and
admirals issued a document on climate change and security
to alert the Pentagon to the implications of instability and
possible conflict prompted by rapid changes in environmental conditions. They recommended that the US government
begin immediately to integrate the consequences of climate
change into 'national security and national defence strategies'. Think tanks and security organizations worldwide
have placed climate change and its political consequences at
the centre of current concerns about the future of conflict.[2]

Yet these anxieties beg the question whether there is a substantial link between ecology and warfare over thousands of years of climate shocks and environmental crises.

The science of ecology is of recent origin (the term 'oecology' was coined in the 1860s by the German scientist Ernst Haeckel), but the idea that a direct and potentially dangerous relationship could be observed between human beings and their environment was most famously argued earlier by the English clergyman Thomas Malthus. His *Essay on the Principle of Population*, published in 1798 and in print ever since, suggested that when the human population outgrew the capacity of the land to support it, a combination of famine, pestilence, and warfare would adjust it back to a level the environment could once more sustain and would always do so through cyclical pressure on subsistence. There was a harsh reality in his view: 'the commission of war is vice, and the effect of it misery, and none can doubt the misery of want of food.' But war was one of the mechanisms that ultimately benefited mankind by reasserting an equilibrium between human populations and the environment they inhabited. Among barbarian peoples, Malthus argued, the victors would become 'great and powerful . . . delighting in war', just as the losers would perish through hardship and famine.[3] War as one of Malthus's three checks on human population growth operated not for its own sake but as an external agent that would help to mitigate an ecological crisis.

Malthus wrote long before it was possible to assess with greater precision whether population growth always outstripped the expansion of food production, and with what consequences. For the future science of ecology, this was a biological issue: every ecosystem depended on establishing an equilibrium for the plant and animal species that inhabited it. The interdependence of these natural elements could be disrupted by environmental shocks, long-term environmental change, or the invasion of exogenous species. Where populations of plants or animals exceeded what the ecosystem could support, natural adaptation would establish a new equilibrium, an argument consistent with Darwin's biological thinking. One solution was to find more 'room' for a species to survive in by changing the size of the ecological niche. The most famous expression of this idea of a larger species territory came from the German zoologist Friedrich Ratzel, who in the 1890s coined the term *Lebensraum* – 'living space' – to describe it.

Ratzel argued that each species in order to survive needed to balance its living space with the size of its population. If this provoked competition for resources, the result was what he called a *Kampf um Raum* (a 'struggle for space'). Ratzel considered the struggle for space, not the Darwinian struggle for existence, to be the critical factor in nature, the struggle for existence being derived from the search for greater space. Each and every species either expanded its space, or ecological niche, or faced natural decline. Although he wrote chiefly about plants and animals, as modern ecologists still do, Ratzel's argument was easily adapted to the human species. In *Der Lebensraum*, published in 1901, he applied his ecological theory to the behaviour of humans as they competed for space: 'In the struggle for existence, space must be given an equal significance in those decisive high points in the struggle between peoples, which we call battles.'[4] Like birds, plants, or other mammals, humans naturally competed, although in their case they did so with conscious violence, not as a natural evolutionary imperative.

The term *Lebensraum* subsequently became notorious as the concept animating Hitler's vision of imperial conquest, which perhaps explains why Ratzel has largely disappeared from any discussion of human ecology. When ecology emerged in the 1960s and 1970s as a key area of debate within wider concerns for the environment, the focus was on the natural history of the world's ecosystems, which human activity threatened to disrupt. Applying ecological science to understanding the human relationship with the environment focused, as Malthus and Ratzel had done, on the issue of population pressure on inadequate resources of land. This raised the question whether or to what extent there was a historical relationship between food scarcity, rising population levels, and human conflict as the earlier theories had suggested. Modern theory describes this issue as 'land carrying capacity' – the extent to which the existing territory of a human population can provide enough food essentials and resources to sustain it. This is a concept easily translated back through time when humans were more reliant on foraging or hunting or on less productive forms of agriculture. Increasing population density could threaten the stability of the ecological niche in which past communities lived, while environmental pressures (changing climate, natural disasters, and so on) might do the same, either slowly or through a sudden environmental shock. For example, the massive eruption of the Ilopango volcano in Central America in 536 CE produced according to one contemporary account 'a sun in eclipse' in the Old World and was accompanied by 'pestilence, and war'. The better-known explosion in 1815 of the Tambora volcano in present-day Indonesia caused a 'year without summer', widespread crop failure, and violent protests across Europe.[5]

Did crises in the 'land carrying capacity' prompt conflict in the long human past? It is difficult to imagine that it did not despite the absence of secure historical evidence for prehistoric and proto-state peoples. Even where populations were sparse, competition for declining food sources – for example, with the loss of megafauna from overhunting – could have prompted conflict as readily as the pressure of a dense and growing population.[6] Large-scale migrations in search of more land meant displacement or challenge for the inhabitants in the reception areas; even movement from one valley to the next could result in conflict, evident in areas as diverse as prehistoric Chile or Neolithic Germany. Across the world, the development of tribal units from the amalgamation of small clans of hunter-gatherers gave rise to fixed territories, although humans almost certainly created notional territories long beforehand even as simple foragers and hunters, like communities of chimpanzees today. Under conditions of territoriality, particularly among sedentary horticultural or agricultural settlements, seizing more territory to exploit or defending existing territories was a signal for violence on some scale or other. If the territory could no longer support the population with adequate food and there was little prospect of improving food yields, or changing subsistence habits, or of moving to uninhabited regions, it was likely that 'living space' would have to be enlarged at someone else's expense.

Conflict would not always result, as can be observed from ethnographic studies of modern tribal populations, but it was implicit in the nature of the choice, both for those seeking to expand their resources and those defending what they had against territorial intruders.[7] Research on contemporary premodern communities has shown that when population density is at its maximum, hunter-gatherers and simple horticulturalists have pursued warfare in 66 percent of cases; among advanced horticultural and agrarian societies, it is 85 percent of cases.[8] In New Guinea, a laboratory for modern ethnographers, a study of twenty-six tribes shows the strong likelihood of warfare for land in nineteen cases where population densities are moderate or high but in only one case where population density is low.[9]

There are many examples from current ethnographic research of ecological pressures that can prompt intergroup violence, but the archaeological record also suggests ecological crisis as a source of conflict when populations tried to resolve the challenge posed by too many mouths to feed, or adverse changes in their natural environment, or simple competition for the same resources of food, water, or forest. The very early evidence is once again patchy, while its significance remains contested because of scholarly distrust of any explanation that suggests environmental determinism. But as human ecology embraces evolution from the very first humans, the prospect that ecological disequilibrium might prompt violence, occasional or persistent, must be a high probability even if it cannot be scientifically demonstrated. Only by the Holocene, in the age of *Homo sapiens*, does archaeology supply some possible examples. One comes from an estimated 10,000 years ago, at Nataruk, west of Lake Turkana in present-day Kenya. Here the remains of a hunter-gatherer group of twenty-seven men, women, and children were uncovered in 2012. They appear to have been the victims of a massacre. Ten of the twelve skeletons still in articulated form had perimortem injuries, some from sharp weapons, some from blunt instruments. They were left where they were killed, at the edge of a lagoon, the six children and four women separated from the men. A number of obsidian blades or points of a type uncommon in the region were found embedded in the skeletal bones, suggesting that this was a massacre perpetrated by another group trespassing outside its own territory, though even in this case the interpretation is hotly contested on the scientific evidence.[10]

Another example, though again far from certain, appears in Eurasia, where migrations of steppe nomads of the Suvorovo culture in the fourth millennium BCE displaced the flourishing Tripolye culture, which had established many large settlements in southeastern Europe and the Black Sea region. The adoption of the horse by the nomads around 4000 BCE allowed them to operate much larger herds of sheep and cattle but also created the need for more pastureland, which provoked growing tribal violence as the nomads pressed westward from the Caspian steppe. At the Verteba Cave in southern Ukraine another massacre was uncovered, with twenty-five identified crania of men, women, and children. There were eighteen perimortem blows to the head, most to the back or top, suggesting that the victims were slaughtered lying face down or kneeling. As these were the years when the local culture of what is called Old Europe was destroyed, it seems plausible to suppose that the killing at Verteba Cave was the result of a raid by nomads pressing into the fertile regions of the Tripolye. By 3300 BCE, the large settlements had been abandoned. Evidence of other massacres at Hotnitsa in northern Bulgaria and at Yunatsite in the upper Balkans, the latter where forty-six skeletons of women, children, and the elderly were found scattered on the floors in the destroyed settlement, suggest an intensification of violent raiding as the Suvorovo culture transformed a settled agricultural region into sparsely populated pastureland.[11]

In more recent times, the impact of environmental stress and food scarcity is a key element in explaining the evidence of widespread violence in the central and southwest regions of the United States in the period between 900 and 1300 CE, caused partly by severe climate change and partly by the tension between hunter-gatherers and settled agriculturalists in competition for land and food as populations increased. Subsistence stress worsened as groups migrated in search of more arable land or were forced onto less productive, marginal agricultural areas where the cooler, drier climate undermined carrying capacity. The frontiers between tribal groups were evident flashpoints under declining environmental conditions and territorial defence. The well-known mid-fourteenth-century massacre at Crow Creek in South Dakota, described in the prologue, was one consequence of a probable tension between migrant newcomers, driven to the area by environmental pressures, and the resident population. The small township was attacked, burned down, and more than 400 people massacred, dismembered, and scalped by the raiding party. A similar fate overtook a settlement along the Missouri River at the Fay Tolten site, also in South Dakota, where bodies were excavated lying on the floor of their houses, among them a scalped child.[12]

Farther west, in southwestern Colorado, Pueblo settlements in the twelfth century were the site of raiding and violence at a time when bioarchaeology has shown evidence of severe food scarcity. The flourishing Chaco culture in the Mesa Verde collapsed by mid-century. Massacres and evidence of cannibalism have been discovered at a few of the sites, including one where seven men, women, and children had been killed, disarticulated, and eaten, probably by a local tribe protecting its frugal territory. The Colorado Plateau was a scene of warlike violence as the ecological context deteriorated down to the fourteenth century, when it was largely abandoned by its human population.[13] In all these cases, there is a growing consensus among archaeologists that ecological pressure from climate change, population growth, and food stress shaped much of the warfare in major areas of North America long before the arrival of Europeans.

There is also a solid case for ecologically driven warfare by the Maori of New Zealand. The islands were first colonized between 800 and 1200 CE, and for an estimated 300 years or so, the Maori lived as hunter-gatherers, exploiting the thirteen species of giant moa birds until they were hunted to extinction. Competition for food prompted the first evidence of intergroup violence. As the megafauna died out, the Maori faced the problem of extensive deforestation and rising population. The turn to horticulture and food storage solved an immediate ecological crisis, but it also prompted persistent violence. The stores of food were protected in fortified settlements, or *Pa*, which were elaborately constructed for defence. Competition over land and stored food was intense so that war between the chiefdoms became endemic in the effort to overcome ecological constraints. Cannibalism was widely practised from the late prehistoric period, perhaps as a supplement to a diet now starved of the giant birds. When in 1542 the Dutch explorer Abel Tasman sent a boat crew ashore on South Island, the unfortunate sailors were promptly killed and eaten.[14] Whether this was 'nutritional cannibalism', as it is called, or ritualized sacrifice cannot be known with certainty, but eating people for food was common in Polynesia and in other contexts where food stress became an ecological problem. At a site in the Cook Islands, prehistoric archaeology shows evidence that humans of all ages and both sexes were eaten, almost certainly a result of chronic food stress.[15]

Eating other humans is perhaps the most extreme evidence of ecological crisis, where the territory can no longer supply adequate nutrition. There has been resistance among anthropologists to acknowledge the extent of cannibalism, but osteoarchaeology provides extensive early examples, and the practice is present in the historical record, as the fate of Tasman's sailors attests. The nature of cannibalism has provoked much argument, because there are cultural explanations for cannibalism as an element in religious ritual or postconflict celebration or in honouring the tribal dead rather than as a form of nutrition. The chief distinction is between what is called endocannibalism (eating kin for the sake of observing the rites of the group) and exocannibalism (eating the flesh of captives secured in conflict). This latter form can be divided again between ritual consumption of the enemy 'other' and feeding for subsistence, or nutritional/gastronomic cannibalism. In either case, the captive victims could only have been taken as the result of some form of conflict, whether a sudden raid, an ambush, or a predatory homicide, so that exocannibalism is closely linked to patterns of warfare.

The extent to which any cannibalism was for subsistence purposes remains uncertain, except perhaps in those cases where excavations have revealed discarded human remains butchered like animals, with cut marks, broken bones, and evidence of bone-marrow extraction. One of the earliest possible examples comes from the Klasies River caves in South Africa where cranial fragments show evidence of butchering and burning from an estimated 115,000 years ago.[16] Other examples are more recent. In the Frontbrégoua Cave in France, the butchered and disarticulated remains of up to fourteen people from the early fourth millennium BCE show the same treatment as the other fauna found at the site. At Herxheim in Germany, excavation of a Neolithic village from about 5000 BCE has found a mass of disarticulated human bones where the marks of defleshing, fractures, and the extraction of bone marrow and brains indicates deliberate consumption for food.[17] At the El Mirador Cave in Spain, the butchered remains of six men, women, and a child have been found obviously eaten for nutrition, with evidence of human tooth marks on the bone, quite distinct from the tooth marks made by carnivorous scavengers.[18] In medieval Europe, at least a dozen French and German chronicles written between 793 and 1052 CE describe cases of cannibalism prompted by major famines.[19] In the Mesa Verde killings in Colorado, the evidence suggests that the victims of raids were eaten at a time of extreme food stress; in thirty-two of forty sites excavated, there is evidence of cannibalism during the twelfth century, but by the next century there is almost none, suggesting a temporary subsistence crisis.[20] By contrast, the discovery of cannibalism on a wide scale in sites excavated in Arizona and New Mexico from the Anasazi culture, which flourished from approximately 900 to 1300 CE, seems to have been promoted more by ritual practices borrowed from Mexican cultures, as rich faunal remains suggest that hunger was not a driving motive. Even this case of possible ritual cannibalism occurred in the years when southwestern America experienced a period of increasing environmental stress and food scarcity, so that the possibility that some of the cannibalism was nutritional cannot be ruled out.[21]

Ecological factors are more easily demonstrated by ethnographers and anthropologists in the study of modern tribal communities, though there is persistent debate over whether population pressure, food scarcity, or a shortage of 'living space' is the real trigger for war rather than embedded cultural practices or social-political objectives. Defending the ecological niche is clearly important, because that niche is the source of subsistence, not necessarily to be shared with others; intruding or trespassing in the food territory of other tribes can itself be a cause of warfare. Among the Eskimo and Athapaskan speakers of western Alaska, an area sparsely populated but with limited food supplies, warfare was common in defence of territory or food sources;

men were always armed, posted sentries for hunting parties and settlements, wore armour of ivory, and carried bows and arrows and clubs for long-range or face-to-face killing. Revenge for trespass on territory was a common motive, and raiders usually slaughtered the entire settlement. Fighting to extinction allowed the victors to exploit the captured territory. Ferocious struggle for hunting territory also occurred farther east in the sub-Arctic when the Inuit population of Hudson Bay in the sixteenth and seventeenth centuries began to move south into the territory of the Lowland Cree in search of marine resources of fish, birds, and seals. In one legendary raid, the Inuit cut off the breasts of nursing mothers and threw them into what is now called 'milky lake' (*Wabagamushusagangan*), in this case symbolically reducing the enemy population so that the Inuit could exploit the ecological resources for themselves.[22]

This last case illustrates the way that tribal societies could engage in demographic regulation through warfare, either to keep down an enemy's population or to build up a population that had suffered decline through disease or conflict. In many accounts of tribal raiding in the historic period, the object of the raiders was to seize women and young children in order to improve the demographic profile of the aggressor. The same Lowland Cree slaughtered by the Inuit later engaged in raids in which all the men and old women were killed and the women and children taken captive. The Iroquois tribes east of the Great Lakes waged savage war against neighbouring tribal groups in the seventeenth century so that severe demographic losses among the Iroquois caused by epidemic diseases from Europe could be made good. Territory was cleared of rival groups and the men killed as the Iroquois population revived through the capture of women and children.[23] In the tribal warfare in South and Central America, in which entire settlements could be massacred, young women and children were often spared to replenish the tribe's own gene pool. Archaeological evidence suggests that this was a practice with a long history. Many of the massacre sites from the Neolithic and Mesolithic have a disproportionate number of male skeletons, indicating that the women were taken as demographic booty. In other cases, the entire population, both sexes and all ages, was killed to reduce competition for resources needed by the assailants and to promote their net ecological benefit.

Like defence of territory and food resources, demographic manipulation has an obvious ecological motive, but it is particularly territorial trespass that has often elicited a violent response. Among the indigenous peoples of Australia, intruders could be met with night raids designed to exterminate their settlements; a lone intruder might be murdered on his path. The Mundarucú tribe of Brazil, dependent on the peccary for protein, made exterminatory war on local villages when the animals declined in numbers to restore their local monopoly to hunt them. Enemy trophy heads were taken, because each head symbolized more game for the tribe, less for the villagers under attack.[24] The Karimajong of Uganda cooperated in sharing cattle and grain between their groups but reacted with extreme violence when any non-Karimajong tried to cross the tribal perimeter.[25] At the same time, violence might be avoided if agreement could be reached over territorial rights or in cases of intertribal trade. Among the Eskimo of western Alaska, it was possible for an outsider to be given temporary right of transit, even one-time use of food resources, as long as permission was formally sought. In Australia, aboriginal groups could negotiate a right to enter and settle in another tribal territory, but only if a 'greeting ceremony' had been carried out.[26] Without evidence of formal greeting, encroachment was met with violence. In many cases where defence of territory and food and water resources provoked conflict, there were cultural traditions that governed the response and social conditions that could determine the degree of violence, but the root cause was disruption to the ecological niche.

It is more difficult to make out an ecological case for warfare in the historic period, though climatic change, discussed later in the chapter, undoubtedly provided stimulus for conflict in Eurasia, the Americas, and the Mediterranean basin. The emergence of empires, settled kingdoms, or chiefdoms, where warfare has complex anthropological and historical explanations, obscures the direct link to ecological pressures, though they certainly existed throughout the historic period, as Malthus understood. Famine, environmental degradation, and lethal diseases are commonplace in the narrative of the more recent past. Nevertheless, worldwide population expanded for thousands of years, with occasional, sometimes serious setbacks, until it finally exploded from the nineteenth century onwards without Malthusian checks holding it back significantly. Larger political and social units found ways to expand food production, or to trade more regularly, or to exploit colonial territories as did the Roman Empire and the later overseas empires of European states. The wars of colonial conquest that resulted could be classified as 'ecology wars' only by ignoring the many other factors that drove territorial expansion.

An exception lies in the twentieth-century embrace of the idea of *Lebensraum*, when Ratzel's ecological theory of species evolution was hijacked by nationalist politicians and their military supporters to justify violent territorial expansion. Hitler's view of the German future derived directly from the popularization of the 'living space' concept among German geographers and biologists in the 1920s. In his unpublished 'Second Book', written in 1928, Hitler presented a clear ecological outline of the relationship between population, territory, and war:

> A people's struggle for survival is determined primarily
> by the following fact: Regardless of a people's level of
> culture, the struggle for daily bread is at the top of all vital
> necessities . . . But the bread that a people needs in order
> to live is determined by the *Lebensraum* that is available
> to it . . . the management of the relationship between the
> population and the land area is of the utmost importance
> in the existence of a people . . . Now, in the life of a
> people there are several ways to correct the imbalance
> between population and land area. The most natural is
> the adaptation of the territory from time to time to fit
> the growing population. This necessitates decisions for
> battle . . . from the distress of war, grows the bread of
> freedom.[27]

Hitler concluded that the search for more land when a population could no longer be fed adequately obeyed 'the laws of nature', which for millennia had impelled humans to extend their territory.

This analysis owes much to Ratzel, whose work was introduced to Hitler by the German geographer Karl Haushofer during his regular visits to see Hitler and Rudolf Hess in Landsberg prison in 1924 after Hitler's failed attempt at a coup d'état in November 1923.[28] Throughout the early years of the dictatorship, Hitler returned to the idea that his chief ambition was to secure living space for the German people: in February 1933, he told military leaders that taking more territory was his ultimate aim; in November 1937, he outlined his plan for seizing Austria and Czechoslovakia as living space; and finally in May 1939, in plans to invade Poland, he told his generals that the purpose was the extension of German living space. The subsequent invasion of the Soviet Union in June 1941 was the final stage in securing the space needed for survival, where food and land would be found in abundance on a continental scale. The expansion of territory and food supplies had a biological motive as well, captured in the popular slogan 'Blood and Soil', as it would provide the area for unrestricted German population growth, like Ratzel's plants and fauna. Heinrich Himmler, head of the SS and in 1939 appointed Reich Commissar for the Protection of Germandom, shared the ecological vision of a Eurasian space in which the German species would survive at the expense of others. He imagined that in a few hundred years, the new territory would support a population of 600 million Germans, while the Jews and Slavs who currently inhabited it would be killed off or starved to death long before. This was a grotesque ecological fantasy, but the attempt to transform the physical context that supported the German people was a clear, if distorted, imitation of the ecological imperatives in nature.[29]

The wars waged by Japan and Italy in the 1930s and 1940s were also justified as wars to secure the future life of a population starved of sufficient land and food. The Italian version of *Lebensraum* was *lo spazio vitale*, a direct translation of the term. Mussolini's imperialism in the 1930s was crudely designed to give more land for agriculture to an overpopulated Italy. The Italian conquests in Libya and Ethiopia were supposed to provide land for at least 6 million Italian farmers; Albania was annexed in April 1939 to supply space for 2 million more.[30] This, too, was biological space for the Italian people, whose gene pool was to be protected by strict apartheid rules. For Japan, densely populated by the early twentieth century and facing an agrarian crisis, the appeal of living space seemed self-evident. The seizure of Manchuria by the Japanese Kwantung Army in September 1931 was only the start of a programme of territorial expansion, designed to support the emigration of 5 million Japanese farmers and to expand the space available for the development of the Japanese race at the expense of those already occupying the land.[31] In the case of all three states, there were additional motives at work, which feature later in this book, but the acquisition of territory designed to provide enough 'land carrying capacity' for populations with allegedly too little territory and with anxieties about food supply was above all an ecological ambition.

It was also a colossal failure. Since 1945, the developed world understands that the pressure of population growth and food supply can be mediated easily through trade and agricultural improvement, as was already the case in practice even when Malthus was writing. The relationship between environmental pressure and conflict has been more evident in the less developed world since 1945, where degradation of the environment through deforestation, water shortages, declining fish stocks, or overuse of arable land provide a context in which conflict, particularly at a local level, becomes a possibility. Above all, rapidly rising population suggests, as neo-Malthusians argue, the probability of famine, the spread of epidemic diseases, and increased conflict in areas of the globe where there exists resource stress of one kind or another (although according to Malthus's theory, population should never have been able to grow so fast in the first place). One example might be potential conflict over access to water as demand rises exponentially – by 2030, the demand for fresh water is predicted to be 64 percent higher than in 2009 when the Water Resources Group, sponsored by the World Bank, first reported on the future of fresh water supply.[32] In areas where there exists potential conflict over access to river water – for example, tension between Uzbekistan and Kyrgyzstan over the waters of the Syr Darya, needed by the one for irrigation, by the other for hydroelectric power – the disagreements have not yet led to armed conflict.[33] Among the 310 international river basins, shared by 150 different states, cooperation over water regulation is widespread, while conflict has been found to be limited or induced by other factors.[34] Where high demand for groundwater from wells coincides with restricted access and a lack of other water sources, conflict has occurred between pastoral and farming areas in Africa and the Middle East, but tensions have also been mitigated through initiatives by local communities or the state.[35]

The example of water shows that there is much ambiguity in assessing whether environmental crisis will lead to more violence. The Environment and Conflicts Project based in Zürich argued in the mid-1990s for a direct relationship among environmental degradation, ecological pressures, and the likelihood of conflict, particularly in communities living in economically marginal areas that have poor or unpredictable access to resources. It has been claimed that scarcity, whether induced by excess demand, or limited supply, or unequal access, makes civil war 20 percent and armed conflict 45 percent more likely. Such statistics are difficult to verify historically, even with plentiful evidence of episodes of violence in states less able to cope with the changes to the environment. Critics of the current neo-Malthusian ecological explanations for conflict find little direct connection among resource scarcity, population growth, and violence, a conclusion that undermines the core arguments proposed by Malthus two centuries before.[36] This is almost certainly an overoptimistic assessment. Conflict in the Horn of Africa and community violence in Bengal and Bangladesh are just two examples evidently driven in part by problems of environmental crisis, even if there are as yet no 'water wars' or violent pursuit of additional living space.

*

At the centre of the arguments over environmental crisis and conflict sit the consequences of climate change (or, more correctly, climatic change). Changing climate, either long-term transitions or short-term climatic shocks, has contributed to ecological crisis in obvious ways over the millions of years of hominin existence: a long decline in temperature combined with greater aridity could undermine the availability of staple foodstuffs, reduce areas of woodland and tropical forest, expand grassland, and change the distribution of local fauna; alterations in monsoon cycles could produce devastating floods and destroy the riverine environment; melting ice from glaciers and the two poles could cause a significant rise in sea levels, inundating coastal lowlands or covering over land bridges inhabited by farmers and hunter-gatherers. During periods of advancing glaciation, human populations in the Northern Hemisphere had to survive in the tundra, adapting to a radically different environment. From about 3 million years ago, a cycle of glacial and interglacial periods, roughly every 100,000 years, challenged humans and many other species to survive by adapting to the changes or perishing. In between the cycle there were severe weather oscillations that could bring a short-term climatic shock. At times human populations shrank, and areas of habitation were reduced in response to climatic change. By approximately 40,000 years ago, *Homo sapiens*, the last hominin survivor, certainly in Europe, was forced to navigate yet another long cooling period and the last glacial maximum, which occurred some 20,000 years ago. By 10,000 years ago, the global human population was tiny, estimated at 4.6 million, spread by then to every continent.[37]

A more predictable, wetter, and warmer climate set in approximately 11,600 years ago, following the last very cold, dry period – known as the Younger Dryas – which drove down human population levels and reduced areas for foraging. From that period on, until the recent onset of man-made climatic changes, the climate overall has remained relatively stable, with short-term shocks of cooling, aridity, and drought, or excessive precipitation, or the occasional catastrophic impact of major volcanic activity, which could cool the globe for years. Much is now understood about past climatic conditions through advances in paleoclimatology, thanks chiefly to the climate scientist Hubert Lamb, whose Climatic Research Institute at the University of East Anglia, founded in 1972, focused on linking climate and history together.[38] But exactly how human communities responded in evolutionary terms to shifting climate is open to interpretation. Whether adaptation to changing conditions encouraged conflict between challenged communities or between different hominin lines is largely speculation, though it is not implausible, particularly in contexts such as Europe 40,000–45,000 years ago. There the cooling climate increased competition for declining stocks of fauna between *Homo sapiens* and *Homo neanderthalensis*, whose extinction is now thought to have occurred during this period of transition rather than during the last major ice age. For more demonstrable links between climatic change and conflict, it has proved necessary to focus on the past few thousand years, where it is possible to measure climatic changes alongside the archaeological and historical evidence.

The conflicts already described between nomads from

the Eurasian steppes and the Tripolye culture in the fourth millennium BCE coincided with a sharp climatic change – the Piora Oscillation – that led to a colder climate, declining sunshine, floods that eroded river plains, and, from 3960 to 3821 BCE, a long period of bitter cold. The archaeological evidence shows increased settlement fortification, new weapons, and many burned or abandoned sites. For the nomadic raiders reliant on forage for their herds, climate may well have prompted the violent move westward. Farther east, on the Ural steppe, climatic change also affected the local populations as arid, cooler conditions reduced forest and marshes and increased grassland. Herders needed access to marshlands for winter forage, and as the marshes shrank, access had to be defended. From about 4,000 years ago, settlements of the Sintashta culture in the Tobol River and Ural River valleys began to be heavily fortified with high walls and towers, new weapons were developed (including the first chariots), and a warrior class emerged, evident in the rich quantity of weapons buried with adult males.[39] Here it is possible to chart archaeologically the connection between a changing climate and the evidence of intensified warfare as one means of survival in an altered environment.

Similar evidence that climatic change might encourage greater warfare can be seen in the conflicts between the nomadic tribes of east-central Asia and the Han Chinese populations over the past 2,000 years. It has proved possible to date the major periods of temperature change to show long time spans that were considerably cooler and more arid. The change affected nomadic tribes reliant on imported food stocks and on fertile pastureland. They inhabited a fragile ecological niche, susceptible to sudden climatic shocks.[40] The poorer climate reduced herd size and led, at times, to severe drought and famine conditions. Mongol and Manchu invasions of China coincided with periods of climatic crisis when the carrying capacity of increasingly arid territory declined, and raiding or migration to the south became necessary for survival. The cooler climate also encouraged domestic conflict within China, when the large population could no longer be supported by double-cropping of rice during the year. The consequence was tax revolts and local insurrections in response to famine conditions, the last of which, the Taiping Rebellion in the 1850s, saw China's population decline from 440 million in 1850 to 360 million fifteen years later.[41] Over the course of 1,000 years of Chinese history, it has been demonstrated that the 453 years of cold phases produced a total of 603 wars of all kinds, but the 459 years of warmer climate produced only 296. Warfare associated with climatic change contributed, so it has been argued, to the collapse of three of China's major dynasties, the Song, Ming, and Qing. Famine and low temperatures perhaps pushed the Manchu to seize Beijing in 1644 and found their own dynasty.[42]

The environmental degradation that led to warfare in western North America also had a major link with climatic crisis. Between 800 and 1350 CE, the region experienced extensive and prolonged droughts as the Medieval Climatic Anomaly produced an arid and periodically waterless climate. The hunter-gatherer and horticultural economies of the area were highly sensitive to sudden shifts in climate. As subsistence became more challenging, so settlements were abandoned, migrations attempted, and conflict increased, while population growth was reversed. One set of tree-ring evidence shows severe periods of drought in 1020–70, 1197–1217, and 1249–1365, while evidence of high temperatures and frequent forest fires confirms a dramatically changing climatic picture. The increased competition for resources, particularly access to water, drove higher levels of warfare, evident in defended settlements, skeletal trauma, and the spread of the bow and arrow technology. The Colorado Plateau was abandoned along with other southwestern territory as the climate undermined local subsistence patterns and reduced population levels; in central and southern California, the archaeology shows that drought conditions provoked a similar mix of abandoned settlements, increased evidence of weapons, and declining trade between regions.[43]

In all these historic cases, the effect of climatic change, while real enough, has to be reconciled with other factors affecting the decision for war. There is much debate about whether environmental deterioration alone pushed nomadic tribes west from central Asia over the 5,000-year period in which the migrations can be charted or promoted the 2,000-year conflict between the nomads of eastern Asia and the settled civilization of China. Other regions also demonstrate that a cooling climate coincided with higher levels of warfare – in Europe during the late medieval period of the so-called Little Ice Age – but the causal pathway is not easy to detect, partly because the climatic change often covered several hundred years rather than prompting an abrupt shock that might more easily account for a particular conflict. A study of European warfare and climate over the past millennium finds a correlation between colder periods and conflict, as in the case of China, but the relationship is weak as an explanation and disappears as European states modernized in the nineteenth century. A case can certainly be made that the classic Malthusian checks operated in the fourteenth century, as evidenced by famine, plague, and warfare during the early stages of severe cooling in the Little Ice Age, and in the 'General Crisis' of the middle years of the seventeenth century, when the three demographic checks were again widely in evidence against a background of deteriorating climate.[44] Nevertheless, historians remain wary of explaining warfare as a result of climatic change, which can seem too deterministic. When Hubert Lamb summarized the impact of climatic change at the end of his pioneering study of climate and history, there was no mention of warfare as an 'impact of the first order'.[45]

A similar difficulty in understanding the mechanisms that relate climatic change to conflict exists with analysis of the current state of the global climate. It is widely assumed that environmental crisis sparked by a rapidly warming climate will at some point lead to conflict either between states or between substate actors responding to conditions of increasing danger. But as with the evidence of man-made environmental degradation, the extent to which climate as such, rather than social, political, or institutional factors, induces conflict is open to wide interpretation, not least because of the argument that long-term climatic change (the macroprocess) and short-term weather shocks (weather variability) should not be confused when explaining ecological pressures.[46]

The search for evident links between climatic change and conflict goes back to at least the 1970s, when the dangers to the environment were highlighted as a coming security problem, but official concern is a phenomenon of the twenty-first century. The UN Security Council has debated climatic change and security regularly, in 2007, 2011, 2013, 2020, and 2021. In the third discussion, the German delegate claimed that climate posed 'a grave threat to peace and security'. In the debate in September 2021, the secretary-general, António Guterres, warned that the link between climatic change and conflict 'was indeed a code red for humanity'.[47] The Intergovernmental Panel on Climate Change (IPCC), established by the United Nations in 1988, has reported six times on the main issues raised and in the Fifth Assessment Report in 2014 dealt directly with the question of whether climatic change has promoted or will promote higher levels of conflict, though with largely negative conclusions.[48] The first director of the International Geosphere-Biosphere Programme (IGBP), set up in 1987 by the international science community, suggested that 'most conflicts have something to do with the climate.' The IGBP published findings in 2006 on climate and history and concluded rather obviously on past evidence that if the human ecosystem was forced out of balance, 'an outcome could ultimately be an environmental collapse', as it had been for civilizations before.[49]

Official pessimism was not entirely consistent with the way the science community has viewed the relationship. Research interest in the link between modern climatic change and conflict predated and partly encouraged the official recognition of the possibility, but it has now become a major strand of research across the human sciences. The focus has been not on potential interstate violence, for which there was negligible evidence, but on local conflicts in areas where the problems of economic development and resource stress are likely to be exacerbated or even caused by short-term variability in weather patterns or longer, persistent alteration of the climate. Some of these conflicts cross state borders but have not spilled over into interstate confrontation. Most studies rely on evidence from Africa, particularly East Africa, where irregular rainfall and rising aridity have undermined an already fragile ecological system, or from South Asia, where variable precipitation has caused intercommunity violence, or from the Philippines and the South Pacific, where communities are dependent to a high degree on marginal agriculture, and so are disproportionately affected by sudden weather shocks. In the cases usually studied, there is a lack of institutional, financial, and social capability to deal with the results of crisis: weak states are by far the most vulnerable.

There is nevertheless serious disagreement about whether climate really does generate violent conflict. To illustrate the division of opinion, a 2016 survey of the academic articles published on climatic change and conflict found that precisely 62.3 percent argued for such a connection, while the remaining 37.7 percent claimed that social, political, and institutional variables were more significant than the weather.[50] Of all the local studies, the African case has attracted most investigation and the most argument. Here the discussion has concentrated on the violent cattle-raiding that takes place between tribal groups on the borders of Kenya, Ethiopia, Somalia, and Sudan. This can involve violence on a considerable scale: in the 109 conflicts recorded between 1978

and 2009, there were 1,307 deaths and the theft of an estimated 20,000 cattle by raiding parties that could number
as many as 500. In Turkana and Marsabit, the raiding occurred most frequently in periods with persistent drought
or with months drier than normal, when raiders searched
for pastureland and water or seized more cattle to compensate for their own losses. Only one group, the Borana, raided
in wet weather, but this was the only one to rely on agriculture rather than a pastoral economy, and raiding in this
case seems to have been linked more to initiation rites for
each new warrior cohort, a cultural rather than an ecological
choice. Although in the East African case, climatic change
might not directly explain the resort to violence, it must be
considered a contributory factor, perhaps the major one, in
conditioning the decision to take violent action.[51] The same
seems true of the long-running civil war in Sudan, where
warming temperatures and regular droughts accompanied
the conflict and fuelled competition for water resources
among the pastoral farmers of the region. One calculation
suggests that weather variability influenced a quarter of the
violent events recorded, while environmental crisis played
a part throughout. But climate was evidently one compon-
ent among many in explaining a war that has lasted for more
than twenty years and has so far cost the lives of an estimated 1.9 million people.[52]

Even in the African example, conclusions are subject
to dispute. Some researchers have found that raiding is
more closely identified with exceptionally wet conditions,
though the consensus now favours rising temperatures,
drought, and desertification as the main drivers, certainly in

sustaining existing conflict rather than causing new ones.[53] There are also significant differences between tribal areas because of diversified cultural practices and social norms, so that reaction to climatic change will not be universally the same. A similar ambiguity has been found in studies of the four ongoing insurgencies in the Philippines led separately by the Communist New People's Army, two Islamic movements, and the Moro National Liberation Front from the southern islands of the archipelago. Violent incidents follow either exceptional precipitation and typhoons, which damage agriculture and reduce food supplies, or drier years, which have a similar effect on yields. Insurgent recruitment can increase in years of damaging precipitation, but in other cases it can reduce a willingness to run risks while subsistence is threatened. For three of the four groups, there are ideological explanations for insurgency and a poor link with climate. A more reliable variable has been the willingness of the Philippine counterinsurgency forces to recruit and fight after precipitation shocks, when volunteers were more likely to come forward. Excessive rainfall in either case coincides with an increase in violent incidents involving battle deaths and casualties. Here water rather than drought is regarded as the trigger.[54]

If there remains doubt about how direct the link is between climatic change and violence, forecasts for the future about the rapidly warming and drying planet suggest that the link will become more evident. One calculation made in 2015 based on analysis of conflict since the 1950s suggests that with every 1 degree centigrade added to the earth's temperature, there is an 11.5 percent increase in intergroup

conflict. Extrapolating these figures to account for predicted temperature increase, there is said to be a likely increase of 54 percent in African conflict and 393,000 further
battle deaths by the year 2030.[55] The one variable that most
researchers agree on is the role of rainfall or its absence in
prompting conflict. Extreme rainfall disrupts crops, causes
severe flooding, and spreads disease, while drought destroys
crops and livelihoods and encourages conflict over shrinking
water supplies, particularly for pastoral societies and self-
sufficient farmers. Study of forty-seven African states from
1991 to 2007 shows that in years that experience very high
or very low rainfall, there is an increase in the number of
conflict events between local communities or between pro-
testers and the government.[56] The issue of conflict, however,
relates closely to the level of economic development and institutional robustness in any state; where climatic change
can be met by shifting technologies, investment in research
and innovation, and state-based initiatives, conflict is largely absent. While in the premodern world, climatic change or
weather shocks affected every kind of society, the adverse
effects in the twenty-first century are unevenly distributed.

The ecological contribution to the question 'Why war?' is
far from straightforward, despite the commonsense view
that food scarcity, population pressure, environmental degradation, and changing climate seem obvious triggers for
potential violence. Across the greater part of the human
past, the evidence is simply lacking, even if the prospect of
conflict over food supplies or protection of territory or environmental migration must certainly have occurred, as it

occurred in the past 10,000 years where the archaeological and climatological evidence is at least available, if often sparsely so. Climatic change from the penultimate glacial maximum about 120,000 years ago to the onset of the Holocene 10,000 years ago happened so slowly that human communities had thousands of years to adapt to the changing environment. A firmer case can be made for defence of the ecological niche when environmental pressures created friction between human populations. The impact in this case was far greater on small social units, whether kin groups or tribes, whose threshold for subsistence was much more fragile than for later settled populations, and it is in this context that ecology was (and still is) more likely to prompt warfare. In pre-state cases as far apart as the tribal societies of New Zealand and Alaska, violent and often savage defence of territory and food stocks against competition for a particular ecological niche was common. In these circumstances, conflict over ecological resources would have been one of the critical keys to survival for tribal peoples. The anomalous experience of the 'living-space' wars of the twentieth century shows, however, that even in the modern age, ecological restriction could be taken as a justification for violent expansion.

On climatic change, the link with violence is more tenuous. On more recent evidence, it seems likely that a sudden climatic shock – a drought of a few years, or a volcanic 'year without summer', or persistent heavy rainfall – would promote conflict as resources suddenly dried up or were destroyed and had to be found by raiding others or securing *Lebensraum* by trespassing on another community's territory. In the historic period, climate-induced famine routinely prompted violent civil protest. In other contexts – for example, the centuries of conflict between China and the nomadic tribes of east-central Asia – regular droughts and encroaching desert fuelled violent efforts by nomadic tribes to find more food or pasture. Even in this case, it was sometimes possible to reach accommodation rather than resort always to warfare. When they could, the imperial Chinese authorities could use food stocks or prestige goods to buy peace from the nomads or allow nomadic tribes to settle on Han territory, thereby blunting the impact of any climate shock.[57]

The best that can be said is that the ecological context has contributed in a variety of ways to the circumstances that might trigger violence, in some cases directly, more commonly indirectly. The difference between human populations and Ratzel's animals and plants is that the decision to pursue more living space or to raid others for food or women was a conscious decision, not a natural response. The ecological pressures were understood and sometimes acted upon, when it seemed necessary, with some level of violence. In the present, climatic change presents the most challenging ecological conditions, as it has done in the past, but the possibility for international cooperation to cope with its effects has reduced, and may continue to reduce, the possibility of 'climate wars' except in those regions of the world most challenged by climatic shocks and least able to mitigate their effects.

PART TWO

CHAPTER 5

Resources

What one does not have, but needs, one must conquer.
— Adolf Hitler, June 1941[1]

Few wars in the modern age were so blatantly about seizing resources – land, minerals, oil, among others – than the German invasion of the Soviet Union launched on June 22, 1941. In a meeting with senior commanders on January 9, 1941, Hitler gleefully reminded them of the 'immeasurable riches' that conquest of the Soviet area would bring.[2] In this he was consistent with views he had held since at least the late 1920s. In the 'Second Book', in which he explained the ecological necessity for living space, he concluded that 'this space can only lie in the East.'[3] The empire he planned to build in Russia was an empire of exploitation that would use the Slav population as so many helots while the German rulers sent back to the German people a stream of resources as befitted an imperial people.

The quest for resources through violent conflict has an exceptionally long pedigree. Indeed, one of the principal explanations for the long history of human warfare has been the ambition, as Hitler put it, to take what is needed – or simply coveted – by conquest. In a cross-cultural survey of 186 societies conducted in the 1990s, Carol and Melvin Ember found that fear of resource scarcity accounted for an overwhelming majority of conflicts. Among non-state, tribal societies, victors took resources in 85 percent of cases and appropriated land in 77 percent.[4] The ethnographic evidence can be traced back by analogy to the known wars of the historic period and by implication to the conflicts of prehistory, where the evidence is more difficult, but not impossible, to find. The materialist, or economic, basis for warfare has been and continues to be a widely favoured answer to Einstein's question, as it was when he posed it.

The economic argument for war – engrossing resources in the broadest sense of the word – differs from the ecological explanation of 'resource stress' explored in the previous chapter. Ecological conflict involves natural resources essential to sustain life in a particular environment, and it emerges when a scarce but vital resource is controlled by others, thus limiting favourable access; or when resources once abundant have been reduced by overhunting or climate change; or when a population surge eats up the necessary resources, which must be found elsewhere. But in cases where resource stress is less obvious, the battle for resources, like Hitler's invasion, is designed to bolster imperial, or national, or tribal power at the expense of others. It is the predatory nature of the material ambitions underlying warfare rather than the pressures of ecological crisis that forms the subject matter of the current chapter. Much of the discussion as a result focuses on the past 10,000 years, when there was something worth taking, whether raw materials, treasure, slaves, or tribute. The pursuit of resources by resort to wars – either for plunder or to exert economic control or to extract a profit – has about it an explanatory simplicity. Material motives appear both rational and demonstrable, whether in a skirmish between hunter-gatherers, a tribal expedition, or modern mass warfare.

Hitler's material motives dominated the strategy he pursued in 1941 and 1942 against the advice of his generals. While they wanted an attack on Moscow in autumn 1941 and destruction of what was left of the Red Army, Hitler insisted on pushing south to seize the rich coal and iron region of the Donbas first; in summer 1942, his military leaders wanted to renew the conflict against Soviet forces in central Russia, but Hitler wanted to move farther south to complete seizure of the Donbas and take Russia's rich oil deposits in the Caucasus region. In this case, the ambition to seize resources drove strategy, though in the end the oil was never captured, and most of the Donbas was lost a year later. Even the ambition to extract grain and foodstuffs for the German home population failed because the huge armed forces in the east consumed most of what was available. To the extent that the German invasion of the Soviet Union was a predatory 'resource war', it failed on every front.

If the obsession with resources frustrated German commanders, it was well understood as a motive for war by the communist enemy. It was orthodox Leninist theory that capitalism, as a result of the contradictions inherent in the economic system, would be compelled to wage war. Stalin understood the economic and political crisis of the 1930s as 'a *general* crisis of capitalism' and assumed that 'things are heading towards a new imperialist war', consistent with Lenin's view in *Imperialism: The Highest Stage of Capitalism* (published during the First World War) that capitalist imperialism explained the origin of modern conflict.[5] The Marxist-Leninist argument that the causes of modern war could be found in the material motives of an economic system that searches for resources to exploit, markets to dominate, capital gains to be made, and territory to conquer became an orthodoxy of the political Left worldwide by the mid-twentieth century and has remained an active explanation ever since. Peace, so it has been argued, was only possible once the proletariat or its political vanguard had replaced the bourgeois state with a socialist alternative in which resources were shared rather than accumulated by the rich.

The Marxist interpretation of the reasons for war owed little directly to Marx, who, like his contemporary Darwin, was little interested in war as such. His focus was on historical materialism, explaining the long-term development of forms of class struggle in the different economic ages of human history, first the classical slave economies, then feudalism, and finally bourgeois capitalism. 'Is our theory that the *organization of labour is determined by the means of production*', wrote Marx to his collaborator Friedrich Engels in 1866, 'anywhere more brilliantly confirmed than in the human slaughter industry?'[6] But after Lenin, economic predation as the cause of war was taken for granted. 'Remember the imperialist war' was the first appeal to the European working class by the newly founded Communist International in 1919. At the international's Seventh World Congress in August 1935, the Italian communist Ercole Ercoli (the political alias of Palmiro Togliatti) gave a long speech analysing the communist explanation for why wars occur. The concentration of capital into huge trusts and corporations sharpened the struggle to control markets and resources through imperial conquest. The crisis caused by the contest between rival capitalist blocs, Ercoli continued, prompted the most reactionary elements of the bourgeoisie to accept that war was at certain times the 'best means', sometimes 'the only means', of overcoming it.[7] Most Marxists assumed that war was as a result inevitable. In another book titled *Why War?*, published two years after the Freud–Einstein correspondence, the British socialists Ellen Wilkinson and Edward Conze answered Einstein's question by the argument that 'capitalist imperialism produces war as inevitably as an explosion of oxygen and hydrogen produces water.' For communists, the war prompted by Hitler's aggression against Poland, and later against the Soviet Union, was no surprise. It was only necessary, wrote Wilkinson, to understand the 'deep, underlying economic factors . . . whatever the momentary excuse may be'.[8]

Historical materialism could be applied to wars both past and present, because throughout history warfare has depended, according to Marx, on 'the character of the class interests and the relation of class forces engaged in it.'[9] Marxist analysis has been used to explain wars in the ancient world to secure slaves to service the classical economy, which was dominated by an exploitative landowning and urban elite. There are Marxist accounts of the Aztec seizure of war captives for mass sacrifice as an instrument to demonstrate the power of the ruling class.[10] Marxism can be used to explain why the feudal ruling class engaged in persistent conflict to seize land and the serfs needed to work it. Later, early capitalism, as it transcended the feudal age, used violence to control overseas resources against competitors and to crush indigenous resistance in the territories exploited globally by Europe's rich merchant class. There are Marxist explanations for the outbreak of civil wars, where economic class interests clashed, as they did in the American Civil War between rival capitalists or later in the postrevolutionary civil war in Russia between the proletariat and the bourgeoisie.

It is nevertheless the later historical era of monopoly capitalism, emerging from the late nineteenth century, that has provided the basis for the Marxist-Leninist view not only of the cause of war in general but also of the cause of particular wars. On this interpretation, the First World War was the model for how conflict was driven by the material greed of the rich. 'This was an *imperialist war* from first to last', wrote the British historian and communist Dona Torr in 1942, 'because on each side the forces which dominated and conducted the war were the *capitalist classes* of each country, who were concerned only with their rival aims of plunder and colonial oppression.'[11] The Second World War in 1939 was again defined as a contest between two rival 'imperialist groups' until Hitler's invasion of the Soviet Union turned it into a hybrid conflict, part imperialist war, part war of socialist liberation. After 1945, the official Marxist-Leninist line continued to insist that there existed a general crisis of capitalism, 'a decaying and moribund' system, whose growing aggressiveness in Korea or Vietnam was driven by the most extreme imperialist wing of monopoly capital, whose militaristic strivings were 'incessantly growing'.[12] The more evident the crisis was, the more capitalists, above all those in the United States, pressured governments to spend heavily on the military and pursue an aggressive foreign policy. The wars in the Persian Gulf were the result, according to two neo-Marxist economists, Shimshon Bichler and Jonathan Nitzan, of the power of 'dominant capital', the 'Weapondollar-petrodollar Coalition' (the biggest arms and oil corporations), to pressure the White House into accepting conflict so that the corporations' profits would rise in step with the onset of war, as indeed they did.[13] For modern Marxists, the contradictions in a failing economic order once again have provoked war and will do so again. 'Capitalism does not go to war for its own sake', wrote the organizer of the Committee for a Workers' International in 2006, 'but to conquer markets, increase its income.'[14]

The communist explanation that wars are caused by economic forces driven by the contradictions in any given economic system does not exclude the idea of just wars waged by the oppressed to free themselves from economic oppression and enable them to take over the resources of the oppressor. Wars of this kind can be explained as the rejection of current class relations by the victims of the prevailing economic stage, such as the Roman slave revolt in 73–71 BCE led by the gladiator Spartacus, often taken by Marxists as an example of early class struggle. Stalin in his gloss on Leninism distinguished between just and unjust wars; the latter were wars to shore up a system of economic exploitation, the former were wars for liberation. In either case, class relations and class interests explain the origin of conflict. The Cold War, according to Soviet theory, was a clash between the

communist social system and the declining system of capitalist imperialism; if it became a real war, it would be a war of
liberation for the progressive forces of mankind, a class war
on an international scale. In the event of a nuclear war, the
task of progressive forces everywhere would be 'the destruction of the entire system of capitalism, which cannot exist
without wars'.[15] Although the Cold War has been viewed in
Western eyes as a war of ideologies, the consistent communist view claimed that ideology was and always would be secondary, a 'derivative of economic contradictions'.

The Marxist explanation for war as an expression of prevailing economic and social reality has barely survived the
collapse of the Soviet system in Europe in 1990–91. Communist, or more precisely Soviet, ideology on the relationship
between war and capitalist imperialism is widely regarded as
theoretically flawed, too prescriptive and one-dimensional
to be convincing; to continue to argue the case that wars are
always the result of 'the basic economic sources' is also em-
pirically problematic. Capitalism, for all its current issues,
has not demonstrated a general crisis leading to its collapse
in war, any more than was the case between 1939 and 1945.
The argument that the dominant class in different economic
systems fights wars to seize additional resources has an obvious plausibility, but it suggests an economic determinism
that not only undermines any idea of human agency but is
also difficult to demonstrate historically except in prescriptive terms too general to be useful. Nor can it account satisfactorily for warfare before the onset of the state, when
resources might be seized by communities that were egalitarian rather than based on distinct social classes.

The era of 'monopoly capitalism' is perhaps the most problematic for the Marxist interpretation, because the burden of proof that specific wars were engineered by big business has proved persistently difficult to find, despite the presence of powerful industrial and financial organizations dedicated to military production and research. It was not the armaments barons who pushed Europe into war in 1914. Hitler's later invasion of the Soviet Union was driven by a radical nationalist agenda, not capitalist ambition; Germany's major business leaders, though they might hope to profit from victory, did not force Hitler's hand. The argument that the 'Weapondollar-petrodollar Coalition' conspired to provoke the Second Gulf War can only be inferred, not proved. In the end, military production, from flint arrowheads to machine guns, makes wars possible by encouraging use of the weapons produced, but it is state and non-state actors who over the long historical past have decided when and for what reason the weapons will be used. The suggestion that capitalists have only hesitated to press for nuclear war because they know it will destroy their markets and kill their customers is unconvincing: they want to avoid nuclear war for reasons that are obvious.

It is, of course, not necessary to be a Marxist to explain warfare in materialist terms. That there can be economic motives at work in the predatory aspiration to seize or exploit resources through war is an unexceptional argument. There have been few conflicts in which resources have not been appropriated by the victor at some stage, even if taking resources was not the proximate or principal cause but a consequence of victory. For humans before the Holocene, fighting for resources almost certainly applied principally to natural resources needed in ecological terms as populations grew, or climate undermined subsistence supplies, or drought affected access to water. Before fixed farming settlements, it is likely that raiding to capture grazing livestock was possible, but too little is known about early human communities as herders or hunters to be certain. Predatory livestock raiding appears with greater certainty in the Eurasian steppes from the fourth millennium BCE where cattle were central to the economy and social structure of the tribal communities that inhabited them. According to Indo-European mythology, the figure Trito (the 'Third' or 'the Warrior') raided cattle belonging to a giant serpent because the auguries confirmed that they were his by right. In this cosmology, Trito was the first warrior, killing the monster and taking the cattle but at the same time defining cattle raiding as a legitimate function for all the warriors who followed him.[16]

Fighting to take or to control material resources is more readily demonstrable only with the onset of farming, the shift to larger tribal communities, then the emergence of cities and the first proto-states or states. From that period on, looting materials or plundering enemy settlements was common and geographically widespread; the loot was one way to reward soldiers and motivate their participation. Tribute could also be exacted to fill the victor's treasury even when peace had resumed. There were conflicts over control of trade routes, access to or control over valuable materials such as salt or mineral sources such as copper ore or jade, and finally the seizure of slaves or sacrificial victims, which seems to have been almost universal until only the past few hundred years. With the development of the first large tribal polities and then the first states, resources also meant treasure – gold, gems, prestige goods. For modern states, resources can mean territory to supply consumer needs to home populations, or control over a key energy source, such as oil, or, as in the case of German conquest in the Soviet Union, a captive labour force.

For pre-state communities there is heavy reliance on archaeological evidence to uncover potential violence to take or defend resources. In Neolithic Europe, the pattern of settlement and destruction suggests conflict over scarce minerals, particularly flint and other hard stones, salt, and metal ores. In Slovakia and Moravia, in central Europe, evidence of fighting coincides with the site of copper ores in the Nitra River valley, while trade in prestige goods – weapons, beads, ornaments – seems likely to have provoked conflict between neighbouring communities over the control of the routes. Among warrior skeletons, perimortem trauma is more evident in the areas containing copper ores.[17] By the time of the metal cultures in the last three millennia BCE, first copper, then bronze, and finally iron, fighting for control of valuable resources or their supply contributed more obviously to an endemic pattern of warfare, including the seizure of land where resources or rich pasture were available. The pattern of weaponry, armour, and horse equipment suggests that violent raiding became common. In Italy, trade and wealth became increasingly important by the Copper Age and early Bronze Age, and the major routes through Liguria or Veneto were protected by heavily fortified coastal towns.

Sea raiding was also carried out along the Italian coastline to seize slaves, livestock, and valuables.[18]

A similar pattern emerged with the regular warfare evident in China and in the New World. In warfare among the early Chinese proto-states, control of key metals, particularly copper and tin, played a role. An early inscription at a Shang site in Anyang (dating from the second millennium BCE) records frequent warfare to gain land, labour, portable goods, and victims to sacrifice. In one case, 300 of the Qiang people were captured for sacrifice to the ancestors of the Shang.[19] The same number of victims, stripped, mutilated, and killed, was depicted on stone blocks at Monte Albán in southern Mexico, where the Zapotec culture, established about 500 BCE, exercised a brutal domination over neighbouring peoples, exacting tribute, slaves, and captives for sacrifice and destroying villages that resisted the demand to provide material goods and wealth.[20] Among the Maya, on the Yucatán Peninsula, warfare meant seizure of slaves and control of valuable trading routes and key resources, particularly salt. Like the Zapotec culture, Maya warfare also involved destruction as well as appropriation. Rival centres were burned down and their populations killed or enslaved if they did not provide tribute.[21]

In South America, more recent pre-state cultures engaged in acquisitive warfare on a regular basis. In the Cauca valley in northern Colombia, chronic warfare between chieftains had clear material motives in seizing slaves, sacrificial victims, and concubines, or controlling trade, or taking land. The Tairona fought for control of fishing rights, seizing women (who would be distributed among the warriors who took part) and plundering the goods of neighbouring villages before burning them down and killing their inhabitants. The Cueva chiefs of Panama fought over fishing and hunting grounds, over trade, and for gold and concubines.[22] Control over traded goods was almost certainly a major motive, even more so once contact with Europeans from the sixteenth century onwards provided a supply of prestige goods made of metal. The notorious Yanomami of the Upper Amazon raided more intensely, it has been claimed, when there were disputes over access to or distribution of steel goods and guns or because of competition with middlemen. The Jívaro tribes of Ecuador, particularly the Shuar, also intensified warfare and head-hunting in the late nineteenth century as Western goods became more available, even trading shrunken heads, regarded as a prestige product, for guns, a bizarre commerce that continued well into the twentieth century.[23]

The systematic spoliation of conquered peoples was brought to a new level through the emergence of the first major civilizations in the Near East and the Mediterranean basin. The best example is republican Rome in the first millennium BCE, where the seizure of treasure and resources and the exaction of annual tribute reached an exceptional level. Rome's early expansion was based on raiding local towns and villages. Warfare provided not only the prospect of exacting tribute but also goods to distribute among the soldiers taking part, a key element not just in Roman warfare. Warfare was necessary to fuel the capacity to make war. Early Roman treaties with defeated enemies specified in detail the spoils to be provided, both material and human. The defeat of Carthage in 202 BCE brought booty on a grand scale, to be divided between the Roman state, the military leaders, and the ordinary soldiery. In the Roman wars in Dalmatia and Greece, a primary motive was to ensure the security of the rich Adriatic trade, which Rome sought to dominate, against the pirates along the Illyrian coast. Expansion into Greece, though prompted by political ambitions, yielded further riches. It has been estimated that the wealth seized in the wars between 229 and 167 BCE amounted to 70 million *denarii*, in addition to the artwork and statuary looted back to Rome. In the conquest of Epirus, 150,000 captives were taken and sold as slaves to make money for the Roman treasury. The conquering Roman general Lucius Aemilius Paullus provided so much wealth to Rome that the Senate suspended direct taxation of Roman citizens indefinitely. When Corinth continued to resist, it was sacked in 146 BCE, its people killed or enslaved and its antiquities looted systematically.[24] The predatory nature of Roman warfare was central to its imperial strategy. Warfare made Rome, the Roman elite, and Rome's generals wealthy. The failure to bring resources back from campaigns was a sign of dishonour, aside from the challenge of buying off soldiers who had expected a share of the plunder.

The Roman Republic and the Roman Empire set a pattern that survived across the historic period. Warfare for the next 2,000 years was not universally about material gain and predatory strategy, but there are endless examples of wars in which economic motives played some part whatever the political, ideological, or security interests involved. In much medieval warfare, the promise of booty in the absence of regular pay was the only way of keeping the army or militia focused on campaigning. If kings or princes had their own motives, for many ordinary soldiers, material interests mattered most. Some of the Swiss mercenaries who joined foreign armies in the fourteenth century did so without pay but expected to take a share of the loot as recompense.[25] The Ottoman sacking of Constantinople in May 1453, following a seven-week siege led by the sultan, Mehmet II, who wanted to eliminate the one remaining barrier to Muslim domination of the Near East, was a model of plunder warfare. Under Islamic law, three days of looting were permitted, but Mehmet, hoping to make the city his capital, permitted only one. His army, which had been close to mutiny as the promise of booty faded away during the prolonged siege, only needed a day. Anything portable was taken. Thousands of women and children were bound together in small groups to be dragged away by their captors to a life of slavery and concubinage. The rest of the population was slaughtered.[26]

These scenes could be repeated from any historic period and would fill volumes. The museums and galleries of the Western world are full of antiquities and treasure appropriated through centuries of violent imperial expansion. Cities or major towns were almost always the target, as that was where wealth was concentrated. The vast cultural heritage of Beijing was ransacked by invading European and Japanese armies as they crushed the anti-Western 'Boxer' Rebellion in 1900. Once the Chinese rebels were defeated, there followed what one paper called 'a carnival of loot'. As soldiers and diplomats wandered through the Forbidden City, centre of Chinese imperial rule, they stuffed their pockets with anything they could find. 'Every day looting parties go out', wrote one Englishman to his mother, 'I have done some splendid looting already.' The looting soon became systematic. The Japanese army found the Qing treasury and sent the bullion back to Japan. The British authorities set up loot sales in the city every day except Sunday, a practice that continued into the following year without any sense of impropriety. The proceeds, which reached $330,000, were divided up among the British servicemen still in Beijing based on rank and race.[27] Looting was evidently a consequence of victory rather than a cause of the campaign, but little effort was made to stop it then or in more recent conflicts.

In the Second World War, looting was widespread and regarded as unavoidable, even when it came to looting from allies or from enemies with little to plunder. In Russia, German soldiers ransacked the villages but found little of value. The imminent occupation of Moscow late in 1941 was greeted by men on the front line as a moment of opportunity at last to find something worth taking, but Moscow was never captured. In the Pacific war, looting consisted of extracting the gold teeth of dead or dying Japanese soldiers; marines and soldiers kept the teeth in little gold pouches, to cash in when they returned home. Modern warfare was no less short of economic opportunity than warfare in the classical or medieval past, even though much twentieth-century warfare was destructive on a large scale rather than acquisitive. This was chiefly the result of bombing from the air, which laid whole cities to waste as thoroughly as a medieval sacking. But it also resulted from scorched-earth strategies in the Soviet–German war and the war between China and Japan, which were intended to deny resources to the enemy. More common in areas of Axis domination was the introduction of virtual slave labour for conscripted workers, or concentration camp inmates, or in some cases prisoners of war. Human resources were seized and used as they had been for thousands of years throughout the human past.

Human beings as a 'resource', or property, or commodity represented a particular kind of resource exploitation. This mode of predation has taken various forms historically. The hunt for human trophies – heads or body parts – has an ancient history, though probably in most cases predation was dictated by ritual practices and customary enmity. The same was true of raiding for captives to sacrifice, which was widespread in pre-state and early-state societies, but this was again a resource in only a limited sense, as the victims provided no labour or value beyond their ritual murder. The key form of predation for human beings as a resource was enslavement. Slavery in its many distinct forms and phases was not always a consequence of warfare, whether major campaigns or minor raids. Slavery in the Indian Ocean region or China could also result from indebtedness, or poverty, even voluntary enslavement; in many cases, slavery is difficult to distinguish from forms of enforced labour or serfdom. But in most areas where a slave trade supplied the human resources, the slaves were initially seized violently, even if their subsequent treatment or social experience differed widely between those sold on to other cultures and those kept to service the society that captured them.[28] How slaves were captured, however, has been much more difficult to reconstruct than the life of slaves once they had their place defined as commodities to be retained or traded. Slaves that were sold or exchanged – like the slaves taken across the Sahara for centuries to feed demand from the Islamic states of North Africa and the Middle East, or the estimated 9.5 million African slaves moved to the New World between the sixteenth and nineteenth centuries, or the estimated 1 million or more Europeans captured and sold by the Barbary corsairs between 1630 and 1780 – were almost all in the first instance the victims of violent expropriation.[29]

The capture of humans to use as slaves has no clear starting date. It probably happened among the early chiefdoms as they jostled for power and prestige, but there is no way of knowing with certainty except to look at more modern ethnographic examples. Archaeologists have found Mesolithic 'Venus' models of women with their hands bound, including one from Kostenki on the Don River, dating back 25,000 years, though this cannot indicate slavery with any certainty.[30] The first evidence historically can be traced back to the earliest known polities in the Middle East and China. In the cuneiform script of the first Mesopotamian cultures, there are words that seem to denote slave, like 'man, head' and 'woman, head', usually used to list livestock; sometimes these are associated with the word for mountain, suggesting that slaves were captured from the mountainous regions to the north in present-day Iran. A 'wisdom text' from the Babylonian kingdom of Hammurapi in the first millennium BCE warns readers not to go to the mountains if they wanted to avoid the slavers. In ancient Egypt, in the second millennium BCE, there is evidence of slaves captured in the Upper Nile region or from other Middle Eastern kingdoms as a result of warfare, and by the first millennium BCE, slavery was fully established in pharaonic society.[31]

There is more certainty about the Hellenistic and Roman world, where slavery was embedded in social structure and practices. In the Greek states, slavery was essential to the economy and the generation of wealth. Slaves were seen as a commodity, to be the subject of exchange and commerce. In the first century BCE, the Greek geographer Strabo described meetings between Greek merchants and nomads around the Sea of Azov in southern Russia, where hides and slaves were traded for wine and cloth. The slaves were seized somewhere in the Eurasian interior, but the merchants could also benefit directly from Greek warfare if large numbers of captured enemies could be bought, parcelled out, and sent on to Greek cities for sale. Some warlike raids were deliberately aimed at obtaining human commodities, such as the fifth-century BCE raid by the soldier-historian Xenophon in Bithynia in present-day Turkey, designed to net slaves for capital gain. Few Greeks seem to have become slaves, as trading, raiding, or warfare along the Greek periphery provided a regular supply.[32]

Much the same pattern prevailed in the period of the Roman Republic, when entire enemy populations could be enslaved. The third war against the Samnite people to the east of Rome, which ended in 293 BCE, netted between 58,000 and 77,000 slaves; the First Punic War between 264 and 241 BCE netted a further 100,000. Julius Caesar's claim to have captured 1 million slaves in his conquest of Gaul in the first century BCE cannot be verified, but mass enslavement was characteristic of Roman warfare. Merchants (*mercatores*) accompanied Roman armies, buying up captured slaves at once for sale in the markets of the empire.[33] The great appetite in Rome for slaves encouraged tribal societies beyond the frontier to fight each other for victims to feed the slave trade along the arteries of commodity supply to Italy. In Iron Age Britain in the first millennium BCE, there existed what one historian has called a 'predatory landscape' in which raiders seized slaves and sacrificial victims to be traded with the Roman Empire or used for slave labour by local chieftains. In parts of Essex in southeast England, there is archaeological evidence of abandoned settlements, possibly due to depopulation caused by regular slave raids and trading across the region.[34] One rough estimate suggests that about 100 million men, women, and children (though usually far fewer males, who were often slaughtered instead) were enslaved during the age of Roman imperialism.

The link between slavery and violence is less easy to demonstrate in other contexts, because most of the historical record deals with slaves when the initial violence was over and they were captive. This is true for slavery within Africa, which was widespread long before the start of the Atlantic slave trade. Little is known of the warfare or raiding that resulted in enslavement or of the different forms that slavery took. Only with the onset of large-scale shipping of slaves across the Atlantic from the late seventeenth century onwards is there more information, though little of it detailed, about where and why the slaves were seized, although many were intended for slavery within African societies, not for export. Warfare between African kingdoms or Islamic warfare against unbelievers contributed to the trade because slaves could be exchanged for Western goods coveted by Africans. The sale to Europeans of males captured in war also eliminated them as a future threat to the tribe that captured them. The Asante wars in West Africa from the 1680s, warfare between the Kongo kingdom and its neighbours in the eighteenth century, and the *jihād* wars of West Sudan all resulted in a sudden upsurge of numbers captured and sold on to European traders. Raiding became endemic practice until Atlantic slavery finally ended in the 1880s.[35]

In a few cases there is historic evidence of exactly how raiding for slaves was conducted. Seventeenth-century Portuguese and Dutch demand for slaves on the island of Timor and its surrounding islets relied on indigenous initiative in finding and trading slaves, usually from remote areas or mountain terrain where communities were peripheral or hostile to the local power holders. On Suva, local cavalry hunted in the hills for captives; on Solor, mountain people were captured and handed on. The Europeans also conducted their own raids, often with a punitive purpose. In 1665, Mateus da Costa attacked the kingdom of Wewiku-Wehali, seizing captives to send on to Portuguese enclaves at Goa and Macau; in 1676, on the island of Suva, the Dutch defeated the Suvanese of Dimu and seized 240 people as slaves, to be sent on to Batavia (Jakarta) or elsewhere in Southeast Asia.[36] In another case, the frontier area between Burma and Thailand in the early nineteenth century, two British officials provided a record of raiding for slaves by local tribes. In the mountainous and forested regions outside state control, slave raiders from the Karen people and from the kingdom of Chiang Mai, in what is now northern Thailand, carried out operations designed exclusively to capture people for sale or exploitation. Local words for slave, *kha* in the Tai language and *that* in Khmer, also meant 'war slave' to indicate the cultural link between violence and enslavement. In 1839, one British witness reported that a party of 7,500 soldiers from the kingdom of Chiang Mai attacked three towns and captured 1,815 people of both sexes and all ages for slavery.[37] Although recent interpretations have tried to show that the condition of being a slave in the Old World was often less coercive and penalizing than plantation work in the Americas, the fact remains that many, perhaps the majority of slaves over the past four millennia, began their condition as a victim of warlike violence.

The problem in explaining the economic, or materialist, source of warfare is to separate out other motives from the simple act of predation. There is no general rule. Wars in prehistory or the early civilizations are easier to see as predatory conflicts because of the evidence of what was seized. Some conflicts over mineral sources or trade routes could be regarded as resource wars if that was the chief object. Fighting to seize slaves or sacrificial victims could also be the main motive in raids from prehistory to the nineteenth century. But in many cases, the economic gain was a bonus or value added to a raid or a campaign, something hoped for but not the principal cause. Even in the case of Rome's predation in Greece, there were political and security issues to explain the Senate's decision, first to weaken a rival monarchy in Illyria, then to conquer Greece to prevent empires farther east from exploiting the peninsula as a jumping-off point for war against Rome, as Pyrrhus had done in support of a Carthaginian campaign in southern Italy and Sicily in the 270s BCE. In medieval and early modern warfare in Europe, plunder was certainly expected and needed to satisfy both commanders and men, but it was not usually the first reason the armies or navies were in the field. Even the link claimed between raiding and the supply of metal goods in explaining Yanomami and Jívaro warfare ignores a long tradition of raiding for territory or human heads or vengeance, which was intensified by contact but not necessarily caused by it. Already in the sixteenth century, Spanish observers described a particularly bellicose region of Jívaro territory as *tierra de Guerra* ('land of war'). In the later historic period, pursuit of resources was a variable strategy, but it regularly went hand-in-hand with other intentions.

Some sense of the ambiguities present in any economic theory of warfare can be found in two examples from the modern age that have been popularly regarded as war over resources: the South African War (or Second Boer War) from 1899 to 1902 and the 'Chaco War' between Bolivia and Paraguay from 1932 to 1937, the former over gold and diamonds, the latter over oil. In both these cases, the alleged intervention of capitalists was taken as evidence that material ambition must explain the conflict. The conspiracy theory of capitalist complicity was first publicized for the South African War by the liberal journalist J. A. Hobson in a book published in 1900. He claimed that war was brought about by a 'small confederacy of international financiers' who wanted to take power in the Afrikaner republic of Transvaal where they had interests in the rich gold-mining area of Witwatersrand.

Years later, the British historian Eric Hobsbawm echoed Hobson when he argued that 'whatever the ideology, the motive for the Boer War was gold.'[38] In the Chaco War, the idea of a capitalist conspiracy was opened up by the US senator from Louisiana, Huey Long, who in four separate Senate speeches in 1934 and early 1935 made out that 'imperialistic finance', in the form of his bête noire, the Standard Oil Company, had deliberately fomented war to promote its interests in Bolivian oil. The conspiracy theory lingered on long after the end of the war to become embedded in Latin American folklore about the reasons for its outbreak.[39]

Neither case has stood the test of time. Detailed research on the origins of the South African War has found no evidence that the mine-owning and investing circles, though certainly capitalist in outlook, exerted pressure on the British government to resort to war or that British politicians were ambitious to control the production and flow of gold from Witwatersrand. If anything, the mining interests in Transvaal wanted to avoid war, though they did hope the British government would pressure the Afrikaner government of Paul Kruger to adopt policies that would benefit the continued modernization of the economy and pay more heed to the needs of the non-Dutch *Uitlander* ('outsider') population. What was at stake were British imperial ambitions for the whole of southern Africa, represented by the High Commissioner at the Cape, Lord Milner. The priority for the government in London was political rather than economic, to assert British suzerainty across the region, including Transvaal, and to secure British strategic interests against the imperial competition of other powers, particularly Germany, in what was regarded as a key geopolitical area. The growing confrontation between the Kruger regime and the British in the years leading up to the outbreak of war derived from British demands for reform and recognition of British paramountcy, which undermined the desire of the Transvaal Dutch to remain as independent as possible from British intervention. Otherwise, wrote the Afrikaner politician Jan Smuts, 'Africa will be dominated by capitalists without conscience.'[40] By 1899, the Transvaal was fast becoming the major military and economic power in southern Africa. War came to be seen as the only way to rein in that power and reassert British ascendancy. The mine owners were a means for the British colonial establishment to insist on reform and political ascendancy, but protecting the interests of capital was not the end point of the conflict.[41] Little of the gold ended up in the bullion supplies of the Bank of England, either before or after the conflict, because it was not central to British requirements. Resources were not the root of a conflict that stemmed instead from the imperial appetites of Britain's governing classes.

In the Chaco War, economic motives were more evident, but the belief that the war was a product of capitalist manipulation was a fantasy, driven by the need to find someone to blame for a conflict that proved disastrous for the Bolivian regime of Daniel Salamanca, who had pressed for war in 1932 as a solution to social and political crisis at home. It was certainly the case that Standard Oil had negotiated a deal with the Bolivian government in 1924 for a fifty-five-year concession to exploit Bolivia's small oil reserves and to explore for more in the eastern, lowland half of the country, but the company made only half-hearted efforts to do so, and when oil prices slumped later in the decade, it had little interest in adding to the global glut.[42] Oil mattered to the Bolivian government because it promised to relieve heavy dependence on the trade in tin, especially when tin prices also slumped after the global economic crash in 1929. As Bolivia is landlocked, access to the Atlantic to export oil would be possible only by securing a port on the Paraguay River, which meant crossing the Chaco Boreal, a semitropical and arid region plagued by disease, its ownership contested for decades between Paraguay and Bolivia. At several flashpoints in the 1920s, the two countries almost came to blows in the Chaco, where they both had military outposts, but peace was kept through international arbitration. When Salamanca became president at the height of the economic slump, war was seen as a means of diverting social crisis and possibly of opening a route to the ocean if Paraguay could be pushed aside.[43] In April 1932, the two armies clashed at a small lake in the Chaco Boreal, and when Paraguay retaliated two months later, a full-scale war developed, supported on both sides by a popular jingoism deriving from the ongoing confrontation over who owned the inhospitable area.

In all of this, Standard Oil played no part, although in Paraguay and Argentina the press made great play with the idea of oil imperialism driving Bolivia's decision. The company declared itself neutral in the conflict and moved equipment to Argentina for safety. When company trucks were commandeered by the Bolivian army, Standard Oil sued the government for the loss. Instead of expanding output in the few wells that the company owned, the flow was restricted until the Bolivian government insisted on expansion and took over refineries to ensure that more oil needed for the war effort would be supplied. In contrast to the view abroad, the Bolivian regime actually accused Standard Oil of sabotaging the war. Paraguay soon controlled almost the whole of the Chaco Boreal, with oil supplied from Argentina (some from Standard Oil's operations there), and was only stopped at the Andean foothills by the determined defence of a small Bolivian oilfield by units soon nicknamed the 'Defenders of the Petroleum'. The ceasefire and subsequent agreement that Paraguay could take over most of the Chaco was followed by a Bolivian decision in 1937 to nationalize Standard Oil's assets in the country, the first state nationalization of a foreign company in South America's history.[44] Although the myth persisted that Standard Oil had engineered a war to take over territory for oil exploitation, the company's noncooperation with Bolivia's war effort and subsequent expulsion from the country tells a different story. Bolivia did see the war as a means of rescuing a failing economy by appealing to popular nationalism, but the decision was as much political as economic. It was an oil war only indirectly, as Bolivia already possessed the oil, and Paraguay had had no plans to take it. No oil has ever been found in the Chaco.

The idea of 'resource wars' has nevertheless become a central argument to explain warfare in recent decades, particularly violence between non-state actors in civil wars or insurgencies. It has also become, like 'climate wars', a way of predicting what may happen in the future as the potential tension between high population growth, global consumer demand,

and the declining supply of nonrenewable resources – oil is the best known – prompts conflict between or within modern nations. The term 'resource wars' was first used in the 1980s to describe possible struggle over resources as part of the Cold War, but it was used much more widely in the 1990s to explain persistent civil conflict in areas rich in non-renewable resources, such as Nigeria or Sierra Leone. It has since been applied less discriminately to any conflict where control over the production, distribution, or international trade of both nonrenewable and renewable resources is con-tested violently. The World Bank in a 1999 report found that states dependent on what are called 'lootable assets', such as timber, diamonds, or scarce minerals, were four times more likely to experience conflict. 'The wars of the future', wrote Michael Klare, author in 2001 of *Resource Wars*, the seminal book on the subject, 'will largely be fought over the posses-sion and control of vital economic goods.'[45]

The modern resource war has something in common with conflicts from a much earlier age, where control of trade routes or mineral sites or the capture of humans to enslave or sacrifice might be the main cause of fighting. But in pre-history the resource range was limited and resources in prac-tice abundant. The context for modern resource wars is the stark reality, predicted by the World Resources Institute in 2000, that by 2050 there will be 9 billion humans supplied by a fourfold increase in industrial production eating up not only nonrenewable mineral and energy resources but also those resources that are renewable, such as forests, which disappear more rapidly than they can be replenished. In this scenario, eventual conflict over resources might seem

unavoidable.[46] A 2009 report of the United Nations concluded that eighteen of thirty-five conflicts during the previous
decade concerned exploitation or control over natural resources, and they did not include the 2003 Second Gulf War,
in which regulation of oil supplies was indeed a major factor.
Nevertheless, as the political ecologist Philippe Le Billon
has pointed out, resources themselves do not cause conflict:
violence has political and commercial motives, involving
control over the regional source, or the flow of commodity
trade, or the export destination, and it is political ambition,
or commercial greed, or in some cases military activity that
makes a commodity something to fight over.[47]

In any assessment of the modern conflict-resources argument, it is important to distinguish between different
kinds of resource, different kinds of conflict, and different
geopolitical conditions. Most resources are traded peace-
fully and legally, even where there is tension between sup-
plier and consumer. Many resources are abundant enough
not to merit conflict over their supply. The resources associated most closely with conflict are to be found in areas of the
world where political or ethnic tensions or social grievances
already exist. These include diamonds and other gemstones,
old-growth hardwoods, rutile (or titanium ore), copper deposits, rare animals or animal parts, and, above all, oil. Their
association with conflict is found overwhelmingly in former
colonial areas or areas where the imperial powers, most no-
tably Britain and France, held a dominant political and commercial position: the Middle East, colonial Africa, southern
Asia, the Pacific. These are not the only places – there is tension over oil supplies in the Caspian region and in the oil

regions of Latin America – but they are sites of the civil wars, insurgencies, and outside military interventions usually regarded as part of the resource wars repertoire. The conflicts vary widely in scope and ambition, but they are not usually simply about taking or controlling resources. In some cases, they are associated with demands for secession, as in the case of the Biafran War or the insurgency on the Pacific island of Bougainville; in other cases, resources are needed to fuel an ongoing rebellion or a civil war, as in Sierra Leone or Angola. Sometimes, control of a resource is motivated by material greed; at other times, civil conflicts result from the damaging effect that resource dependence and environmental damage imposes on the large fraction of the population that enjoys no benefit from the resource revenues.[48] The human cost of resource conflict also varies widely but can be extremely costly. The civil war in Sudan from 1983 to 2002 saw an average of 3,000 combat deaths a year; in Biafra, the war cost an estimated 70,000 deaths in four years.[49]

Where resources are used to fuel conflict rather than to cause it, there is high dependence on international businesses willing to turn a blind eye to the looted nature of the asset in order to profit from the gems or minerals or timber on offer from rebel groups or unofficial sources. Without the possibility of selling the resources, usually illegally, there would be no point in controlling them. Resource wars where foreign sales are essential depend on networks of intermediaries, some criminalized, in order to realize the potential profit from commodity sales. In some cases, there has been little incentive to end a rebellion or civil war if that resulted in a loss of revenues, as was evident in the struggle to control the diamond regions of Sierra Leone across the period of civil war from 1991 to the final peace brokered in 2002. The West African conflict has provided a model for the study of resource wars, but the civil war was not about seizing control of the diamond mines as an end in itself but about using diamond revenues (and other valuable minerals) to sustain an insurgency against a government widely regarded as corrupt and insensitive in what was one of the world's poorest states.

The insurgency launched by Foday Sankoh in 1992 against the regime of General Joseph Momah was prompted by social protest over the way diamond revenues had been syphoned away from helping the people of Sierra Leone. Sankoh's Revolutionary United Front (RUF) quickly seized the diamond region in the southeast of the country and used diamond smuggling to provide weapons for the movement and to buy off opponents while choking off the government's source of diamond revenues. Sankoh got help from Charles Taylor, rebel leader in neighbouring Liberia, who needed diamond revenues to help his own insurgency. The RUF also controlled the rutile mines as another source of funding. The region was seized back again by the government in 1997 with the use of a private mercenary army operating from South Africa, Executive Outcomes, but two years later in a negotiated agreement signed at Lomé in Togo, Sankoh was made vice president and given virtual control of Sierra Leone's key commodities. In 2002, the president, Ahmed Kabbah, secured intervention from British forces, and Sankoh's revolutionary career was brought to an end after a decade of savage violence that cost the tiny country an estimated 50,000 dead. A similar link between diamonds, minerals, and conflict emerged in the civil war in Angola between the rival movements Movimento Popular de Libertação de Angola (MPLA) and União Nacional par a Independêcia Total de Angola (UNITA), where sales abroad were used to buy weapons in a war that cost in this case an estimated 1 million dead. This war, too, was fuelled by sales rather than caused by greed, but resource exploitation here and in many other cases both prolonged and intensified warfare while making corrupt appropriation of the profits more likely.

A very different example of conflict over resources existed in the insurgency on Bougainville. A mountainous, tropical island, Bougainville was administered by the Australian Territory of New Guinea through a mandate granted in 1919 when German colonies were redistributed. After 1945, the island became part of a UN trusteeship administered from Papua New Guinea. A concession was granted to a subsidiary of the British mining corporation Rio Tinto Zinc to establish a huge open-cast copper mine on Bougainville, the Panguna, which provided generous revenues to the company and the government but next to nothing to the islanders. After Papua New Guinea won independence in 1975, mine revenues continued to prop up the government, but the mine, covering an area of 8.75 square miles, produced severe environmental damage on Bougainville. In 1988, the Bougainville Revolutionary Army seized the mine, stopped production, and two years later declared independence. After a protracted fight with the Papua New Guinea defence forces, agreement was finally reached in 2000 on making the island an autonomous region; a 2020 referendum found 98 percent in favour of independence, to be achieved by 2027. Once again, battles involving resources proved costly, with the loss of 20,000 on both sides.[50]

A similar secessionist insurgency in 1976 in the Indonesian province of Aceh, on Sumatra, was also based on concern over resources and resource revenue. The region was almost entirely Muslim, and it had a history as an independent monarchy until it was brutally annexed by Dutch colonizers in the 1890s. This sense of difference partly explains the desire in Aceh to demand the right to secede from Indonesia. The discovery of a huge natural gas field in the province in 1971, exploited by overseas capital and the central government together, provoked the formation of the Free Aceh Movement (Gerakan Aceh Merdeka; GAM), led by Hasan di Tiro. As the gas boom developed, President Suharto revoked Aceh's limited autonomy, and the revenues generated by the gas were taken by Mobil Oil (later Exxon-Mobil) and the central government, putting little back into Aceh. The movement called for national liberation and an end to the neocolonial economic exploitation that characterized the new industrial complex built around the gas field. A military insurrection followed, with fighting between the Indonesian security forces and the GAM. After a lull when di Tiro went into exile, conflict resumed in 1989, and by the end of the century violence was also directed at Exxon-Mobil workers and the gas installations. In 2001, onshore production was temporarily shut down by GAM guerrillas, prompting a vigorous response from a government anxious not to lose its substantial share of revenues. By 2003, GAM dominated about 80 percent of Aceh and raised its funds through ransoms, extortion, and 'taxation' of the large industrial corporations that now populated the industrial zone. There followed a new counterinsurgency operation that inflicted severe damage on the rebel forces, and in 2005 a peace agreement was achieved under the terms of which Aceh was granted autonomy within Indonesia as a 'special territory' and the right to live under Islamic Shari'a law. As in Sierra Leone, natural resources were not the immediate cause of the armed confrontation, but control of revenues became a central issue, while resource exploitation by foreign companies was used to justify continued insurgency.[51]

The one resource in the twentieth and twenty-first centuries to have produced interstate warfare, rather than conflict at substate level, is oil. Together with natural gas supplies, widely exploited only from the 1960s, oil plays a critical role in supporting the industries and lifestyle of the developed world and increasingly of the developing world as well. More discoveries have been made to compensate for rising consumption, but for every two barrels of oil consumed, only one new one is discovered. Global oil production reached the midpoint of known available reserves about 2010 and is widely predicted to run out at some time between 2040 and 2060.[52] Natural gas can still be found in large quantities, but much of it is poorly accessible, and its extraction will depend on the evolution of technology capable of retrieving it. For the most oil-dependent states, in Europe, East Asia, and the United States, oil security has been a major strategic priority, not least because a high proportion of oil reserves is to be found in areas with a long history of conflict and potential instability, particularly the Middle East, or in areas where colonialism has left a legacy of ethnic or religious conflict and democratic failure, as in Libya, Sudan, Nigeria, or the Congo basin. Oil lay at the heart of the so-called Carter doctrine, announced by US president Jimmy Carter in 1980 after the Islamic revolution in Iran: that deliberate interruption of the flow of oil from the Persian Gulf would be 'repelled by any means necessary, including military force'. General Robert Kingston, the first commander of US Central Command, covering the Middle East, understood that his role was 'to assure unimpeded flow of oil from the Arabian Gulf'.[53] In the year 2000, Russian military doctrine, endorsed by the recently elected president, Vladimir Putin, specified maintaining the security of Russia's territorial waters, continental shelf, and exclusive offshore economic zone with its potentially rich resources of oil and gas.[54] In 2007, two Russian submarines planted the Russian flag 4,000 metres under the North Pole, where large deposits of natural gas and oil are known to lie, as a preliminary to laying claim to the Lomonosov Ridge, an underwater mountain range linked, it is claimed, with Russian territory. The claim remains contested by Canada and remains a potential site of conflict.

The history of the interstate war for oil in the twentieth century is well known. In the Second World War, some 90 percent of natural oil output was controlled by the Allies; the Axis states, Germany, Italy, and Japan, controlled just 3 percent of output and 4 percent of refining capacity. Germany dominated the supply of its ally, Romania, but that provided too little to satisfy the military and economic demand of German consumers. The invasion of the Soviet Union had a range of motives, ideological and material, but seizing and exploiting Soviet oil in the Caucasus region was a priority, even though German industry lacked the technology and expertise necessary to extract the oil rapidly, even if it had been captured. For Japan, where oil dependence was even more pronounced, the sanctions applied by the United States in the summer of 1941 tipped the balance in the strategic arguments of Japan's armed forces in favour of confronting the United States and the colonial powers, Britain and the Netherlands, whose Southeast Asian colonies had large supplies of oil. Like the German case, the conflict with the West was a more complicated affair than simply the search for oil, but no other motive was more significant in the Japanese choice of strategy taken in the summer of 1941 and in the planned direction of advance. Alongside the oil, there was also the prospect of other resources that the Japanese war effort needed: iron ore, bauxite for aluminium production, and manganese ore. The result was not what had been intended. The oil was captured, but three-quarters of it was used to fuel the Japanese war effort in the Pacific theatre rather than the Japanese home islands, while most of the large Japanese tanker fleet, including new tanker tonnage of 1 million metric tons, was on the ocean floor by 1945, destroyed by the US submarine fleet. For the Allies, heavily reliant on air power, ground mobility, and long oceanic sea-lanes, oil was almost never a problem. When an Iraqi rebellion occurred in 1941, threatening the flow of oil to the British Empire's Middle East armed forces, the rebellion was rapidly crushed and Iraq occupied for the duration of the war.

Since 1945, at least three wars between states involved the security of Western oil. The first, in 1956, involved the Egyptian decision to nationalize the Suez Canal, jointly managed by Britain and France. Because this threatened the security of the flow of Middle East oil to Europe, the two states together with Israel launched a war to take back the canal. Only Soviet and American intervention – in the United States' case because of fears that the war itself might genuinely destabilize the supply of oil – prevented the recapture of the canal and brought the brief war to an end. The two Gulf Wars in 1991 and 2003 were – despite vigorous protest from some of the political actors in the West that there were other more important factors at play – evidently linked to anxieties about sustaining the supply of oil from the world's largest area of oil reserves. The decision by the Iraqi dictator, Saddam Hussein, to take over the tiny oil state of Kuwait, which shared the oil basin of southern Iraq, followed a draining eight-year war against Iran, in which control of frontier oil resources also played a part. Acquisition of Kuwait would have given Iraq control over one-fifth of global oil reserves; pushing on into Saudi Arabia would mean putting an even larger fraction of the oil under the control of an unpredictable autocrat. Although the ostensible ground for expelling Iraqi forces was to restore Kuwaiti sovereignty, the US armed forces had already created an operational plan for an Iraqi–American war, OpPlan 1002-90, to be activated by US Central Command in the event of military crisis. When Saddam invaded Kuwait in August 1990, this operational plan was activated, and four months later in the First Gulf War, Operation Desert Storm, overwhelmed and expelled the Iraqi army. Relations remained tense throughout the 1990s as Saddam Hussein struggled to retain his legitimacy and power, and in the Second Gulf War in 2003, Operation Iraqi Freedom, the West pursued regime change as the only way to provide greater security for an area essential for Western economic interests. The ostensible claim that Iraq possessed weapons of mass destruction and would use them if pushed was regarded at the time, and demonstrated subsequently, to be without foundation.

The Second Gulf War ended as swiftly as the first but involved the overthrow of Saddam Hussein and occupation of Iraq by an international alliance, including British forces, which had a long tradition of oil security operations in the region. What followed was not the clean break the West hoped for, with a secure and increasing flow of Iraqi oil, but instead the onset of what Mary Kaldor has called one of the 'new oil wars'. These wars are not about sustaining oil security for the rich states that need it but about utilizing the oil revenues to serve sectional and local interests. In Iraq that meant Kurdish demands for control over revenues and distribution from the major oil centre of Kirkuk, or syphoning off oil revenues to fund Islamic terrorism or anti-Western insurgency, or criminal diversion of oil via the Persian Gulf or Turkey for private profit. The cost for Iraqis is an estimated 600,000 dead from the postwar violence. The 'new oil war' has a mix of motives, some political, some religious, some avaricious, so that the warfare that has characterized the long pacification in Iraq since 2003 is not simply about oil revenues. Like most modern resource wars, there is no simple or straightforward linkage between control of the resource revenues and the fact of violence.

Much the same could be said of the 'new oil war' in the Niger delta, which has a long history of ethnic conflict and political fragmentation. For most of the first three decades after independence in 1962, Nigeria was subject to military rule that was harsh, corrupt, and incompetent. The discovery of rich oil resources in the Niger delta produced a situation in which large oil revenues were appropriated by the military regime, distributed through a complex patronage system, and reinvested hardly at all in the delta areas where oil produced wide environmental degradation. The major international oil companies collaborated with the regime, which needed their expertise and investment. Oil undermined an economy previously based on the export of primary agricultural products so that by the beginning of the twenty-first century, cash-crop production in Nigeria had been all but destroyed while oil contributed half of GDP and 95 percent of foreign exchange earnings.[55] During the long oil boom, the number of Nigerians below the poverty line increased from one-quarter in 1980 to two-thirds by 1996. The result has been persistent local protest in areas most affected by the oil industry, where a lack of local investment and services has prompted popular resentment. A demonstration by the people of one village in 1990 at a Shell installation resulted in a police action that killed eighty people and destroyed 400 houses. The same year a Movement for the Survival of Ogoni People, one of the ethnic peoples damaged by the oil industry, began a programme of peaceful protest that prompted a similar harsh response and eventual elimination. The Ijaw youth movement, another ethnicity from the delta, in 1998 promulgated the Kaiama Declaration demanding economic justice for the region and the redistribution of oil revenues to the areas where the oil came from. Youth violence against the oil multinationals prompted a further round of repression. Although Nigeria moved to constitutional rule after 1999, there were still 1,000 deaths a year in the delta during the period before the 2003 election.[56] The argument over oil revenues, which fed the political system, was not resolved, and the delta remains one of the most unstable areas of oil extraction, marked by regular attacks on oil pipelines and installations and illegal 'bunkering' of oil for criminal profit.

Interstate tensions over oil and gas may well surface again as the supply shrinks. The war between Russia and Ukraine was not over resources, but the widening of the conflict to include surrogate warfare by NATO opened up a crisis in oil and gas supply from Russia to Europe. The war was a reminder that the 'new oil wars' are not necessarily confined to the Middle East and Africa but may surface anywhere that energy supply and revenues have the potential to become objects of political or military confrontation. Most predictions about resources and future conflict play on the gap between the supply of, principally, nonrenewable resources and the nature of the control – local, national, or transnational – exercised over them. Historically, resource wars have taken many different forms, and the resources embedded in conflict have wide differences depending on whether they are lootable or fixed assets. As with ecological crisis, the future may be one of further technical breakthroughs in energy supply, extensive substitution of scarce minerals or metals, or international agreement over production and distribution. Most resources today are still traded outside the circle of violence.

*

There is no doubt that all through recorded history, and earlier still, resources have been a direct object of many different forms of warfare. It is plausible to argue that they must have been an object of violent predation even before the historical record, once there were stocks of animals, goods, or established trade that were worth fighting for or defending. Trade in humans probably also predated the growth of more organized chiefdoms and states. There is much in common between the tribal conflicts over material gain or loss and the modern resource wars, where weak states can do little to prevent conflict over the revenues flowing from goods with ready international markets. The chief difficulty in describing warfare as the consequence of material ambition is separating out the desire for gain from the other motives that prompt conflict. If, for the regular soldiers and leaders, plunder was a necessary corollary of warfare, often the only means of maintaining loyalty, the campaigns in which they fought might nevertheless be principally for political advantage, religious imperatives, or dynastic ambition, in which predation was a satisfying by-product, but not the product itself.

Certain kinds of violence can with greater certainty be ascribed principally to material gain. Viking raiding in northern Europe, for example, if not for settlement, was about taking resources to serve Viking interests in securing commodities, from slaves and concubines to salt and gold. The Annals of Ulster record regular raiding on the coasts of Ireland. In 821 CE, they 'carried off a great many women into captivity'. Raiding in ninth-century Brittany was carried out to seize human commodities and salt. A raid on Seville in 844 provided a great many captive women and children, some of whom would have been sold on through Viking trade networks down to the Arab and Byzantine territories in the Middle East.[57] This form of what might be called 'commercial warfare' has existed in all times and places, but it is one facet of historical warfare, to be balanced against motives that are ideological, political, or strategic. Oil has been the chief modern example. It is vital as a resource, but only because without it the modern military cannot function and civil communication would break down. The resources that have through time attracted predation do so because of the value that is attached to them culturally, economically, and politically by the predator. The construction of value explains why wars are fought for resources, from slave raiding in the classical world to looting the diamonds and oil of today.

CHAPTER 6
Belief

You who believe, fight those of the disbelievers who are near to you, and let them find harshness in you, and know that God is pious.
— Sūrat Al-Tawbah, The Qur'an, 9:123[1]

With what reproaches will the Lord overwhelm us if you do not aid those who, with us, profess the Christian religion! Let those who have been accustomed unjustly to wage private warfare against the faithful now go against the infidels and end with victory this war.
— Pope Urban II, November 27, 1095[2]

Belief as a driver of war is not a general characteristic of all warfare past or present, but religious faith or supernatural beliefs or political ideology can clearly explain the decision for war in a variety of different contexts across thousands of years of human history. When Pope Urban II used the Council at Clermont in November 1095 to upbraid those present for fighting between Christian communities, he had in mind a call to defend the faith whose Holy Places in Palestine, and much else, had allegedly been defiled by Muslims. The age of the Crusades was launched that year and continued for hundreds more. In response, the Muslim conquerors of the territories surrounding the Holy Places eventually fought back, as the Qur'an required them to do. The Muslim concept of *jihād*, poorly rendered as 'holy war', has often been blamed for centuries of Muslim violence. Though subject in Islamic law to interpretation, the idea of *jihād* did permit defensive conflict of a quite uncompromising kind against those who violated and threatened the religion of Islam or who acted in bad faith or who suppressed the *da'wah*, the call of the Prophet Muhammad.[3] In both cases, Christian and Muslim, defence of religious interests has come to define the confrontation historically, even though other, more secular, aspirations and appetites accompanied that ambition.

Belief as a motivator for war goes well beyond the historical confrontations between Christianity and Islam, the two most bellicose of the world's religions. Whether in the cosmologies of tribal societies or the political religions of the twentieth century, belief can mobilize popular engagement in warfare and justify its necessary excesses. To wage war on these terms, it is not necessary that belief be held with the same degree of intensity by all those participating, but the cause is usually shared between leaders and led. Nor does belief necessarily result in conflict. Belief, whether ancient faiths or modern ideologies, has a plastic quality. Where warfare results, it is often short term, a result of heightened enthusiasm whose force ebbs away after the first spasms of violence: the conquered may well abandon one faith and adopt another; belief can be abandoned or scaled down if the gods seem not to favour the warriors fighting in their name; modern ideology can be shed remarkably quickly, as National

Socialism was in Germany after 1945 or Leninism-Marxism after the collapse of the Soviet Union in 1991.

Partly for these reasons, modern Western history, predominantly secular in outlook, has evolved a sceptical attitude to expressions of faith as a cause of war. It is commonly assumed that belief is used to mask real motives that make greater sense in a self-consciously rational and post-Enlightenment age – class interest, or political ambition, or predatory greed, or material necessity.[4] The British historian Christopher Hill, writing in the 1980s against the idea that the English Civil War was a 'war of religion', gave preference to economic and constitutional explanations, as many historians have done: 'religion', he argued, 'was not a self-sufficient motivating factor' but simply a convenient idiom for the bourgeoisie to mask its political and social ambitions.[5] Belief can certainly be manipulated for other ends, as it has been in the civil war in Northern Ireland or the second civil war in Sudan from 1983 onwards, where Islam was appropriated by the political elite to justify the conflict, but even in these cases religious difference was not artificially created.[6]

Anthropologists are less inclined to view the peoples they study as sheltering behind a façade of belief, because understanding cultures in their own terms is what they do, but even anthropology can turn belief upside down. Aztec cannibalistic sacrifice has been interpreted as a result of protein shortage in central Mexico or as a symbol of ruling-class power.[7] Neither suggestion works for a people rooted in a culture of warfare sanctioned by profound religious imperatives. Belief is not merely an epiphenomenon of human communities but also the way diverse cultures give meaning to the world and what lies beyond, both natural and supernatural, spiritual and mystical. Human societies in the past have all displayed some form of cosmological explanation, and many still do. However exotic or fantastic many beliefs seem to a modern audience, it is necessary to understand them from within, in what anthropologists define as 'emic' meaning, rather than through evaluation of external, universal, or 'etic' terms. Attached to many such beliefs is a commitment to warlike violence that cannot be understood separate from the faith, or belief, or ideas that generate it. Without recognizing the power of belief in mobilizing and permitting violence, explanations for many kinds of warfare will be incomplete or poorly understood.[8]

There is perhaps no better example than the medieval Crusades for illustrating the problem of reconstructing the mentality and the worldview of those who participated on either side. There has been a tradition in historical writing on the Crusades to see them as a result of material ambition for land and loot, led in many cases by men whose Christian credentials were hard to detect but whose material motives and lust for power seemed easier to accept. Recent historical writing has reversed this view of crusading culture.[9] Without ignoring the evidence that crusading knights seized booty from the areas they conquered and jostled for position in the new kingdoms of the Near East that they founded, there is now much greater emphasis on the religiosity of the crusading movement, and in terms understood at the time. This was particularly true of the First Crusade, launched by Pope Urban II in his sermon at Clermont. The pope had his own motives as one of the eleventh-century church reformers:

he was trying to end warfare between ostensibly Christian princes in Europe and to direct their energies against the enemies, pagan and Muslim, that threatened the survival of the Christian world. His predecessor, Gregory VII, even hoped that intervention in the Muslim east might result in Rome exercising spiritual leadership over the whole Christian world, Orthodox Byzantium included. Preaching crusade was consonant with a broader desire to confirm church authority and reinvigorate a Christian tradition of sacred warfare.

It is a fundamental paradox that Christianity was founded on the pacifist injunction to love your neighbour and renounce violence, but after the first few centuries came to endorse warlike defence of the faith. The holy warrior, armed and armoured for God's purpose, became a central figure in medieval Christian culture and can be seen still in numerous effigies and windows in Europe's Christian churches. The link between Christian faith and warfare emerged with the fourth-century conversion of the Roman Empire to Christianity under Emperor Constantine. Although war was still formally regarded as sinful, if it was waged in a just cause – in this case defence of the faith against pagans and heretics – it was no longer tainted. Saint Augustine, writing in the wake of the Roman conversion, claimed that the biblical commandment that forbade killing 'was not broken by those who have waged war on the authority of God'.[10] In the late fourth century, Bishop (later Saint) Ambrose of Milan, a major contributor to early doctrine, found no difficulty in reconciling Christianity with sacred violence because in his view, following centuries of persecution, all Christians were obligated to defend the faith when challenged. For Ambrose, church and state had a common responsibility to wage sacred war, and the model monarch was an armed and militant Christian.[11]

From this period on, Christian zealots and ascetics, many among the early monastic orders, resorted to the torture or killing of those they regarded as heretics or hypocrites, patrolling the religious borders with what was regarded as justified violence. 'Torturers are terribly clever', wrote the early fifth-century Greek bishop Synesius approvingly, 'at refuting pretence.'[12] Christian warriors, however brutal or worldly in fact, could become saints and martyrs for the faith and heroized as such, like the East Anglian king Edmund, killed in war with the Vikings in ninth-century England and soon canonized. Through the Carolingian empire of the eighth and ninth centuries, sacred warfare was waged to defend and expand Christian Europe. Warriors for Christ, according to the ninth-century pope John VIII, won remission of all sin for 'the defence of Christendom'.[13] Over the next 200 years, Christianity fought against major threats from pagans in the north and east of Europe and the Muslim invasion of Mediterranean Spain and France, but only during the period of church reform in the mid-eleventh century did the concept of 'holy war' become a central church ambition. When Urban II preached the crusade, the ground was already laid for the injunction that Europe's princely and warrior elite ought to be fighting the infidel rather than each other.

The First Crusade was part military campaign and part pilgrimage. An estimated 70,000–80,000 European Christians responded to the appeal in the first year by 'taking the cross' – patches of material with a cruciform image to be worn on armour or clothing. The stated purpose was entirely religious. Those who took up the cross would win remission of all their many sins.[14] The object was to free the Holy Places in Palestine from control of the 'Saracens', the general term used to describe the mix of Arabs and Seljuk Turks occupying the Near East. Muslim Arabs had captured Jerusalem in 638 CE and turned it into a holy city of Islam. In 1009, the Muslim caliph of Cairo ordered the destruction of the church of the Holy Sepulchre. For Christians, the city was the site of Christ's crucifixion and resurrection; there were eschatological writings that suggested Jerusalem would be the site of the Last Days predicted in the biblical Book of Revelation. The capture of the city was expected to be a moment of transformation. The abbot of the monastery at Cluny, addressing knights destined for the First Crusade, saw the campaign as fulfillment of the Old Testament passage in Isaiah in which all who were to be saved should come 'to the mountain of Jerusalem'. The apocalyptic atmosphere was captured in contemporary poetry: 'Rivers of blood flow / In these hours / While the race of error dies / Jerusalem, rejoice!' ran one, written in the city following its violent Christian liberation.[15] On the way to the Holy Land, the crusaders were accompanied by priests and monks who provided the liturgy, devotional practices, fasts, and masses to sustain the religious character of the procession. New liturgies were established along the way (one was the 'Feast of the Invention of the Holy Lance'), and before each siege or battle, the crusaders fasted, prayed, confessed, and attended mass.[16] At home, church authorities insisted that Christians support the crusaders with prayers of divine intercession, fasting, and charitable acts, all of which were designed to create the idea that the Crusades were the responsibility of everyone in Christian Europe.

The path to Jerusalem was long and laborious, punctuated by regular battles and sieges. The crusaders and pilgrims were worn down by disease, dehydration, and the ambushes and ruses used by the enemy. The perseverance of the First Crusade says much for its intended religious cause, as there was no other obvious reason to be struggling far from home across hostile desert and hills with high casualties and at considerable personal cost. Jerusalem was finally reached in June 1099, and after a brief siege it was captured. The crusaders, who had been subjected to years of propaganda about the coming of Antichrist in the city, systematically massacred the Muslim population, burned to death the Jews of Jerusalem in the main synagogue, and tortured Eastern Christians into revealing the whereabouts of what was left of the True Cross on which Jesus was crucified.[17] The crusaders sent back or returned with sacred relics and many souvenir pieces of the True Cross. The stories of their exploits were expressed in letters and sermons. Count Bohemond, who became ruler of the captured city of Antioch, told a congregation in France on his return that the archangel Michael (from the Book of Revelation) came to the aid of the crusaders with a host of angels. Those many who died on the crusade 'Michael will lead exultantly into paradise.'[18] This was the idiom within which the crusade was conducted. The extreme violence the crusaders displayed was redeemed by their service to God's purpose and the divine providence that delivered Jerusalem into their hands. Belief seems paramount in explaining the origin and character of crusader warfare, and its ultimate object.

The response of Islam to a completely unexpected invasion, whose purpose Muslims found hard to understand, was incoherent and ineffective. Any history of the religious character of the wars waged to expel the crusaders from their new kingdoms in Antioch, Edessa, Jerusalem, and Tripoli on the Syrian coast must begin decades after the crusaders had achieved the papal goal. But like the Crusades, Muslim warfare eventually came to focus on waging war in the cause of Allah to recover Jerusalem, a symbol of the religious contest between the two sides. There was much less difficulty in reconciling religion and warfare in Islam, as the establishment of Muslim territory relied from the outset upon the willingness of Muslims collectively to defend and enlarge the faith. In Islamic tradition, the Prophet Muhammad during the period of his life known as 'the raids' engaged in twenty-seven campaigns and authorized a further fifty-nine (thirty or thirty-eight in some accounts) for his followers. A collective obligation on Muslims to engage in war to defend the faith dated from the seventh century CE and was built into Shari'a law by Islamic jurists over the following centuries.[19] The root of holy violence lay in the sacred texts of Islam, both the Qur'an and the *hadith*, the sayings of the Prophet Muhammad produced after his death. In *sura* (chapter) 9 of the Qur'an, Muslims are enjoined to combat idolaters: 'Fight them! Allah will chastise them at your hands, and will lay them low and give you victory over them.' Among the *hadith* sayings of the Prophet Muhammad is his declaration, 'I have been ordered to fight the people [unbelievers] until they say: "None has the right to be worshipped but Allah.'" Defence of the faith, according to another saying, brings the greatest of rewards for 'the gates of Paradise are under the shadow of the swords.'[20]

The term used to describe defence of the faith is *jihād*, 'to strive/make effort in the way of Allah', but the meaning depends on the context. The 'greater *jihād*' means personal inner struggle to become a better Muslim; the 'lesser *jihād*' is struggle against non-Muslims and is a collective obligation on the faithful to defend the 'House of Islam' (*Dar al-Islam*) against the 'House of War' (*Dar al-Harb*). The spread of Islam across the Middle East, North Africa, and Spain over the next two centuries was based on this lesser *jihād*.[21] War to defend the faith was waged on the frontiers of pagan central Asia and the Byzantine Empire and against Christians in southwest Europe. It could be declared only by established authority, either political (the caliphs) or religious (the imams). Like Christian just war, Muslim warfare was permitted only when Islam was threatened by nonbelievers, particularly through trespass on the 'soil of Islam', but like early medieval Christian Europe, the Muslim lands saw regular conflict between Muslims, particularly along the fault line between Sunni and Shi'ā Islam as it emerged in the seventh century after the death of Muhammad. By the time of the Crusades, the concept of *jihād* had declined, both in its pietistic sense and as a justification for war, but the example of the faithful warrior for Islam, the *ghāzi*, fighting on the religious frontier from his *ribat* base remained part of Islamic culture and was revived in response to the arrival of the crusaders, or the 'Franj' (Franks) as the Arab world described them.[22]

War to defend the faith took decades to mature in a div-ided Muslim world, undermined by rivalry between the Sunni caliphate at Baghdad and the Shi'ite caliphate at Cairo and the intrusion of the Seljuk Turks into the region. Muslim leaders who fought the crusaders were sometimes hailed in these terms, as was Prince Barak of Aleppo, killed in 1124, whose tomb was inscribed 'sword of those who fight the holy war . . . vanquisher of the infidels and polytheists', but there was no collective Muslim response of *jihād*.[23] The religious leaders of Islam, like the popes of eleventh-century Europe, blamed the failure to wage war for the faith on a lack of piety and true religion. The concept revived only under two Turk-ish leaders, Imad al-Ding Zengi and his son Nūr al-Din. Zengi recaptured the first of the crusaders' new kingdoms, Edessa, in 1144. His son spent much of the time fighting other Mus-lims in order to unify the Near East, but Nūr al-Din forged a close alliance with Muslim clerics to cleanse Islam and revive its mission, and he eventually became an ascetic model for other Muslim leaders.

The symbolic ambition was to take back Jerusalem, which was the third holy city in Islam after Mecca and Medina, the site of Muhammad's 'journey into the heavens' and of the sacred al-Aqsā mosque; as in the Christian tradition, Jerusa-lem was also central to Muslim eschatology, the place where the resurrection and the 'Last Day' would happen. By the 1160s, the Islamic tradition of the 'merits of Jerusalem' was revived as propaganda for its reconquest. Nūr al-Din died before he could lead the *jihād* to take back the city, but his adopted follower, the Kurdish leader Salah al-Din (Saladin), committed himself to wage war for the faith and retook the city in October 1187 following the decisive battle of Hiṭṭīn. His son recalled that before the battle, Saladin had declared 'Satan must not win!' A sermon subsequently preached in the restored al-Aqṣā mosque invoked Allah as the source of victory and Saladin's forces as the army of Allah.[24] By the time the crusaders were finally expelled, with the fall of the port of Acre in 1291, militant *jihād*, in the words of the jurist Ibn Taymīyah, produced either 'victory and triumph or martyrdom and paradise'.[25]

The capture and recapture of Jerusalem was warfare based on religious ambition to own a site sacred to both Christianity and Islam. For both sides, the warfare involved a revival of religious traditions of holy violence and the shaping of religious identities to match the revival. The conflict also involved issues of diplomacy, power politics, and personal ambition, but only belief ultimately explains why the crusaders were there and why they were eventually expelled. Crusading continued in the Near East and Africa for several centuries more without permanent success, while the Ottoman Turks later pushed the frontier of the Muslim world deep into southeastern Europe, to survive until the twentieth century. In the sixteenth and seventeenth centuries, the Christian world descended into a series of internecine conflicts between Catholics and various Protestant denominations over the substantial issue of church reform. The 'wars of religion' that followed the reformers' challenge to established Western Christianity have been subjected to the same kind of scrutiny applied to the Crusades over the extent to which religion was the primary cause of the conflicts rather than diplomacy, dynastic politics, and popular rebellion. This remains, as it does for the Crusades, an unhelpful distinction. These were religious ages in which politics, social structure, and religion were elements of a common worldview. What makes the wars of religion different from other late medieval conflicts is simply that in this case, belief predominated as the motivator of violence. They were wars, or in most cases civil wars, fought because the enemy was defined in terms of religious beliefs, practices, and affiliation. Mobilization of support for conflict depended above all on networks founded on religious identity.[26]

The 'wars of religion' lasted from the mid-sixteenth to the mid-seventeenth centuries: in France, with lengthy interruptions, from the 1560s to the 1630s; in the Netherlands, from the 1560s through the next eighty years; in England, in the civil wars of the 1640s; and in conflicts in central Europe as part of the Thirty Years' War. The theological differences, which were profound, became politicized by the involvement of kings and princes in defence of one confession or the other or to suppress religious rebellion, but the enmities were held with extreme zeal by local religious communities who willingly participated in the violence, each side seeing the other in terms of idolatry or heresy or devil worship. In France, Protestants (popularly known as Huguenots) clung to the Gospels as the truth and paraded through streets calling out 'Long live the Gospel!' while the Catholic mass was derided as 'vile filth'. Catholics saw their Protestant enemy as the instrument of chaos, polluting the social order and desecrating the holy, even, it was rumoured, engaging (of all things) in nighttime bacchanalia, drinking and whoring. Protestants murdered in Normandy and Provence sometimes had pages of the Bible stuffed into the mouths of their corpses to show what little power the Gospel had to save them. In Paris, a baker who made the wafers for Catholic communion was surrounded by a group of Huguenots telling him to call on his God before beating him to death. Much of the civil war violence was taken out of elite hands as the confessional division widened, and Catholics and Huguenots alike took law into their own hands.[27] There were other sources of urban violence in sixteenth-century France, but most historians now agree that religious conflict was about religion.[28]

In the late 1560s, Catholic militants formed the Holy League to combat, violently if needed, the reform Protestants. They rejected any attempt at compromise: 'shall we, then, have to be neutral between God and the Devil?' League supporters saw their enemy in terms of the biblical Last Days, to be purged in order to avoid God's wrath. Catholic preachers stoked the fire of confessional hatred with biblical injunctions: 'kill the false prophets without sparing a single one.'[29] On August 24, 1572, the Holy League, led by Henri, Duc de Guise, massacred the Huguenot leaders and followers gathered in Paris on Saint Bartholomew's Day to celebrate the wedding of the French king's sister to Henri of Navarre, a fellow Calvinist. Catholic crowds followed the lead with a savage militancy against any Protestants they could find. Catholic rhetoric surrounding the massacre echoed that of the Crusades: 'The Catholic Christian rejoices in the death of the pagan and of the heretic, since in it God is glorified.'[30] In more than a dozen other French cities and towns, local Catholic zealots imitated Paris by slaughtering the Huguenot communities; in some cases, royal officials tried to prevent disorder by putting the Protestants in prison, but enraged crowds broke down the doors and lynched those inside.[31] The papacy approved the massacres, in terms usually reserved for the Muslim unbelievers. Indeed, the search for the presence of Satan or Antichrist by those who viewed themselves as true believers re-created the eschatological moment of the opening Crusades.

An even more ferocious religious conflict was waged in the Netherlands, where the Spanish king, Philip II, heir to the Habsburg legacy in the Low Countries, would brook no compromise for confessional tolerance. When rebel Calvinists occupied major cities in Brabant and Holland, the Spanish governor-general, the Duke of Alba, permitted his troops to slaughter many of the inhabitants of each town they overwhelmed, until on December 2, 1572, the same year as the Saint Bartholomew's Day massacre, the entire population of the small town of Naarden – men, women, and children – were put to the sword.[32] The degree of violence exhibited here and in France demonstrates the extent to which confessional differences informed profound hatreds of an enemy seen not just as rebellious or politically dangerous but as an enemy of the true God, to be fought against to protect the confessional boundary, like the earlier medieval boundaries between Christian, heretic, pagan, and Muslim. The iconoclastic violence of Calvinist crowds against church images in France and the Netherlands was a popular effort to reinforce the boundary, 'more God's deed than human'.[33]

Something like the same intensity of religious belief underlaid the conflict in England ostensibly between King Charles I and the English Parliament over issues of constitutional and legal right. Historians of the English Civil War, in this case too, have come to take the religious dimension of the origins and course of the civil war as the missing link in explaining the descent into armed conflict. Puritan iconoclasts took seriously the beliefs that led them to civil war in 1642 to protect England from a conspiracy to reintroduce 'popery' and undermine their branch of reformed, Calvinist Christianity, even when the constitutional issues seemed close to resolution. There were also mainstream Protestants who doubted the king's willingness to defend what the Declaration of Lords and Commons in August 1642 called the 'true religion'.[34] Little distinction was made between the temporal and the sacred; the bishops accused of subverting the true reformed church were seen both as ungodly and as agents of a tyrannical king who failed to maintain a religion whose character had been rooted in law at the time of the sixteenth-century English Reformation.[35] The result was division along religious lines, and it was this distinction that made the resort to war possible. In February 1642, the Puritan preacher Stephen Marshall addressed Parliament in a lengthy sermon in which he exhorted his listeners to join a war to save the true faith or suffer the fate of the biblical city of Meroz (Judges 5:23), which was destroyed by God's curse for the failure of its inhabitants to help their embattled neighbours. As Marshall put it in the published sermon, 'The Lord acknowledges no *neuters* . . . It is Christ's rule, "He who is not with Me is against Me."' The sermon was preached countrywide more than sixty times.[36]

The warning entered mainstream preaching to encourage partisan support for Parliament against the king, the 'militant church, triumphant over the dragon', as a later sermon put it. If Puritans campaigned against the king's alleged challenge to liberty, their priority was defence of the true religion, and it was this rhetorical summons that attracted supporters to the parliamentary cause. When prisoners were questioned by a royalist chaplain about why they had joined the parliamentary army, they replied, according to his later account, that they 'took up armes against *Antichrist* and *Popery*'. Like zealots in the French wars, they adopted the biblical view of the Last Days, widely publicized even before the war began, that 'the whore of Babylon shall be destroyed by fire and sword.'[37] In *Babylon's Downfall*, published in 1641, William Bridge urged that there was 'nothing cruell which God commands', and the subsequent war was waged with biblical sanction for merciless violence, a 'bellum sacri' as some called it. In another pamphlet, Jeremiah Burroughs explained that once God had drawn his sword, 'he many times will not put it up again, until it be bathed, filled, sated, drunk with blood' of the idolators and ungodly.[38] In 1644, *The Souldiers Catechisme* enjoined the parliamentary troops 'not ever to look at our enemies as Country-men or Kinsmen or fellow Protestants, but as enemies of God and our religion . . . and so our eye is not to pitie them, nor our sword to spare them'.[39] As in France, local communities took the violence into their own hands as preachers and pamphleteers drove on the ambition to cleanse and purify the body politic and the sacred body together. It was an often confused and vicious conflict, with much ungodly behaviour on both sides, but the initial conflict was shaped by pursuit of true religion. As one Puritan pamphlet explained, 'God is . . . *a man of warre.*'[40]

When the Scottish leaders signed the Solemn League and Covenant in September 1643 to help the English Puritans, the General Assembly of the Kirk of Scotland declared that this was done to help in the fight 'betwixt the Lord Jesus and the Antichrist with his followers'.[41] Those swearing the covenant were 'to endeavour the extirpation of Popery, prelacy' but to do so as an act of personal spiritual reformation, to match the effort to recover the original Calvinist reformed church. Emphasis on the religious content of the English Civil War does not mean separating religion from politics, for here, as in France or the Netherlands, religious issues melded with political demands and political solutions, often inseparable in the minds of those striving to defend a religious position. One of those who supported the execution of Charles I in 1649, John Cook, wrote a pamphlet under the lengthy title *Monarchy no creature of God's making, etc., wherein it is proved by Scripture and reason, that monarchicall government is against the minde of God . . .'* to explain the way religion and politics were bound together.[42] The role of belief from the Crusades to the English Civil War was to privilege it over temporal ambition. In all these cases, war resulted from the desire to reform or purify existing religious belief; sin, Satan, and salvation were common tropes in conflicts with a powerful eschatological core. Jerusalem's population would not have been massacred, nor confessional dissenters burnt at the stake, nor religious communities butchered, if belief were not a driving force behind the carnage.

*

How far back in history can the relationship between belief and warfare be traced, away from the conflicts between and within Christianity and Islam? Archaeological evidence for early symbolic cultures indicates that archaic communities constructed a view of the world around them that was more than materialist, but their cosmologies are lost, and there is no possibility of reconstructing them. The best evidence that remains are archaic funerary practices that date back before the arrival of *Homo sapiens*, but the practices of burial give no clue to whether these hunter-gatherer communities had a belief system that involved a god or gods or no god at all. And until the Bronze Age, when elaborate graves were granted to leaders and warriors, accompanied by their weapons, there is no way to tell whether death was the result of conflict or not.[43] For the period from the Neolithic onwards, there is much more archaeological and iconographic evidence about belief systems, though arguments remain about how to interpret it. From contemporary ethnographic observation of tribal peoples and early states, dating back to the first European contact, there is much more certain reconstruction of the cosmological traditions in which their cultures were rooted and the link between cosmology and warfare.

There are common features of many cosmologies, even if they unfolded in specific ways in different cultures. There are foundation stories for the cosmos, usually associated with the sun and the earth, whose beneficence must be rewarded with sacrifices to prevent calamity or to guarantee the continued fertility of the land. Among some Amazonian tribes, killing an enemy enhances the fertility of the warrior and his kin by absorbing the identity of the victim. The trope of decline and rebirth or renovation involves ritual that must be precisely observed, often in the form of human sacrifice or blood offerings to appease the gods and ensure their continued protection. In many cases, war and warriors are integrated with the myths. Few ancient cultures did not have a god or gods of war, or warrior cults where the imperatives to warfare were divinely sanctioned: Thor, Wotan, Mars, Athena in Europe, Huitzilopochtli in Mesoamerica, Trito in Indo-European Eurasia, and many more. War was waged always with the blessings of the gods; failure was attributed to a lapse in ritual performance that incurred divine wrath. Seizing captives to appease the gods gave warfare a sacred purpose, and their sacrifice ensured the cycle of cosmic renewal. In early Chinese cultures, endemic warfare was rooted in religious practice and an all-embracing cosmology where the social order was deemed to depend on waging war and sacrificing captives, who were dedicated to the ancestors. At the Anyang complex in China's Henan province, the remains of 13,000 sacrificial victims have been found from a 250-year cycle of killing. Wars were planned in ancestral temples, where altars of grain and soil were dedicated to ensure that war would replenish the earth. If victorious, the left ears of the defeated soldiers were brought to the altars as a blood sacrifice. Combat itself was governed by strict ritual behaviour in order to satisfy cosmic processes that would determine victory or defeat.[44]

The story of the Indo-European mythic warrior Trito, introduced in the last chapter, provides a particularly useful example of the link between cosmic myth and war.

Indo-European myth is rooted in the fragility of the cosmos and the sacrificial rituals necessary to sustain it. At the creation of the world was a priest (Manu), a king (Yemo), and an ox; the priest sacrificed the king and the ox and distributed their body parts, creating the material universe and the human race. They were joined by the 'Third' (Trito), who was the model warrior whose challenge was to overcome an alien three-headed serpent that had stolen the warrior's cattle. With the providential assistance of a war god, 'Third' slew the serpent, paradigm of the enemy 'other'. The model became a central one in Indo-European myth, justifying centuries of raiding and conquest. Before each raid, priests invoked the help of the gods, libations were poured, and animals or humans were sacrificed to repeat the myth of creation by distributing the body parts to ensure that the material world would be replenished. This myth was, according to the historian Bruce Lincoln, 'one of, if not *the*, most historically important narratives in world history' because it drove the warrior culture that led to Indo-European migration and conquest of an area stretching from India to Ireland in the last millennia BCE.[45]

These stories could be repeated for most known cultures, but the example commonly cited for the link between cosmology and war is the Aztec Empire of Mesoamerica in the two centuries before the Spanish invasion in the 1520s. Many earlier American cultures had war and sacrifice integrated through a particular view of the world and its origins, some of which the Aztecs borrowed. The Moche Empire of Peru in the first millennium CE waged ritualized warfare to capture prisoners for sacrifice to link the natural and cosmic worlds. Victims were bound, their throats slit, and the blood was gathered in goblets for the deity Ai Apaec. Iconography shows warfare, capture, decapitation, and dismemberment with cosmological images of earthly largesse and fertility. The nature of Moche warfare and its symbolic meaning is nevertheless still open to interpretation.[46] The difference with the Aztecs (or Mexica as they called themselves) is the fortunate extent to which the elaborate cosmology can be understood and reconstructed from their own records and images. It was also a culture chronically committed to warfare in every area of daily life, for both the elite of Aztec society and the commoners who participated in war or watched its brutal consequences. Cosmology and warfare evolved in a powerful symbiotic relationship expressed through complex rituals, behaviour patterns, and social relations.[47]

Aztec violence is conventionally viewed in terms of mass sacrifice on the platform atop the pyramid in the great temple of Tenochtitlán, dedicated on its completion in 1487 to Huitzilopochtli, the Aztec god of sun and war. To celebrate the dedication, current estimates suggest that 20,000 captives from neighbouring regions were killed, climbing one by one the pyramid steps, to be greeted by five priests, four to hold the limbs over the sacrificial slab, and one to excise the heart with the *tecpatl*, a flint or obsidian knife. The heart was held up towards the sun while the body was pushed back down the steps, past the next clambering victim, to be flayed, decapitated, and dismembered before distribution to the families of those warriors who had taken prisoners.[48] This particular sacrificial ceremony was exceptional, which is perhaps why it has attracted so much attention, but sacrifice long predated the inauguration of the temple – indeed was widespread throughout Mesoamerica. There were other smaller temples or sacrificial sites spread across the city in each *calpulli*, or city ward, which local inhabitants regarded as their link to the Aztec cosmos. It has been calculated that sacrifice occurred somewhere in the city on an average of once every four days. When they captured the city, the Spanish invaders counted 136,000 displayed skulls.[49] The seizure of victims on this scale was a product of Aztec war, which derived from the nature of the Aztec cosmic vision.

The Aztec worldview was shaped by fear of the end of things. Myth related that there were five ages, four of which had already passed, while the last might well end in a cataclysm. To stave off this transformation, the earth deity Tlalteotl needed to be replenished with human blood ('the most precious water') to nourish both his body and the land. The Fifth Age was dominated by the Aztecs' patron god of the sun and war, Huitzilopochtli, who also had to be appeased with offerings of hearts torn from human sacrifice, an act that in the Nahuatl (Aztec) language meant 'spread out' or 'set in motion' to suggest that the blood released would secure the renewal of the cosmos. There were many other gods and many gods of war, including Xipe Totec, god of battles and fertility, for whom the skin of the first captive in battle would be flayed and worn by whoever was the commander on the day, or Mixcoatl, god of war and hunting, and his siblings Mimixcoa, brave warriors who sacrificed themselves to nourish the sun and the earth.[50] These myths cemented the idea that life was born of death, the cycle of renewal requiring a permanent supply of victims, like the unfortunate bound captives thrown live into a fire, then pulled out still alive to have their hearts cut out to ensure that the fire god would continue to supply fire. Men from the *calpullis* would then grab a brand and run to their quarter to show that fire had indeed been replenished.[51]

The warrior and warrior culture were central to Aztec society, expressed in everyday life. All boy infants were regarded as potential warriors. At birth they were raised to the sun as a symbol, and the umbilical cord was buried by a warrior in the grounds where warfare was practised. Boys were scarred by priests as a sign of commitment to Huitzilopochtli and began warrior training along with training for the other occupations they would hold. They entered fraternities where rules were strict and any failure would bring demotion. The object of every warrior was to take captives alive in war. Novices would fight as a group of six, and if they took a captive, a senior warrior would apportion parts of the body to each boy, to reclaim when the victim had been sacrificed. Distinction in battle earned new insignia or clothing to indicate exceptional bravery. Each warrior household would share in eating its allotted body parts after the sacrifice, although the warrior himself by tradition did not; instead, after the sacrifice, the warrior would run to his *calpulli* with a gourd filled with blood, covered with the flayed skin of his captive, to be honoured ceremoniously by his kin.[52] The most determined warriors would wear jaguar pelts (*ocelotl* in Nahuatl) as members of the elite jaguar fraternity, a group dedicated to an animal that represented the warrior's strength and aggression. The fraternity was associated with the supreme deity Tezcatlpoca, whose nighttime guise was a jaguar/warrior.[53]

Aztecs engaged in two distinct forms of warfare, but both served the cosmological landscape. The first were wars to subdue local cities or regions and to extract tribute, part of which might consist of victims for sacrifice. The thousands of prisoners taken in these wars were marched back to Tenochtitlán to be kept in cages in each of the *calpulli*, guarded and fed by the local population until their collective sacrifice. The second form of warfare, known as the 'flowery wars', were ritual encounters with warriors of other cities, where battles consisted of one-on-one combat in order to take a prisoner of high status. The flowery wars were entirely dedicated to finding sacrificial victims of rank to feed the sun god's insatiable appetite. Warfare was a formal affair, waged only in the war season of half an Aztec year, between the festival presaging the harvest and the festival of the first planting (the 'Feast of the Flaying of Men').[54] The flowery wars gave warriors from all classes the chance to shine and so rise up in warrior rankings. Their high-status captives were forced to fight in gladiatorial combat with the best Aztec warriors until they collapsed, when their hearts were offered to the sun god as with all other captives.[55]

The Aztec belief system consisted of complex and intertwined strands, but the cosmology was central to the Aztec pattern of warfare, while the thorough integration of warfare in everyday social, economic, and religious life reflected the priority to keep going through the Fifth Age in order to postpone as long as possible the movement towards the end. Human life in Aztec philosophy was fleeting and fragile, which explains the systematic search for sacrificial victims and the elaborate rituals that surrounded their capture and killing.[56] Warfare was about the survival of the Aztec universe. It is difficult to see in these beliefs simply an elite strategy to maintain social power and political domination of the empire, though this is still a current interpretation, perhaps because it makes the gory spectacle of mass sacrifice somehow more comprehensible in modern terms. Nevertheless, the elite were bound to the system, too, and suffered rigorous tests to become priests or the senior warriors, while commoners could share in the culture of war not simply as passive onlookers but as participants. War and sacrifice were the essence of Aztec society, and the empire project helped to sustain the cosmic necessity of fighting and killing. When the conquistador Hernán Cortés and his small army returned to Tenochtitlán in 1521 to capture the Aztec capital, a leading warrior was dressed as the sun god Huitzilopochtli to go out alone to confront the Spaniards. The subsequent destruction of their empire was viewed by the Aztec survivors as evidence for the cataclysm at the end of the Fifth Age that they had tried to stave off. The lone warrior's gesture exemplified the extent to which belief animated the warring cultures not just of the Aztecs but of Mesoamerican cultures for thousands of years before the conquests.

Belief in the modern age is less obtrusive as a driver of war, but it has not disappeared. The nineteenth-century struggles for national liberation were led by idealists who developed an ideology of entitlement to nationhood that justified the wars waged in its name. In the twentieth century, movements that developed in Europe in the years after the First World War were committed to an ideology of social reconstruction and rigid political conformity. Communism, Fascism, and National Socialism have come to be regarded, in a term coined by the Italian historian Emilio Gentile, as 'political religions', which are as demanding of their members as any puritanical church.[57] They have been bracketed together as totalitarian movements, bent on controlling every aspect of the lives of their people. These were experimental systems whose symbols, myths, and rituals mimicked those of religion; they made a distinction between true believers and heretics that justified in the eyes of the ruling elite a reign of terror against the unbelievers. In the Soviet Union, the trial of those defined as heretics ('enemies of the people') resembled medieval practice, first torture followed by forced confessions of heresy, followed by execution. In Hitler's Germany, the religiosity of the regime was expressed in the taking of oaths to a worldly saviour or suffering exclusion from the racial congregation. Even the title chosen by Hitler, the *Führer*, suggested a guide or prophet, leading the German people to a future promised land of racial empire, purified of those who polluted the racial body – Jews, the so-called asocials, and Roma 'half-breeds'. The earthly paradises promised by the political religions were certainly not the same, but like the major monotheistic religions, there was a necessary shared belief, a political faith in the achievement of a communist utopia or a pure 'people's community', an end point in time, or 'eschaton', when the world would be made anew.

Much academic effort has been devoted to trying to

demonstrate that the ideology driving these political religions led inevitably to warfare against external foes who resented or feared the new faiths, but the evidence is at best ambiguous. Bolshevik warfare in the aftermath of the First World War, particularly the invasion of the new state of Poland in 1920, could be said to be driven by the desire to expand the communist revolution, but defeat outside Warsaw turned the Soviet Union into a defensive state, fearful of the war plans of others, with regular 'war scares' in the 1920s and 1930s. War against Poland and Finland in 1939 had strategic and security aims as much as any desire to spread communism. In the two fascist states, war and militarization certainly constituted an element in the ideology both proclaimed, but Italian and German expansion in the 1930s against Ethiopia, Albania, Austria, Czechoslovakia, and Poland was driven not by the sacralization of politics but by material ambitions to build new territorial empires and economic blocs to underline their great-power status and identity. The colonizing ideology they shared was not so different from the form of imperialism conducted by European powers and Japan from the last decades of the nineteenth century onwards.

The one clear exception was the unique, asymmetrical war waged by Hitler's Germany against the Jews of Europe and beyond. This war was central to Hitler's distorted vision of world history, developed in the early years of his political activity. In his speeches from the early 1920s, as leader of the tiny National Socialist Party, Hitler spoke of a 'life and death struggle', a real war 'between Jew and German' in which only one could triumph while the other went under.[58] This apocalyptic fantasy shaped the ideology of the regime and many of its supporters as they sought to eliminate Jews and Jewish culture from Germany. The ideology focused on the alleged existence of a worldwide Jewish conspiracy to dominate the world and eliminate the German people by provoking war, just as the Jews were said to have acted throughout history.[59] There was an eschatological dimension at work here too in defining the Jew as historic enemy. 'He who contends with the Jew, contends with the devil', claimed a book on 'Jewish criminality' published in 1937.[60] The final showdown with world Jewry was supposed to usher in a new age. When war broke out in September 1939, Hitler blamed it on the Jews for driving Britain and France to declare it; when he unleashed German forces against the Soviet Union in June 1941, it was to destroy the 'Jewish-Bolshevik' enemy; when he declared war on the United States in December 1941, it was against a state whose leader was in the thrall of New York Jews. For Hitler and the cohort of extreme anti-Semites around him, Germany waged two wars, one against the Allied powers, one against the Jews wherever they could be found. The ideological drive to eliminate Jews from Germany and Germany's new-won empire in Europe ended with mass extermination, carried out with guns, machine guns, and poison gas, as if the Jews really were a militarized enemy rather than the fearful, disoriented, and powerless victims they actually were. The transition from ideological fantasy to genocide was a complex one, but of the wars Hitler waged, this was one rooted in murderous belief shared widely by those who carried it out.

Ideology did play an important part, however, in explaining opposition to the new political religions. For the Christian West, the challenge they posed presented a profound conflict of ideals, which in the end justified the waging of war. The Christian denominations in Europe regarded the new totalitarian regimes as a direct challenge to centuries of Christian belief, even to religion itself. Soviet state atheism and the hostility of the Hitler regime to the German churches were seen as evidence that Christians faced the gravest threat in the history of their faith. 'The mystical dogma of Class, Race, Blood, Nation, Force and War', wrote the editor of the French *Revue de Christianisme Social* in 1937, 'are everywhere replacing the mystical dogma of the Gospels.'[61] An ecumenical conference at Oxford the same year unanimously rejected 'any deification of the nation or the state' and the quasi-religious cult of personality. There was an overwhelming sense of doom pervading much of the discussion – 'Mankind has never faced a greater crisis', wrote the American philosopher Melvin Rader in 1939, '. . . as nations plunge downward towards barbarism.'[62] Roger Lloyd, canon of Winchester Cathedral, thought that the final battle of Armageddon predicted in the Book of Revelation, a regular reference point in medieval eschatology, was about to be unleashed by the totalitarian Antichrist.[63] It is significant that Neville Chamberlain in his declaration of war on Germany on the morning of September 3, 1939, justified the decision in terms taken from this discourse on war as a moral crusade: 'For it is evil things that we shall be fighting against, brute force, bad faith, injustice, oppression, and persecution. And against them I am certain that the right will prevail.'[64]

This sense of a conflict that had to be fought to restore the values of the Western world against the menace of totalitarianism derived from the liberal internationalism that emerged as a major ideological current before the First World War, favouring the spread of democracy, liberal freedoms, capitalist economics, and above all peace. Woodrow Wilson brought the United States into the First World War at least in part on this vision of a future warless world. The internationalist worldview did not always constitute a coherent ideology, and despite the antiwar rhetoric characteristic of many liberal internationalists, war was seen as one way – by the late 1930s perhaps the only way – to prevent further war. The result was a paradox. War in the mid-twentieth century could only be waged with destruction on a vast scale, but through destruction it was hoped that a finer future could be constructed based on liberal values. It has been argued that this paradox reflected the long historical tradition of Christian suffering that had been accepted as necessary in order to justify salvation. War was waged, despite its catastrophic nature, to ensure further progress.[65]

In the Second World War, the paradox seemed less puzzling, because the enemy, particularly Hitler's Germany, was pictured as the embodiment of evil whose defeat would usher in a new age. This permitted liberal states to embrace a level of violence against the 'other' that strict observation of the laws of war would have prevented. The city bombing of Germany had about it a biblical character of harsh punishment of the ungodly, captured in some of the operational code names – Gomorrah for the attack on Hamburg, Millennium for the 1,000-bomber raid on Cologne, Chastise for the attack on the Ruhr dams. The paradox was spectacularly demonstrated with the atomic bombing of Hiroshima and Nagasaki, apocalyptic punishment before the opening of a new age for the liberal West, and it has persisted in the belief that possession of nuclear weapons is the only way to ensure that the interests and values of the West can be preserved, even under the menace of extreme suffering. Meanwhile, the lead taken by the United States to contain communism in Korea, Vietnam, and through many lesser conflicts reflects a persistent ideology of defending Western liberal values through violence or the threat of its use. For the United States, those values were regarded as universally valid; deeply embedded in American popular culture, they were to be defended whatever the cost to either side. The war in Vietnam cost 50,000 American and an estimated 2 million Vietnamese lives just to hold back communism. Indeed, the Cold War from the 1940s to the 1980s was defined as much by hostility to communist ideology in the West as it was by any Soviet threat to wage war for further converts. In the post-Cold War era, American commitment to a core internationalist ideology, reflecting American national interests, persisted. President George W. Bush in his State of the Union address in 2006 claimed that the United States had been summoned by God and by history to 'end tyranny in our world'. This commitment has resulted in a permanent readiness for war in which ideology remains a central feature in the pursuit of American strategic and material interests.[66]

One of the consequences of the persistence of Western violence has been the emergence of a radical return to the politics of *jihād* in defence of a puritan version of Islam, long suppressed through the experience of European colonialism and the pressure on traditional religion in the face of secular modernization. This is by no means a recent phenomenon:

Islamic militancy in the twentieth and twenty-first centuries has strong continuities with the distant past of Islamic legal and religious life and with the response of Islam to the establishment of colonial empires by Christian powers. The desire to create a purified religion, common to most modern *jihād* movements, has echoes of the response to the Crusades and draws heavily on the eighteenth-century Wahhabist movement, led by the Arab cleric Muhammad Ibn Abd al-Wahhab, for a reformation of Islamic faith. Modern reformers look to the 'pious forefathers' (*Salaf al-Sālihīn*) as a reference point for their renovation of the Muslim world.[67] In imitation of the efforts of Nūr al-Din to mobilize Muslim religious fervor to confront the crusading Christians, the modern leaders of radical Islam appeal to the language of the medieval struggle to justify their *jihādist* movements, 'fighting in the way of God'. The Iranian leader Ayatollah Khomeini saw in the conflict with the West 'the last stage of the historical crusades'; one of the founders of modern Islamic resistance in the 1950s, Sayyid Qutb, invoked *jihād* 'against the crusader spirit which runs in the blood of all Westerners'. The journal of the Islamic State of Iraq and Syria (ISIS) repeatedly invoked the fight against 'the crusader coalition' and hoped to rescue Muslims unfortunate enough to be living 'amongst the crusaders'.[68]

The revival of the ancient tradition of *jihād* dates back to at least the 1950s and 1960s with the rise of the Muslim Brotherhood in Egypt and the broader Muslim hostility to the new state of Israel and its Western supporters. But not until the Soviet invasion of Afghanistan in 1979 and the successful Iranian revolution the same year did the call to defence of the faith become more widespread, and in many cases more strident. The summons of the *mujahidin* from all over the Muslim world to fight against Soviet efforts to undermine Afghani Islam was the first real manifestation of modern *jihād*. This practical violence was supported by Islamic clerics and jurists who returned to ancient texts to justify the violence and explain its purpose. The 1984 *fatwā* of Aballah Yūsuf Azzām, 'In Defence of Muslim Lands', was a major influence; the 1993 treatise on Muslim war by Muhammad Khayr-Haykal, although against extreme violence, was another. Azzām saw Afghanistan as the site of a possible Islamic state to be used as a base for the eventual reconquest of the lands that had once been firmly Muslim, from southern Spain to central Asia. He argued that *jihād* was a requirement on all Muslims, as the original meaning intended, but in doing so he made defence of the faith an individual obligation rather than a collective one, circumventing the traditional Islamic injunction that the call to war could be made only by religious or secular leaders. Azzām thus opened the way to *jihād* waged without formal authorization.[69]

More significant, the failure of Muslim governments and leaders to defend a pure version of the faith permitted war against the apostates of Islam as well as the idolators and polytheists of the modernizing West. One theological response in Islam is to declare apostates, particularly rulers who 'rule by other than God's laws', as subject to *takfir*, or 'declaration of infidelity'. Rulers who pretend to be Muslim will incur the wrath of God as much as the infidels who invade Muslim land.[70] This explains why much of the current wave of Islamic war is waged against other Muslims as well as the 'polytheistic and idolatrous' enemy in the West. Because modern *jihād* can be waged without authorization from above, the number of groups fighting for a purer Islam has proliferated: the Armed Islamic Group in Algeria, which declared all Muslims who worked for the regime as infidels; the Jemaah Islāmiyyah in Indonesia; Ansar Bayd al-Maqdis and Ansar al-Sharī'ah in Egypt; Harakat al-Shabaab al-Mujahiddeen in Somalia targeting apostate Muslims and the infidel enemy; Boko Haram in Nigeria; Taliban in Afghanistan and Pakistan, divided into distinct groups; and al-Qaida, which operated (despite its name meaning 'base') right across the arc of Muslim lands from Afghanistan to Yemen.[71] These groups are linked through transnational networks of Muslim volunteers and activists, many from the World Muslim League set up in the 1970s to campaign for a global awareness of an existential threat to the Muslim *umma*, or 'nation', and to promote through propaganda Pan-Islamist activism in its defence. There is as a result no single *jihād* but rather a range of conflicts dictated by differing circumstances and by differing interpretations of traditional Islamic law and theology.[72]

Much of the current explanation for the revival of Islamic warfare, like the materialist explanations for the Crusades, sees religion as the idiom in which more significant political and social protest can be cloaked instead of taking the religious element of the violence at face value. Social science generally assumes that those who gravitate to radical Islamic groups do so because they are the victims of Western globalization, which leaves them impoverished, marginalized, and resentful (as many indeed are), or because they need a distinct identity in order to challenge the threat posed by violent Western intervention, or because they are attracted by the familiar ideology of Muslim political insurgency. The temptation is to see movements that claim to be based on a historic defence of Islam as sham religiosity, to be exposed by the 'real' motives of those who take part as social and political actors. These are interpretations hard to reconcile with the aims and (extreme) actions of those groups that have declared *jihād*, unless all belief is to be dismissed as so much expedient rhetoric rather than an essential explanation for behaviour that is otherwise difficult to understand once the religious imperatives are played down or ignored. While it is no doubt the case that people can be coerced into supporting a religious cause or join because of social resentment, it must be the cause that counts when explaining religious warfare.[73]

The authentic nature of religious motivation is evident in some well-known examples. The Nigerian Boko Haram movement (literally 'Western Education is Forbidden'), the popular name for the 'People Committed to the Propagation of the Prophet's Teaching and *Jihād*', has been influenced by the writing of the eighteenth-century Islamic reformer Sheha Uthman Dan Fodio, who defined the character of infidelity among Muslims and the apostasy of rulers who ignored the laws of God. Boko Haram has also drawn on traditions of Islamic revivalism in West Africa, which developed under British rule into an apocalyptic vision of the confrontation with the West and with all those accused in Muslim eyes of degeneracy, apostasy, or abandonment of the faith. In this case, *jihād* is waged to purify religion, impose Shari'a law, and punish those who have betrayed the true religion, often with extreme violence against those deemed to be ungodly.[74] The idea of war against unbelievers and apostates reached its apogee with the founding of al-Qaida and then with ISIS. Both are puritanical movements committed to the reconquest of former Muslim lands and the imposition of Shari'a law. Both are Sunni Muslim, which pits them against Shi'ite Muslims as well as the world of 'crusaders' and their apostate Muslim allies, although Shi'ite *jihādists* also began their own version of religious war in the wake of the first Persian Gulf conflict. Al-Qaida's principal figure, Osama bin Laden, published a 'Declaration of War Against the Americans' in 1996, followed two years later by the 'World Islamic Front for Crusade Against Jews and Christians', giving a direct political substance to the waging of religious war and terroristic violence. ISIS went further in the ambition to found a new caliphate as the core of a new Islamic state that would spark a real reform and revival of Islam.

ISIS has pursued a form of Islamic puritanism derived from readings of the Qur'an and the *hadith*. As in all the religious wars described above, ISIS supporters saw themselves as true believers. They also shared an apocalyptic vision of the clash between the Islamic state and the world of infidels and apostates that mirrored the eschatological imagination from the Crusades to the English Civil War. ISIS established a caliphate, revived what it saw as a conquest society initiated by Muhammad, and campaigned for all Muslims to struggle for a global 'Abode of Islam'. Its members believed that the final battle foretold in the Qur'an would take place at the small Syrian village of Dabiq, recorded in the *hadith*, and named the ISIS mouthpiece journal after it. During the final apocalyptic struggle with the forces of Satan, both Jesus and the Mahdi ('messianic guide') were to appear to help defeat the infidel enemy and all Muslim heretics.[75] The end times would be revealed only by God, when *jihād* would be replaced, as the Qur'an explained, by *qitāl*, a state of true war. Violence that killed other Muslims – a suicide bomber, a car bomb – could be justified bizarrely by reference to Muhammad's siege of the town of Ta'if in 630 CE, where mangonels (stone-throwing siege catapults) were used indiscriminately against the people within.[76] ISIS leaders assumed that the conquest society they created would win the conflict with the unbelievers through the divine intercession of Allah. For those fighters for Islam who died in the confrontation, their reward was paradise, a promise that drew on a long tradition in Islamic religious writing.[77]

It is well known that the great majority of Muslims worldwide did not and do not subscribe to the vision of a future world Islamic state or to the extreme violence with which the new warriors for Islam, like the medieval *ghāzi*, hoped to achieve it. In Islam, as in Christianity, there is also a theological tradition of tolerance and peaceability, fragile though it may appear. But historians of the future will look back at the fifty years of modern *jihād* as another period of religiously inspired warfare, whatever political, social, or economic motives might be entwined with it. Islamic militancy is not an aberration but part of a long tradition, going back to the days of Muhammad himself and the founding of the first conquest society, just as Christianity has a tradition of militancy on behalf of one or other variety of the faith.

In all these cases, from the Crusades to ISIS, much of the scholarly analysis of their causes has rested on another belief: that humans do not really go to war for religion or ideology or the supernatural but for reasons comprehensible to the modern Western view of human behaviour, driven by material interests, political ambitions, or social protest. There has been a reluctance to abandon the 'rational actor model' or to accept that there may be other realities for those who choose war.[78] The 'myths' at the heart of all religions and cosmologies can easily be dismissed, as the literary critic David Leeming has suggested, as 'false belief and superstition' in response to the 'scientific-rationalist training' to which modern populations are generally subject.[79] In the past decades, however, historians and social scientists have begun to argue that belief must be injected back into any analysis of warfare where religious or ideological motives can be seen to be paramount. This is almost certainly how many of those fighting 'wars of religion' would have interpreted the events in which they participated. Anthropologists have long understood that the beliefs they observe among the small fraction of human societies still animated by an older supernatural apprehension of the world around them are real enough for the individuals who live by these beliefs. Belief in all these contexts can lead at times to violence, often extreme violence, however disposed a modern observer might be to consider belief extraneous to the 'real' material motives. Belief has never universally resulted in violence, but at points where belief is thought to be under threat or has to be reinforced by conquest or sacrifice, it can be a primary driver that cannot by any measure be rationalized away.

CHAPTER 7
Power

> Keep this fact before your eyes: that if you overcome
> the enemy not only will you be the complete masters of
> Africa, but you will win for yourselves and for Rome the
> unchallenged leadership and sovereignty of the rest of
> the world.
> — Speech ascribed to Scipio Africanus by Polybius[1]

After the Roman forces under Publius Cornelius Scipio Africanus defeated the Carthaginian army at Zama in 202 BCE,
North Africa became another part of the world dominated by
Roman *imperium*, or the right of command. The Roman Republic now became the prevailing power throughout much
of the Mediterranean basin. According to the later Greek historian Polybius in book XV of his history of Rome, Scipio
dangled before his troops on the eve of battle the prospect
that victory would bring world power to Rome and its people.
True or not, Zama was the high point in the long rise of Rome
from a small city-state of the sixth century BCE to a republican empire stretching around the Mediterranean littoral.
It was an achievement, Polybius believed, 'which is without
parallel in human history'.[2] Illyria in the western Balkans and
then Greece were both added to the zone of Roman power

by the second century BCE. Though other motives can also be ascribed to the wars almost continually waged by Rome and its allies, it is difficult not to conclude that the pursuit of power at the expense of other polities, big and small, was the driving force of Roman warfare in the first six centuries of Rome's existence.

Power itself is evidently an elastic concept, difficult to measure and the object of multiple definitions in all languages. So complex is the semantic understanding of power that the American political scientist Robert Dahl, author of one of the first scientific studies of the concept in the 1950s, concluded that for some scholars 'the whole study of "power" is a bottomless swamp.'[3] It is nonetheless a key concept in all discussions of warfare and national policy in the modern age. First used in this sense of national power by the early eighteenth century, the linguistic turn is now a familiar one: great powers, rising powers, declining powers, balance of power, power transition, and military power are the bread and butter of any discussion of the relationship between states and the possibility of war between them. In this context, the original Roman term *imperium*, or the right of command, remains a primary definition, whether applied to society at home or domination over a neighbour or more distant enemy. This was the essence of Dahl's definition of power: 'A has power over B to the extent that he can get B to do something that B would not otherwise do.'[4] This need not involve war or military pressure at all, as Dahl's own example was to explain the 'power' that American senators held when it came to affecting policy. In the case of states, it is more useful when discussing power to distinguish between 'hard power' and 'soft power', the first expressed as military capability, the second the power exercised through political pressure, social hierarchy, economic dominance, or cultural imperialism. To understand the relationship between warfare and power, it is the first version that matters: use of war or its threat to extend and exercise power over others, or what is called 'compulsory power'.[5]

This form of power was central to the formation of the first chiefdoms, kingdoms, and empires. In another seminal contribution, the anthropologist Robert Carneiro claimed that the origin of the state lay in the extension of power by one tribal community over others, usually through men who had distinguished themselves in warfare and now claimed the role of chieftain. The step from 'village autonomy to supravillage integration' was, Carneiro claimed, the fundamental step; everything else that followed, from chiefdom to kingdom to empire, was a change in degree, not kind. The evolution of differing degrees of power over others was almost entirely due to warfare, made possible by generating an economic surplus from larger and more concentrated populations. Force, he concluded, was what moved humans from villages to the state.[6] Carneiro did not see this as war only for the sake of power but in response to ecological pressures or resource competition, in which larger and more militarily effective units prevailed over those that were weaker. Power, in other words, was power *for* something – more land, tribute, slaves, resources. Power is not a commodity but a state of being, defining the relationship between those commanding and those commanded. Possession of coercive power makes warfare possible, but the motives for exercising that power are usually what explains the resort to conflict, whether material, ideological, or political.

For most of human existence, the idea of power was absent among small egalitarian communities, where the possibility of migration made physical domination by one group over another unlikely, though it did not rule out skirmishes and raids to secure material needs. The transition to larger polities with more social segmentation, as Carneiro described it, still revolved around access to and competition for resources, but power for emerging elites meant the ability and willingness to coerce others into accepting the unequal distribution of social esteem and material possessions and the legitimacy of their rule. Power in this sense is manifested in two distinct ways in relation to warfare. First, power can be pursued and exercised over external communities through war, a common feature from the first tribal chiefdoms to the historic state. Power here was also the power to defend the community against the threat of others' power, perhaps the most important if neglected manifestation of coercive power. Second, power over the internal community, whether a small chiefdom or a larger state, can in some and perhaps many cases depend on the chief, king, or broader elite conducting warfare to validate their claim to leadership, to be able to reward warriors and followers, to satisfy popular clamour, and, when needed, to propitiate the gods.[7] The pressure on leaders to make war is widely attested in archaic and premodern societies, where the choice to do otherwise was culturally circumscribed. Aztec rulers when they ascended the throne were expected to make war at once to demonstrate their legitimacy; leadership among the small chiefdoms and kingdoms of Europe following the end of Roman rule relied substantially on skill in warfare, usually led in person.[8] Failure to make war, as much as failure in war, could undermine the claim of leaders to rule. Power had to be demonstrated, not merely enjoyed, and for much of the past 5,000 years that meant making war against neighbours, often frequently and regularly.

It is more challenging to find war waged simply to extend power for its own sake rather than for some material, or ideological, or political ambition for which power is a condition but not the motive. In most wars in the historic period, pursuit of power played a part, if only as a description of its outcome one way or the other. To understand the pursuit of power as an aim in itself, it is necessary to return to Scipio and the defeat of Carthage. In describing Roman victory, Polybius teased his readers with the question of why Rome in a matter of decades had come to dominate 'almost the whole of the inhabited world'. Historians have asked the same question. There is a long tradition of seeing Rome's expansion from the fifth century BCE as chiefly defensive, acquiring a vast empire as if pressed to do so by others, rather like the equally unconvincing view of the British Empire as something constructed absentmindedly during the course of centuries of imperialism. This is a view difficult to reconcile with persistent aggressive warfare and expansion that came to embrace the entire Mediterranean basin, North Africa, the Balkans, Asia Minor, and much of western and central Europe; such a history stretches the idea of 'defensive' far beyond any reasonable limit. That is not to rule out wars fought in response to the aggression of others, but the consequence was in most cases the extension of Roman power of command over new peoples. Far more convincing is the argument that Rome was indeed driven by the pursuit of power to secure its ascendancy over what Romans regarded as the *orbis terrarum*, the entire world as they knew it. Throughout this world it was possible to boast by the start of the first millennium CE of the *imperium Romanum, sine fine*, 'Roman command without end'.[9]

To better understand the nature of that power, there are distinctive features of Roman expansion derived from the nature of Roman society and the way in which the Roman elite and citizens viewed it. The 'empire' was not described as such until at least the first century BCE, when the term *imperium popoli romani* first appears, and here again the sense is of Roman command. Roman expansion was based not on an idea of territory – in an age when mapping was still all but unknown – but on peoples conquered and 'under command'. This could also include peoples forced to pay tribute but still politically separate, who were also subject in Roman language to *imperium*, as Carthage was for fifty years after its defeat at Zama until it was attacked and destroyed in 146 BCE for reasons that remain obscure.[10] It was the same year that the Romans sacked Corinth in Greece to stamp their command on the peninsula before embracing Asia Minor and moving on into the Near East. War for power and glory was integral to Roman society and celebrated as such; it was also central to the way the Roman aristocracy and military leadership enjoyed their domestic power. This was true of Julius Caesar in his conquest of Gaul in the first century BCE or of his contemporary Pompey, who left an inscription claiming his subjection of 1,538 towns and forts to Rome when he conquered Spain and the Near East.[11] This was not a planned expansion, nor was there a standard pattern of extending *imperium*, but once achieved republican Rome almost never abandoned its power, which derived ultimately from a military force whose organization, technology, and tactics by the fourth century BCE set Roman armies in a class apart for hundreds of years.[12]

The two consuls appointed by the Roman Republic each year were expected to make war or explain why not. Success for them or the generals they appointed was crowned with an elaborate triumph in which captured chiefs and kings were led in chains to the Forum and in most cases publicly executed as an expression of Roman power over other peoples. The cultural symbols of dominion were essential to the image of Roman power. Roman commanders had arches built to celebrate what they had achieved. At least 300 of them still survive. To achieve success always meant pressing beyond the area already under command, so that power at home and abroad evolved in harness. There developed a sense that Rome could expand indefinitely. In *The Aeneid*, written in the first century BCE, Vergil has Jupiter grant the Romans '*imperium* without end'. By the time Augustus became the first *principes* (poorly rendered as 'emperor') in 14 BCE, expansion was almost over except for the Roman conquest of Britain and of Dacia on the Danube. Inscribed on his epitaph was the following heading: 'Accomplishments of the divine Augustus, by which he subjected the world to the rule of the Roman people'.[13] The spread of Roman *imperium* was traced by the elaborate network of roads, marked at regular intervals, first in the Italian peninsula, then across Greece into Asia Minor, where the markers were in Latin with Greek subtitles. Roads substituted for effective mapping, marking out the regions where the power to command was understood to exist. The Roman sense of unlimited power, driven by the favour of the gods, was also a civilizing mission. It was assumed that Roman expansion was good for those brought under Roman command, and indeed there were advantages for those who maintained faith (*fides*) with Roman power. Those who broke the bond, however, were subjected to merciless punishment.

Rome was not the only aggressive power in the classical age of Roman expansion, but it was the most successful. The idea of creating a universal, one-world system was also not confined only to Rome but was characteristic of the fantasies of a great many warring empires. The Greeks had the idea of a *kosmopolis*, a superpower city, which by the second century BCE Rome came to represent for the Hellenistic world.[14] In eastern Asia, Chinese 'warring states' had visions of universal rule, 'All-Under-Heaven'; the Qin Empire that followed created the title 'emperor' (or 'august thearch' in the original Chinese), to rule the entire known world as the son of heaven.[15] The Japanese imperial house, dating back to the legendary emperors of the seventh century BCE, developed the concept of 'the world beneath one roof', that of imperial Japan. Later, the empire of Chinggis Khan laid claim to universality following the early thirteenth-century CE conquest of much of Eurasia; his name translates as 'universal ruler.' The Mongol Empire rested like that of Rome on regular and destructive warfare in pursuit of power against those who failed to acknowledge the khan's authority. Chingiss claimed a mandate from the sky god, Tengri, to rule the steppe, but as the empire expanded, the mandate changed to embrace the whole world, 'from the place where the sun rises to the place where the sun sets'. An edict declared that on Earth, 'there is only one lord, Chingiss Khan', and Mongol ideology divided the world into two parts, that already conquered and the part still to be subjugated.[16] As a result, waging persistent war was inseparable from the Mongol imperial project, as it has been for almost all known empires at some point in their history, including the British Empire on which, so it was claimed, 'the sun never set'.

The case of Chinggis Khan nevertheless highlights a form of power seeking different from that of Rome or most other classical or modern empires, which were constructed over time by generations of leaders, soldiers, and officials. It is best captured in the term 'hubristic power'; that is, power associated with the personal ambition and achievements of a single individual who, like Chinggis Khan, used warfare to carve out a vast but temporary empire. The ancient Greek term *hubris* suggested arrogant challenge to the gods by a mere mortal, doomed to end in calamitous collapse, or *peripeteia*, but it can be applied without too much linguistic distortion to a great many historical examples.[17] Unlike almost all the other explanations for warfare that feature in this book, hubristic warfare is about individual personalities rather than systems, contexts, and cultures. Their power seeking through war derives from a particular set of historical circumstances; it is aided by others, not least the military; and it can be masked by a variety of alleged motives beyond mere pursuit of power for its own sake. But individual, hubristic ambition is the engine driving the machinery of war.

The best examples of hubristic warfare are well known: Alexander the Great, Napoleon Bonaparte, and Adolf Hitler. Although far apart historically, their careers have some instructive parallels. All three emerged on the fringes of the regions they would conquer, the first in Macedon in northern Greece, Napoleon in Corsica, Hitler in Austria. All three were responsible for creating vast territorial empires in a short time – Alexander in nine years, Napoleon in ten, Hitler in five – which in different ways then collapsed when the central figure died or was defeated. All three never knew when to stop once warfare was started, though all three would blame others for making them wage war continually. Their ambitions prompted wars of the most brutal kind on a huge scale, while their personal authority kept their armies fighting regardless of the cost. They shared a propensity for bouts of vain anger if they suspected deception or resistance among those around them. All three had a sense that they were chosen providentially in some way to fulfill their role. Alexander understood that the claim he might have been fathered by Zeus, king of the gods, could confirm his destiny to conquer; Napoleon was crowned as emperor in 1804 'on the throne on which Providence has placed me'; Hitler developed from early in his career a sense that he alone was chosen, perhaps by God, to rescue Germany through his own efforts. All three, despite an artificial diffidence, were attracted to the reality and symbols of personal power, whether Alexander in his royal tent requiring obeisance from his subjects, or Napoleon creating a sumptuous court despite his republican sympathies, or Hitler in the new Chancellery building seated in a vast study to overawe any visitor by the material image of power. All three survived the demise of their imperial projects through a public fascination with their historical impact. Lives of Alexander began to be written before his early death and continued through Greek and Roman antiquity, up to the present day; Napoleon had fifty biographies written in the first years of his career; the history of Hitler clutters the shelves of bookshops worldwide.

The relationship between power and war that these personal histories demonstrate nevertheless requires a closer inspection; there were evidently many differences between them, dictated chiefly by the unique historical context in which their power evolved. Alexander III of the northern Greek kingdom of Macedon, known not long after his death, but not before, as Alexander the Great, was an exceptionally precocious conqueror: succeeding his father Philip II as king at the age of twenty in 336 BCE, he conquered 2 million square miles of territory in less than a decade before dying aged only thirty-two in June 323. Sources on Alexander are not plentiful, and most were written centuries after his death, derived from earlier and often divergent accounts. But used cautiously, enough can be gleaned both of Alexander's personal history and of the path of conquest. Alexander owed much to his royal father, Philip II, who unified Macedon, defeated threats on the state's borders, and built a formidable military force based upon a phalanx of heavily armed infantrymen who wielded with two hands the *sarisa*, a spear that was five to six metres in length and had a heavy iron blade.[18] Philip used the new force to subdue the warring cities of Greece, and in 336 BCE he planned a campaign against the Achaemenid Empire in Persia, ostensibly to liberate Greek cities on the coast of present-day Turkey and to exact revenge for the damage the Persians had inflicted on Greece a century before. A force of 10,000 was sent across the Bosporus under command of the Macedonian general Parmenion, but before Philip could undertake a campaign, he was assassinated. Alexander inherited the power of Macedon and the plan to invade Persian territory; there is no certainty about Philip's intentions, but it seems that Alexander set out not simply on a war of revenge but on a war to destroy the vast Achaemenid Empire. Before he disembarked on the Asian side of the Hellespont, he is said to have flung a spear into the ground as a symbol of 'spear-won land' that would come from the conquest of Asia.[19] After a visit to the tombs of Achilles and Ajax at the site of Troy, an act to associate the new king with the Greek heroes of the past, Alexander embarked on a campaign that saw major victories over the Persian armies of Darius III at the Granicus River, Issus (both in Turkey), and decisively at Gaugamela in the Mesopotamian plain. In between he conquered the eastern Mediterranean littoral (destroying Tyre in a seven-month siege, massacring the men and enslaving the women) and occupied Egypt.[20]

There is much speculation about Alexander's ambitions. He was brought up in a world of military endeavour, immersed in a culture of military gods and heroes, descended it was claimed from Achilles on his mother's side and from Heracles (Hercules) on his father's, even, so it was rumoured, fathered by Zeus. There were omens at his birth that he would be 'invincible' or 'unconquered'. Later his court seer, Aristander, obligingly provided auguries to cement Alexander's sense of invincibility. A later classical biographer, Arrian, saw Alexander as 'zealous for honor' and having an 'utterly insatiable appetite' for glory, which are certainly not incompatible with his evident thirst for conquest.[21] He was a remarkable battlefield commander, the epitome of the childhood heroes he idolized and imitated. Each victory fed his sense of destiny, and a campaign that began as the liberation of Greek cities from Persian rule became a hubristic campaign to conquer much of the known world. When he arrived at Gordium in Anatolia, he solved the challenge to untie the 'Gordian knot' by simply cutting through the rope with his sword hoping to fulfill the prediction that whoever did so would be 'ruler of Asia'.[22] The scale of his ambition was clear from Alexander's arrival in Egypt, where he was declared to be a new pharaoh. He travelled across the desert to the oracle at Siwa in present-day Libya ostensibly to discover whether his birth was indeed special. The priests are said to have hailed him as son of Zeus or Ammon (king of the Egyptian gods). Some sources suggest that he did not want to be considered a god, but only godlike, which was enough to separate him off from ordinary mortals.[23] If there remains debate about whether he sought divine status, there is more general agreement that by the time he arrived at Siwa, he already sought to be king of Asia in place of the Persian dynasty. His conquest of the Achaemenid Empire was followed by campaigns in Bactria and Sogdiana in central Asia and then his dream of moving on to conquer India, when he and his armies were already more than 1,000 miles away from Macedon.

Clearly Alexander found conquest intoxicating. Arrian again, writing in the second century CE: 'Alexander had no small or mean conceptions, nor would ever have been contented with any of his possessions so far . . . but would always have searched far beyond for something unknown.'[24] The campaign to capture India proved, nevertheless, a step too far for an exhausted Greek army far from home. Arriving at the Hydaspes River, he defeated the local king, Porus, but his troops refused to go farther to the east, having reached the limits of endurance. Alexander's intentions remain an issue of debate, but there seems little doubt that his obsession with conquering power might have led him further had it been possible. Accounts indicate his resentment at having to turn back, when the whole world seemed to be in his grasp. He sacrificed a sheep and found bad omens in the entrails, and he used this as his excuse for what he saw as failure. As it was, he turned his tired forces south for a gruelling trek down the Indus valley, recklessly slaughtering any communities that opposed him. Arriving at the ocean as the limit of the world, he sacrificed bulls to the sea god Poseidon. The return journey through the Gedrosian desert was a source of prolonged suffering for his men, who had gained nothing from following their king's ambitions.[25] On his return to Babylon and Susa, the cities he had captured from the Persians, it seems likely that Alexander was already thinking of campaigns to conquer Arabia or the region of the Caspian, even to move into central and western Europe, but whether the Macedonians and the motley allied armies under Alexander's command would have followed him is a moot question.

By this time, Alexander's pretensions to demonstrative power were alienating many around him. Across his conquests, he built at least twenty towns or forts named Alexandria (including the most famous in Egypt, and Alexandria-Eschate or 'the farthest' on the fragile frontier with the Scythian nomads of central Asia) when no other towns in the Hellenistic world were named after a mortal individual. He even named towns after his horse, Bucephalus, and his favourite dog.[26] After the defeat of Darius, Alexander adopted the Persian style of court set in a vast tent, allegedly with fifty golden pillars, one hundred couches, and a large security guard. Here he restricted access to his person (he had once been more egalitarian and approachable), wore Persian costume, and in 327 BCE tried to introduce the Persian custom of *proskynesis*, or obeisance, to make subjects prostrate themselves before him.[27] This proved too much for the Macedonians in his entourage, but Alexander was ruthless in tracking down opposition and executing those involved. The increasing delusions of grandeur of a man now more king of Asia than of Macedon ended with his sudden death in 323 BCE, almost certainly from disease rather than poison. There was no nominated successor, and within a handful of years the brief empire broke up into different warring kingdoms, leaving only the legacy of Alexander's extraordinary personal ambition.

This was a legacy almost certainly known to the young Napoleon Bonaparte who, by all contemporary accounts, read the histories of the great generals of the classical age with voracious enthusiasm, above all the Greek and Roman conquerors. He had few of Alexander's early advantages. The second son of minor Corsican nobility, he spent ten years of his childhood at a tough military school at Brienne in France, where he was bullied by classmates who found him a surly, lonely cadet who preferred reading to games. Most of the sources on Napoleon's early life (and indeed of the later general, then from 1804 emperor) are secondhand, if often contemporary, but more reliable than for Alexander. They agree that Napoleon was an unusual youth, given to a haughty demeanour, occasional bouts of uncontrollable temper, and ambition to be someone. Power seems to have been central to his view of life. He saw successful action as an artillery commander in the siege of the city of Toulon in 1793, where he showed himself to be both bossy and courageous, but success did not bring any reward. At the trough of his military career in 1794 he told his older brother, Joseph, 'The only thing to do in this world is to keep acquiring . . . power and more power. All the rest is meaningless.'[28] His break came in October 1795 when he took a conspicuous part in suppressing the Vendémiaire rising in Paris against the revolutionary government. He was appointed a major-general and within a year had persuaded the government to let him lead an army into Italy to reverse the military crisis the revolutionary wars had suffered there at the hands of Habsburg armies. The Revolutionary Wars, fought with mixed fortunes from 1792 onwards, gave him the opportunity to shine.[29] His remarkable victories demonstrated that Napoleon had a natural operational flair, and he used them to inflate his reputation in Paris as hero and saviour. He later claimed that victory at Lodi near Milan in May 1796 was a turning point in his own view of the future: 'It was only on the evening of Lodi that I believed myself to be a superior man, and that the ambition came to me of executing the great things which so far had been occupying my thoughts only as fantastic dreams.'[30] There was an evident hubristic streak in a commander always concerned with his own success. 'My power', he later claimed, 'depends on my glory and my glory on my victories.'[31]

Like Alexander before him, Napoleon continually sought to expand the frontiers of his empire with a restless energy. French control was extended into Italy, Germany, the Low Countries, Switzerland, and later into Spain. In 1799, Napoleon conceived an invasion of Egypt, perhaps echoing Alexander ('We must to the East; all great reputations come from that quarter'), and despite defeats on land and at sea, he managed to convince the French people that here was another glorious Napoleonic adventure.[32] Most historians are agreed that there was no particular plan for conquest, perhaps unsurprising given the constant twists and turns of alliance politics among French allies, vassals, and enemies. Napoleon often complained that he was forced to fight by the obduracy of others, which in one sense was true, but resistance was a consequence of the spread of French power and Napoleon's refusal to be curbed by any other state in his way. Once he had become first consul in 1799, the executive head of a new constitutional system, decisions for peace or war were essentially his. He had a profound Anglophobia – because Britain was consistently opposed to his imperial project – and a mix of distrust and contempt for many of the crowned heads of Europe. The peace of Amiens, signed between two exhausted adversaries, Britain and France, in 1802, was quickly broken and war resumed. Victory over Austria and Russia at Austerlitz in 1805 and over Prussia at Jena-Auerstädt in 1806, then Russia again in 1807, allowed Napoleon to redraw the political map of Europe, placing his brothers on the thrones of vassal kingdoms. By 1808 the empire had reached its zenith, but Napoleon was never content without war. Still at war with Britain, he tried to add Spain to the empire and opened up a new front line. Four years later came the disastrous war with Russia, a war that Napoleon did not need to wage save that he would not brook defiance to his power.

Napoleon revelled in the exercise of this power. 'Everywhere I have been, I have commanded,' he told court councillor Pierre Roederer. 'I was born for that.'[33] From early on in his rise to power he adopted the trappings of leadership. His base in Italy at the Mombello palace outside Milan became effectively a royal court where Napoleon began to distance himself from his colleagues, dine separately from his aides-de-camp, and control access to see him. 'I saw him great, powerful, surrounded by homage and glory,' wrote his military secretary, Louis de Bourrienne, but no longer 'equal to equal'. During Napoleon's two years in Italy in the 1790s, no fewer than seventy-six pamphlets were published on his triumph. He was compared favourably with Scipio Africanus, though his opponents compared him less favourably with Alexander, Hannibal, or Caesar.[34] The style of authoritarian command remained central to Napoleon's growing power in France, initially as first consul for ten years, then as consul for life in 1802, and finally as emperor in May 1804, placing him on an equal footing with the other emperors of

Europe or, perhaps more significant for Napoleon, on a footing with the great classical empires, to which his empire was soon widely compared. His coronation was sumptuously prepared and attended by the pope, who handed the crown to Napoleon to put on himself, a gesture to show that he owed his power to no one.[35] The following year he decided to have himself crowned in Milan as king of Italy using the iron crown of Lombardy, handed down from the time of the medieval Holy Roman Emperor Frederick Barbarossa. Significantly, he no longer talked of citizens but of subjects.[36]

Napoleon himself played a part in developing the propaganda that underlaid the evolution of a cult of personality. The regime closely monitored what was published, censoring criticism of the empire, and controlling the information that shaped public opinion. The process was a ruthless one. In 1789 there had been 130 journals published in France; of these, only four remained in print by 1811.[37] The image of saviour and hero was constantly embellished. In 1806 the French Senate voted to erect a monument to 'Napoleon the Great', and subsequently the epithet became more commonly used. In 1802 there was the first mention of a 'Saint Napoleon', and in 1806 Napoleon's birthday, August 15, was celebrated officially as the day of Saint Napoleon, designed to eclipse the Catholic feast of the Assumption on the same day, though many clergy opposed the change. An addition to the Catholic catechism was drafted in 1806 and made compulsory for teaching to children throughout the empire, linking Napoleon with the divine, as Alexander was bracketed with Zeus. Children were asked why they should be attached to Napoleon, and the answer was 'He is the one God created . . . he has become the anointed of the Lord.'[38] There was widespread discussion of 'universal empire' or 'world domination', which Napoleon played to. Whether he did see his power stretching ever farther, to the Middle East and India, and on into Eurasia, is open to debate. In 1811 he told the clergyman Dominique Dufour de Pradt, 'In five years, I will be master of the world. Only Russia is left and I will crush it.'[39]

The invasion of Russia by an army of 610,000 raised from throughout the empire had echoes of Alexander's drive to India, and both ended as futile, hubristic enterprises. There has been much speculation over why Napoleon chose to gamble on destroying Russian power when it made little strategic sense, as Russia could hardly be added to the French Empire. The view that defeat of Russia would somehow pave the way for the final defeat or settlement with Great Britain, an ambition central to Napoleon's desire for unrivalled power in Europe, is plausible but hard to demonstrate. The ostensible motive was to force Tsar Alexander I to ban British trade, but it is difficult not to see the campaign as an expression of Napoleon's own ambition to overcome challenges to his power and imperial grandeur. He saw the Grande Armée in classical terms, as 'an army like that of Xerxes, [which] will perform spectacularly like that of Alexander'. He was warned of the many hazards of fighting in Russia, the problems of logistics, the reality that the army was poorly trained and a mix of nationalities, many of them hostile to the French. Few commanders or rank-and-file soldiers could really understand why they were asked to fight deep in Russia with few supplies and no winter clothing. He regretted that 'few people were capable of grasping his great projects in their entirety.'[40] The campaign proved a disaster of colossal proportions; a wretched sixth of the army returned from Russia. Napoleon was right that his power rested on victory and personal triumph, as did the power of the empire he constructed. The Russian campaign undermined both: within a year, the renewed Allied coalition had destroyed the French armies in Germany, despite a desperate if flawed effort by Napoleon in summer 1813 to regain the initiative, and then the coalition moved on into France.[41] Paris capitulated at the end of March 1814, and Napoleon was sent to rule the island of Elba, where he was still allowed to call himself emperor. He returned to France in 1815 but was finally and decisively beaten at Waterloo. In permanent exile on the island of Saint Helena in the South Atlantic, he reflected on his destiny if he had won in Russia, still unrepentantly self-centreed: 'If I had succeeded, I should have died with the reputation of being the greatest man who ever lived. From being nothing, I became by my own exertions, the most powerful monarch in the world.'[42]

Adolf Hitler had even fewer credentials for taking power and running a war effort than either Alexander or Napoleon. Although he served in the Great War, reaching the rank of 'private, first-class', he had none of the military experience of leading troops in battle in person or running the dangers that combat exposed them to. He was by comparison an amateur strategist. His one brush with violence during the Third Reich was the attempt to assassinate him in July 1944; his survival he immediately attributed to providence. Nonetheless, by this time he was supreme commander of the armed forces, a role he assumed in February 1938 and which he played in full down to the last days of the Third Reich. Hitler, like Alexander and Napoleon, was alone the one who decided on war because the structure of power that he created in the dictatorship permitted nothing else. He waged war to extend the power of Germany, and the more successful he was, the greater the power he wanted to accrue to the new German empire that he created and ruled in Europe. His personal power made war possible, while war confirmed both German imperial power and his own. Hitler, like Napoleon, never doubted that war was the chief and necessary expression of power, which is what made the strategy of both men so dangerous for the rest of the world, not least because they attracted an indispensable and wide circle of soldiers and civilians who endorsed or benefited from the wars they waged.

There was little about Hitler's early life to foreshadow the future dictator and warlord. Most recollections by contemporaries recall an awkward, self-absorbed individual, wont to preach views that reflected an untutored if deep engagement with a broad range of issues that set him apart from his companions in pre-1914 Vienna and in wartime. German defeat in 1918 generated in him a profound hatred for those he blamed for 'stabbing Germany in the back'. It has proved difficult to gauge exactly when Hitler decided that he would be the one chosen by providence to save the German people from postwar misery and disempowerment. At first, he seems to have seen himself as the drummer, making way for a German saviour. But after taking leadership in 1920 of a small fringe party, whose name he changed to the National Socialist German Workers' Party, he began to see himself as the one destined to rescue his adopted homeland. This was a narcissistic ambition, evident in his desire to be a leader unrestrained by others, obliging obedience and inflating his sense of self. Those who challenged his power in the party were shunted aside or, in 1934, murdered.[43] It is no accident that he chose from early on the simple title *Führer* ('Leader') and kept it right through his career to 1945; the title implied a special calling, a unique style of leadership, brooking no rival and demanding absolute loyalty from the led – charismatic in the original sense of the term.[44] No accident either that the book he wrote while imprisoned after the failed putsch against the Weimar Republic was called *Mein Kampf* (*My Struggle*), in which his personal history somehow represented the wider challenge faced by the German people. In the second volume of *Mein Kampf* and the later 'Second Book', written in 1928, Hitler insisted that warfare was a natural consequence of the competition between races. The failure of a race to fight for its preservation was a sign of degeneration: 'Who wants to live, must also fight, and who does not wish for conflict in this world of eternal struggle, does not deserve to live.'[45] War, in Hitler's view of the world, was the key to racial survival and progress, and it dominated his view of the German future when he came to power in 1933.

Chance played a significant part in bringing Hitler to political power, as it had with Napoleon, although Hitler became adept at attributing his rise to the hand of providence, a reference he used regularly during the dictatorship to confirm that destiny both summoned and protected him. On February 3, 1933, in one of his first meetings after he became chancellor, Hitler laid out to the military high command how he understood his exercise of power: first, power to create a united people and to destroy the internal enemies of the German race; then the extension of German power abroad, which could only mean war. Hitler, with a remarkable degree of hubris, explained to the generals that 'you will not again find a man like me, who with all his power stands up for his goal, for the salvation of Germany.'[46] To a considerable degree, Hitler fulfilled that early pledge. He assumed absolute power by August 1934 when on the death of the ageing president, Paul von Hindenburg, he merged president and chancellor into the single title *Der Führer*. He achieved political unity through remorseless terror against opponents; in 1938, he took the title of supreme commander of the armed forces and within weeks began the promised expansion of Germany by occupying and absorbing Austria into the Greater German Reich. Hitler understood that charismatic leadership required constant proof of success. Although with no firm blueprint to guide him, he built up large armed forces from the feeble foundation available when he came to power to enable further expansion. After Austria, he immediately aimed to conquer Czechoslovakia but was prevented from doing so only by British intervention at the Munich Conference, when he had to be content with annexing the areas with majority German populations. That experience he viewed as a defeat, and he determined from then on to not allow other powers to curb his international aims. His will for war led to the occupation of rump Czechoslovakia in March 1939, then the order to prepare for war against Poland, a decision that against his expectations led to war with the British and French Empires six months later. He responded to victory in

Poland in predictable style: 'Providence has spoken the final word and brought me success . . . Only he who fights destiny can be favoured by Providence. I have experienced many instances of Providence in the last years.'[47]

In September 1939, on the day German forces invaded Poland, Hitler pledged in a nationwide speech that he wished 'to be nothing other than the first soldier of the German Reich'. His commitment to war as the means of securing German power meant in his view no compromise or peace that restricted this ambition. He blamed others for forcing his hand, particularly the malign power of 'international Jewry' and a 'wicked and vicious Britain', but in truth it was his hubristic desire for triumph against all odds that found him by December 1941 at war with the British Empire, the Soviet Union, and the United States. This was a combination he could have avoided. Further war was his choice. Among his reflections, recorded in 1945, not long before Germany's utter defeat, was the claim that his fate mirrored that of Napoleon: 'I perhaps better than anyone else, can well imagine the torments suffered by Napoleon, longing as he was for the triumph of peace and yet compelled to continue waging war, without ceasing.'[48] It is not easy with Hitler, as with Napoleon, to grasp the rationale behind apparently limitless military ambitions, but building and defending their empires as a source of power certainly explained the constant warfare that characterized them. Hitler made it clear to those around him in the political and military elite that he was not prepared to abandon a single metre of the soil he had conquered. These were his wars, and he was intolerant of any sign of weakness or defeatism among those who served him.

The lack of realism in his military strategy brought him regularly into conflict with his commanders, but as the war went on, he listened less and less to advice and relied more on the guiding hand of providence. In his view, he had been responsible for German victories, and he alone would rescue Germany from the prospect of defeat or, like Nero, bring it crashing down in flames.

Hitler's power owed much to the development of a cult of personality that not only sustained his domestic authoritarianism but also underpinned his role as the 'first soldier' of the Reich. There was an element of religiosity in the bond between leader and led. Hermann Göring, Hitler's chosen successor, could claim in a speech in 1934, 'When the need was greatest, the Lord God gave the German people its saviour.' In a 1937 diary entry, Hans Frank, later governor of conquered Poland, wrote 'Oh God! How happy you have made us that we can call the single greatest man in world history our *own*.'[49] Some theologians welcomed Hitler as a 'presence of the divine', and they defined Hitler's will to power as the foundation of a healthy spiritual life in the new Germany.[50] There were special celebrations for Hitler Day (his birthday, April 20), for the anniversary of Hitler's appointment as chancellor, and for the party 'martyrs' killed during the putsch on November 8, 1923. The universal greeting, Heil Hitler, was a daily reminder of the special status of the leader. All servicemen had to swear an oath of personal fealty to Hitler as supreme commander rather than swear the former oath to defend the fatherland: 'I swear by God this sacred oath that I will give unconditional obedience to the *Führer*.'[51] Hitler played up to the image of a providential leader in the theatricality of the mass rallies and celebrations. He avoided the pomp of Napoleon or Alexander, emphasizing instead the modesty of his dress and the simplicity of his daily life. ('Imagine the effect . . . if I had myself carried through the streets of Munich in a gilded coach,' he was heard to tell dinner guests, after first criticizing Napoleon's decision to become an emperor.[52]) He was nevertheless regularly compared with both Alexander and Napoleon and by more hostile critics with Chinggis Khan or Attila the Hun or numerous other brutally ambitious leaders.[53] Hitler had a sense of where he might stand in world history, expressed most clearly in his desire to build fabulous new cities to rival Rome or Greece, their ruins to be visited a thousand years hence. From Trondheim in northern Norway to his hometown of Linz in Austria, Hitler planned *Führer* cities as a monument to his remarkable history, all carefully constructed in miniature and deposited in the 'Model Room' in the Reich Chancellery to feed his fantasies of power.[54]

Hitler, Napoleon, and Alexander between them personified what has been called for obvious reasons 'destructive leadership', imposing goals without agreement or regard for the long-term welfare of those the leaders ostensibly represented. The unlimited pursuit of war as the material manifestation of personal power is in each case the result not just of individual will but also of the willingness of followers to accept charismatic leadership and the costs that go with it together with the existence of historical circumstances that make the bid for leadership possible in the first place. This 'toxic triangle', as it has been well described, is the context within which hubristic ambitions can flourish.

This model of leadership reflects a profound selfishness.[55] There is little evidence that any of the three examples here regretted the cost in hundreds of thousands of lives sacrificed to their ambitions. Napoleon tried to turn the defeat in Russia into a pseudo-victory by publicizing the final dramatic crossing of the Berezina River with the retreating remnants of his Grande Armée, during which he narrowly escaped capture, but he showed little concern for the rest of his force lying dead along the line of retreat. Hitler notoriously turned against the German people for failing to live up to his expectation that racial will would see Germany achieve its rightful place. In a sudden outburst of temper while recording a broadcast for the November 8, 1943, anniversary of the putsch, Hitler announced that he would not shed a tear if Germany were defeated because the German people would have only themselves to blame – prudently edited out in the broadcast version. 'Here I am also ice-cold', he once asserted. 'If the German people is not ready to support its self-preservation, so be it: then it should disappear.'[56] Power exploited cynically by leaders to wage war in the name of a providential mission is the most dangerous and unpredictable cause of war from the classical world to the twenty-first century.

Power for power's sake is not the whole answer even in the case of hubristic leadership, though it came to dominate the ambition of these three men. Writing not long after the end of the Napoleonic wars, the Prussian general Carl von Clausewitz famously penned the conclusion that 'war is not merely an act of policy, but a true political instrument, a continuation of political intercourse, carried on by other means.'[57] This much-vaunted claim can say everything or very little. It is of small use in understanding hubristic warfare. Most wars across human history were fought for a variety of reasons, some for directly political objectives but a great many not, and 'by other means' appears to reduce war to a limited instrument of statecraft contrary to the massive and violent dislocation that war in Clausewitz's own time demonstrated. Wars waged deliberately to enhance political power at the expense of other powers, though likely to have either material or ideological motives, more closely fit with Clausewitz's view of the function of war in the modern age, although the precise historical explanation will certainly be more complicated than his simple formula: 'the political object is the goal, war is the means of reaching it.'[58]

The struggle for power, in the sense that Clausewitz understood it, has become a commonplace in discussing the emergence of today's states system, captured fully in Paul Kennedy's seminal volume *The Rise and Fall of the Great Powers*, published in 1988. Kennedy's thesis that economic strength and a corresponding military capability can explain both the rise and decline of great powers (though presumably of many lesser powers too) was appropriate, like Clausewitz, to the international order that arose from the late seventeenth century onwards in Europe, and later to include the United States. The wars between those states defined as great powers have been classified as 'hegemonic wars' in which the power claims of a potential hegemon (whether Louis XIV's France or the Germany of Wilhelm II and Hitler) are challenged in war by the other powers, leading usually to a recalibration of the international power hierarchy.[59] If possible, the great powers attempt a 'balance of power' between near equal states or alliances and thus avoid or postpone a military power struggle. Hegemonic wars are likely to be a product of what is now called power transition theory (PTT), in which rising powers dissatisfied with their place in the international system or declining powers anxious to perpetuate their claim to primacy initiate war for their own power ends. The theory relies on effective measurement of 'power', without which a power transition cannot be verifiable, so that much effort has been devoted in the past half-century to calibrating comparative power measurements, and hence the probability of war.

The assessment of power is associated most closely with the Correlates of War Project established at the University of Michigan in 1963 by the political scientist J. David Singer. Most previous assessments had been based on GDP and rates of military spending, but Singer's project generated a broader measure of power potential in the Composite Indicator of National Capability (CINC) index, which is the measure now most commonly cited. The indicator is based around six measurements: total population, total urban population, iron and steel production, primary energy consumption, military expenditure, and military personnel. The 'scores' are added up, divided by six, and provide a ranking designed to show relative power.[60] The measurement can then be used to indicate power transitions over time, principally among the nations high up in the ranking, and to suggest that they are the sites of possible conflict. The favourite source for evidence of power transition and war is the classic Greek historian

Thucydides, whose account of the war between Athens and Sparta suggests that Athenian power frightened the Spartans into a conflict to save their status. The current term is the 'Thucydides Trap', which describes the difficulty of avoiding war between two states who are rivals for hegemony. It is widely regarded as a trap hard to circumvent. Thucydides believed war between the two Greek city-states became 'inevitable'.[61]

There are many drawbacks to measuring power potential in this way and even more historical objections to the idea that power transitions usually involve war. The use of GDP as a measure is unhelpful because states with very large populations and economies can score highly even if their military capabilities are limited. Per capita GDP is usually a surer indicator of economic strength. The CINC scores suffer from much the same objection (apart from the obvious fact that many states which have advanced military capability no longer produce much iron and steel). Gross resources as a measurement says little about how efficiently such resources might be mobilized in wartime, nor does it take account of shared power through alliances, which alters power capabilities substantially. Nor do gross figures on military spending and the size of armed forces say very much about the operational, tactical, and technical capability of the forces available. The nature and degree of militarization is a measure more likely to demonstrate the possibility of war, particularly if it produces an arms race between states of more or less equal military and industrial capacity. Gross estimates of domestic resources also understate the extent of a great power's global reach. The United States has military bases stretched across the world, and American investment and ownership abroad has produced the remarkable figure that 41 percent of global household assets are in American hands.[62]

The power transition theory is difficult to validate historically. The theory presupposes that a hegemonic power will be challenged by a single rising power; when that power reaches a certain percentage of the power score of the hegemon, perhaps 80 percent, then the rising state may resort to conflict to stake its own claim to hegemonic power. Yet the two chief examples show a quite different picture. The hegemonic power of the British Empire in the second half of the nineteenth century was challenged by the rise of the United States, whose GDP reached parity with that of Great Britain in the 1870s and exceeded it by the 1890s. Yet even though relations between the two states were often brittle and hostile, no conflict occurred between them. By the twentieth century, the two democracies were allies throughout the period of Britain's relative economic and military decline and the United States' rise to superpower status. In the period after 1945, the United States was in turn challenged by the Soviet Union, whose CINC scores later indicated a lead over America in the 1950s and 1960s, even though Soviet GDP never exceeded more than 45 percent of that of its rival. By the mid-1990s, CINC scores showed that China had overtaken the United States, but in both these modern cases no military conflict occurred.[63] Many modern wars in fact involved a major power picking on a much weaker one, prompting intervention from the coterie of other major powers: Austria-Hungary's war against Serbia in 1914 and Germany's war against Poland in 1939 ushered in colossal world wars, but neither trigger can be explained by power transition theory. There are many cases of a weaker power challenging a hegemon even where the decision made no sense in terms of comparative resources – Japan is a case in point, defeating imperial China in 1894, the tsarist Russian Empire in 1905, and then launching an entirely unwinnable war against the United States in December 1941. By contrast, no one using CINC data would ever have predicted North Vietnam's success against the United States or that of the Algerian rebels against metropolitan France. Power in modern conflicts involves imponderable factors that have little to do with evaluating the potential strength of an opponent, which has proved a notoriously difficult thing to do.

The one power transition that has occupied the international relations community more than any other is the potential for conflict between the United States and China, the one a hegemonic power in relative decline (so it is claimed), the other a rising hegemon-in-waiting. This potential for conflict has replaced the analysis of 'unipolarity' in the 1990s following the collapse of the Soviet bloc. In the immediate years after 1991, American leaders assumed that the United States was the sole global power and should remain so. The draft of a Defense Planning Guidance drawn up by the Pentagon in Washington in 1992 concluded that 'we must maintain the mechanisms for deterring potential competitors from ever aspiring to a larger regional or global role.' Although removed from the final draft of the document, the sentiment remained. President George H. W. Bush announced a 'new world order' in 1992, dominated effectively by the United States. Concern that Germany and Japan, then the next two largest economies, might rediscover their defeated ambitions to become hegemonic powers provoked renewed efforts to ensure that neither would become a nuclear-armed state.[64] The evidence for unipolarity was nowhere more obvious than in the statistics of world military spending, where by 1998 the United States exceeded the spending of the rest of the world put together. Although there are other ways of exercising 'power' in the international system, it is military power in all its many forms that ultimately determines the risk of war.

The rise of Chinese economic and military power ought to be a classic case of power transition theory. From a modest position in the 1980s, Chinese GDP has experienced exponential growth since the 1990s; the result has been a larger surplus for investing in military resources. Second only to the United States in GDP and military spending by 2014, China according to theory ought to become sufficiently dissatisfied with its power position relative to the United States to contemplate war as a means of altering the international system in China's favour, while the United States ought to think of war against China to protect its international standing. The media in the West have become obsessed with the possibility of war between the two powers, essentially over the issue of power itself, although Chinese sources have also exploited the perception of American decline and China's rise. Even Thucydides has entered the debate. The Harvard political scientist Graham Allison argued in *Destined for War: Can America and China Avoid the Thucydides Trap?*, published in 2015, that war is more likely than not. The Harvard Belfer Center Thucydides Trap Case File is filled with examples from past ages designed to prove the case for any curious researcher. Xi Jinping, China's leader, has publicly stated that it is important to avoid falling into the trap, given the publicity the concept now enjoys internationally.[65] Academic opinion is sharply divided over how seriously to take the danger of war now that unipolarity seems to be replaced by multipolarity, which may or may not provide a stable platform for a new global order. It is possible to see China as a regional great power rather than as a global power, where the power transition only affects international conditions in Asia and so involves less risk of a power transition conflict, except in the case of the status of Taiwan, which has wider international ramifications. Critical assessment of China's real economic and military potential has demonstrated that there is still a very wide gap between the United States and China militarily and an even wider one between the United States and all the other major powers, so that to talk of power transition in this case is at best premature, at worst an ill-considered provocation.[66]

The whole discussion of a potential conflict between the United States and China based on power calculations begs the question whether a major war between current nuclear-armed powers is conceivable. In 2019, the British strategic thinker Lawrence Freedman concluded that great-power war is a thing of the past because the risks involved in rapid escalation to a nuclear exchange mean that the costs of war will always massively outweigh any possible gains, a bleak reality that earlier hegemonic powers did not have to face. Instead, great powers will resort to proxy wars or sanctions, not mutual destruction.[67] This conclusion relies on the assumption that modern statesmen are rational actors. On past historical evidence, it seems more likely that war for power might again result from hubristic leadership whose emergence and effect are as difficult to anticipate as they were with Napoleon and Hitler; or it may result from the reaction of a leader to internal crisis, loss of international esteem, or the perception of threat, whether real or not; or from the mobilization of domestic support through nationalist rhetoric, emotional appeal, fear, and resentment. The wars of Saddam Hussein and Vladimir Putin's current war in Ukraine fall into this category, driven by leaders who saw and see war as the solution rather than the problem and could carry enough of their population with them. None of these variables can be included in calculations of relative power because they are the product of particular historical circumstances or the ambitions of power-hungry leaders. There are no empirical or theoretical ways to predict the likelihood of wars for power, power transition theory notwithstanding, but there seems no reason to assume that they will not happen again, even between great powers. The use of statistical power parameters to calculate when or where such a war might happen must remain in the realm of imaginative speculation.

Power has proved to be a difficult concept to use in analysing the cause of war. Not only can power be exercised in a variety of coercive ways short of war – through economic pressure, cultural dominance, even in enforcing peace – the concept itself describes means rather than ends. A power relationship exists in all forms of warfare, whether aggressive or defensive, but that will say very little about the motives that caused the power to be exercised, and these motives, not the simple fact of power, are more properly the cause of conflict. Power, and in particular military power, can encourage risk taking if the aggressor perceives, wrongly or rightly, an imbalance in its favour that promises lower costs for warfare. War for power in this sense, whether by tribes, federations, chiefdoms, or states, is recognizable in most contexts and geographic regions. But most of these wars will still be for land, wealth, booty, resources, or to defend or promote beliefs, or in pursuit of glory and esteem, the subject matter of the earlier chapters of this book. The exception to wars that have material or ideological motive can be found in the construction of the world's major empires. Here the pursuit of power develops its own dynamic based upon imperatives from within, like the Roman view that war was willed by the gods and conducted to bring fame and honour to those who pursued it. Rome needed to continue to expand to confirm its own self-image as an expression of power or 'the right of command'. The other variant of war for power, hubristic warfare, waged by a powerful individual to enhance his own status and reputation regardless of the cost, is historically rare, which is why so much attention has been paid to understanding what drove Alexander, Napoleon, and Hitler not only to wage war but also to continue to wage war over years, without recognizing limits when these made rational sense. Hitler was well aware of Napoleon's failure in Russia, but he thought he would do better; Alexander wanted to emulate and then surpass the reputation of Heracles, who had failed to conquer India. Whether Vladimir Putin sees himself in the large shoes of Peter the Great in the attempt to conquer Ukraine remains to be discovered. But these are unquestionably motives that are power-driven first, and in the principal historical cases warfare ends with calamity rather than triumph. The pursuit of power through war, however seductive to an ambitious leader, can all too often be self-defeating.

CHAPTER 8

Security

> But though there had never been any time, wherein
> particular men were in a condition of warre one against
> another; yet in all times, Kings, and Persons of Soveraigne
> authority, because of their Independency, are in continuall
> jealousies and in the state and posture of Gladiators;
> having their weapons pointing, and their eyes fixed on one
> another; that is, their Forts, Garrisons, and Guns upon the
> Frontiers of their Kingdomes.
>
> — Thomas Hobbes, *Leviathan*, 1651[1]

There is a persistent fashion in discussions of warfare to
regard Hobbes's view of human nature and the insecurity of
human existence as an explanation for war. He famously defined life in a state of nature as 'solitary, poore, nasty, bru-
tish, and short' because no one could be certain of his or her
security; even in a system of kingdoms or states, 'continuall
jealousies' between them provoked a permanent 'posture of
Warre'. Even a temporary period of security would, Hobbes
believed, be undermined by continued distrust of potential
enemies sufficient to provoke yet further 'Warre amongst
themselves'. Security for individuals or for polities always
implies someone else's insecurity, encouraging a new round

of violent competition to win security back. Hobbes was no apologist for war; he wanted to explain why it happens, not to endorse it. Indeed his fundamental law of nature was 'to seek Peace, and follow it'. Only when peace could not be secured did men enjoy the right to use the 'advantages of Warre' to defend themselves against threat.[2] The modern neorealist school of security studies still uses a Hobbesian model of the state of nature to explain why states must be in constant readiness to protect their security. Security pacts may help to avert conflict, though neither the League of Nations nor the United Nations has been quite equal to the task. The modern world is massively armed against any threat to security, both external and internal. This contemporary 'posture of Warre' has provoked two global conflicts in the past century, which is why so much effort is currently devoted to understanding security and its fragile history.

It is certainly right that polities throughout history have existed in a Hobbesian state of nature. Individual communities – whether tribes, chiefdoms, kingdoms, empires, or modern states – have a permanent interest in protecting themselves against threat because there is no common source of power to ensure that the security of territory and people will not be violated by some form of warfare. It may be possible to avoid conflict and enhance security through alliances or treaties or institutional collaboration, but the critical factor remains the issue of trust about the intentions of others. As Hobbes pointed out, in a state of nature it is self-interest that predominates, not the interests of others. Even where a strong hegemonic state emerges, it is possible for a combination of weaker ones to bring the

hegemon down, but competition for security continues between them as before. In the words of one of the leading figures in the school of 'offensive realists', John Mearsheimer,
'the best way for a state to survive in anarchy is to take advantage of other states and gain power at their expense.'[3] The
object is not power for its own sake, but for the sake of greater security. A state of nature is constantly in flux as a result,
at one point perhaps in a phase of balance, but always with
the promise of uncertainty. Indeed, an overwhelming sense
of insecurity has led and can lead to preventive or preemptive war to forestall a potential enemy. Where state actions
are governed by anxiety, suspicion, or fear, so the modern
argument goes, then conflict is an ever-present possibility.
This 'misperception realism', as it has been called, 'is a ubi-
quitous motive for war'.[4] In a state of Hobbesian anarchy,
every state, like every man, seeks power to prevent the loss
of security. And power, according to one of the first modern
realist thinkers, the Dutch American Nicholas Spykman, is
'in the last instance the ability to wage successful war'.[5]

It could well be argued that the security dilemma, as it
is now defined, has always existed through both prehistory
and history, even if the theoretical language to define it is a
modern invention. Problems of trust, uncertainty, and threat
were certainly as real for early foragers and hunters as they
were for a later system of nation-states. The resort to violence to remove a perceived threat or to stem anxiety over
the motives of a neighbouring clan or tribe can be corroborated by modern ethnography but must have operated deep
in the past. The search for security, however temporary, is
present to some degree in almost every warlike encounter,

and it is linked to the desire to protect a particular territory and people, whether defined with little precision as in the past or a firm boundary line as in the present. One calculation suggests that 73 percent of all ethnic conflicts between 1940 and 2000 were over disputed territorial boundaries; another suggests that 65 percent of all 'dyadic' wars (between two opposing states) from 1815 to 1945 concerned disputes over territory. Yet a third data set, produced by the Correlates of War project, shows that 80 percent of interstate wars fought since 1815 were between neighbours with a common boundary; the figure for 1648–1814 is 91 percent.[6] Being neighbours does not necessarily lead to warfare, but warfare is overwhelmingly concentrated among states that are, for whom security is likely to be more fragile.[7]

The borders between different polities or ethnicities have been potential zones of insecurity and conflict for obvious reasons. Contiguity has been no guarantee of security, and most warfare has taken place between contiguous communities or states where they are not protected by natural boundaries. The instability of the frontier has long been recognized as a danger point, as Hobbes made clear. The British viceroy of India, Lord Curzon, chose 'frontiers' as the title of his Romanes Lecture at the University of Oxford in 1907. They were, he claimed, 'the razor's edge on which hang suspended the modern issues of war or peace'.[8] Arnold Toynbee, author in the mid-twentieth century of the six volumes of *The Study of History*, covering every known civilization, concluded that frontiers were the major cause of war as states trespassed across them and their victims defended them. Nicholas Spykman defined the frontier as a zone of 'vital importance' where strategy and geography coalesced as statesmen sought a way to defend the security of the state against potential aggressors.[9] The emergence of the independent nation-state across the globe since 1945 has made defence of territorial security a universal phenomenon but has also produced regular flashpoints where bounded territory is disputed or where frontiers prove dangerously porous. These are in many cases disputes that become intractable, even where the territory involved is not otherwise of value either in terms of resources or strategic necessity. The disputes can be symbolic, or a means of signalling to others a reputation for toughness. Where the argument is about an ethnic fraction trapped on another side of the boundary, research has suggested a much higher likelihood of armed conflict.[10]

The frontier, however it is marked, does not cause war directly. It is incursion across a frontier for motives of territorial seizure, or raiding for loot, or to satisfy irredentist ambitions, or simply as a means by which to enhance security that explains why fear of the violation of frontiers has been, and still is, a central security issue. There is no shortage of archaeological and ethnographic evidence to show how prehistoric communities reacted to the threat of insecurity. One way was mutually to accept a buffer zone between tribal communities, a no-man's-land where neither side would hunt or forage and which neither side would violate. Archaeologists have identified an uninhabited zone between polities in Oaxaca, southern Mexico, dating from 700–500 BCE, which most probably served to keep them apart, although raiding still seems to have happened. In the Mississippi valley in the 500 years before European arrival, buffer zones

of up to 30 kilometres between chiefdoms have been identified, although here too, frontiers remained unstable, and
endemic violence undermined whatever shallow security
physical separation was supposed to give.[11] Archaeology in
Europe has also found evidence of neutral zones of territory
between the sedentary farmers that moved across continental Europe in the seventh and sixth millennia BCE and the
hunter-gatherer communities to the north and west. Yet the
existence of an estimated 100,000 small polities in Neolithic Europe made it improbable that territory could be clearly
defined or that conflict between them could be prevented.[12]

The other way to enhance security was to build physical
barriers against potential threat. Pre-state communities certainly built fortifications, often enhanced by the protection
of natural barriers of mountains, rivers, or swampy ground
(see chapter 3). As violence became more widespread on the
American Great Plains after the migration of tribes from the
east in the thirteenth and fourteenth centuries CE, fortification of local communities became widespread, with ditches
and wooden palisades complementing settlement on less accessible geographic features. On these tribal fault lines, fortification posed a challenge to aggressors but also invited
conflict.[13] There is now copious evidence of fortification in
areas of Neolithic Europe where migration and competition
for land and resources created constant insecurity on the
frontiers between cultures. The search for ways of increasing protection spread across much of Europe in the period
from about 6,500 to 1,000 BCE but was most evident in
east-central Europe and the Balkans, where peoples had to
face aggressive migration from the eastern steppes.[14] In the

Bronze Age, the Castro culture of northwest Spain tried to use fortification and inaccessible topography to enhance its almost complete geographic isolation from the warring regions around it.[15] In West Africa, fortification became widespread in the centuries before European expansion into the continent. The kingdom of Benin was protected initially by a wall around the palace and royal enclosure that had an average height of seventeen metres, but eventually a system of banked fortifications was constructed throughout the kingdom, an extraordinary 16,000 kilometres in length, to give security to the entire royal territory and its different townships. The frontier in present-day Nigeria between the Old Oyo Yoruba kingdom and the Nupe kingdom was a classic frontier zone. Constructed in the sixteenth and seventeenth centuries, the boundary consisted of earth and stone barriers of considerable height with smaller outposts along the frontier with Nupe, in an area where allies could be found among local tribal chiefs to help defend the frontier against hostile incursions.[16]

The African example dates from a time when the state in one form or other had become the common form of political organization in much of the Old World and in Central and South America. Indeed, one of the motives for creating larger and more organized polities was evidently to be more secure, as aggregate military strength would defend a geographic area more effectively than scattered clans or tribes could do for themselves. This was security at best merely relative. Insecurity helped to drive the states of first-millennium BCE China to permanent conflict in the period of the so-called Spring and Autumn States or the later Warring States, whose insecurity is captured in the name. The classical period in the Middle East and Europe is punctuated by the collapse of states whose security was destroyed from across the frontier. The Assyrian Empire at its height was the most powerful empire yet created, but on its northern frontier in present-day Iraq and Turkey, there was a persistent threat from the Urartu kingdom. The frontier was not geographically fixed as a modern frontier, but the Assyrians constructed a frontier zone to prevent people they regarded as barbarian from trespassing across it. When the Urartu began to migrate into the valleys of the upper Tigris River, the Assyrian king, Tiglath-Pileser III, defeated them in battle in 738 BCE. He stabilized the frontier by a network of fortresses and the annexation of a buffer zone filled with tribal allies and vassals to keep the main enemy at a distance. The frontier served well enough in the short term, but it was simply too permeable to keep the barbarians at bay, and by 600 BCE Assyria had collapsed as an empire.[17]

The Assyrian example highlights the difficulty of coping with the mass migrations, chiefly from Eurasia, that pushed aside whatever fragile frontiers of culture or military strength existed in the Middle East or Europe. In Eurasia, frontiers had little meaning by the time horse-riding nomads came to dominate the steppe. To their settled, sedentary neighbours they posed a permanent threat to security either because of constant raiding for food, cattle, and women or because of larger-scale invasions, which drove established cultures westward or eliminated them entirely. The nomadic tribes lacked a settled state structure and fought among themselves as well as against other established polities. In this context, insecurity was a fact of life for those subject to regular incursions or larger invasions but also for the chief-doms on the steppe, which jostled for power in a setting that was quintessentially anarchic. Security in terms of protection from military violence, coercion, and economic exploitation was for much of history merely transitory. Frontiers were in most cases meaningless as a barrier to warfare or a source of protection; territory changed hands with predictable regularity as warfare crossed and recrossed notional boundaries between polities and cultures. The exceptions to this rule were the two longest surviving territorial empires: the Roman Empire, which lasted for more than 1,500 years in one form or another, and the Chinese Empire, which endured, through numerous iterations, for more than 2,000 years. In both these cases, there existed a persistent tension between the search for imperial security and the insecurity generated by centuries of defence of a long and vulnerable frontier.

The history of the Chinese frontier has expanded considerably thanks to a substantial increase in archaeological surveying of the long boundary that separated the early Chinese states, then the centralized empire, from the nomadic societies of the northern and eastern steppes in what is now Mongolia, Manchuria, and eastern Russia. Interaction between the two, not always violent, can be traced back to at least the seventh century BCE. The early steppe also featured some settled agriculture, but climate shocks changed the settlement pattern and created largely nomadic communities reliant on animals for food. The nomads became horse riders by the fourth century BCE, adapting warfare to their new mobility and posing a major threat to the northern Chinese states if the nomads chose to raid. The relationship between the two very different worlds was governed by trade. The nomads needed cereals, tea, iron goods, and cloth; Chinese merchants took furs, horses (for the cavalry units founded to combat the nomads), and livestock. Over hundreds of years, the relationship was based on differing insecurities. Chinese states were anxious to prevent invasion by people they regarded as barbarians, while the nomads were uncertain about the flow of goods from China, which were essential not only to daily life but also to the power of local chieftains, who distributed the trade to keep the peace among the nomad community. When the trade was cut off, for whatever reason, the nomads resorted to force to secure what they wanted by raiding and looting. When the incursions occurred, the Chinese states responded either by trying to buy peace or resorting to warfare to drive out the nomads and disrupt their society, which in turn created a spiralling insecurity.[18] Not surprisingly, perhaps, the Chinese records employ a range of words to describe the vulnerability of the frontier: 'looting border areas', 'robbing border areas', 'border encroachment', 'invasion', 'great invasion', 'deep invasion'.[19]

The consequence was a frontier zone with the constant threat of conflict, exacerbated in the Warring States period by the continual violence between the many polities that composed northern and central China. It was during this period that the first 'long walls' (*ch'ang-ch'eng*) were constructed, designed for a variety of possible functions: to give protection at the frontier between states, to allow control and taxation of trade, to monitor the movement of peoples, and to serve as a launching pad for incursions into neighbouring territory. Although the popular view still survives that something called the 'Great Wall' was built along the whole northern frontier by the first Qin emperor, Ying Zheng, at some point in the late third century BCE, the archaeology and early records suggest that there was never a single 'Great Wall' built either then or later. The long walls were built at different times from at least the fifth century BCE onwards, a total of perhaps 20,000 kilometres. From the recent archaeological record, the first long wall appears to date from around 440 BCE, a length of 600 kilometres from the Taishan mountain massif to the sea, designed to protect the Qi state from invasion by other warring states, although there is also on record a wall along the Yellow River built by the Qin between 467 and 417 BCE. All seven of the main warring states constructed frontier walls, forts, and watch stations. Only with the victory of the Qin in 221 BCE were the northern walls linked together to form a longer wall against the nomadic tribes in inner Asia, made chiefly of stamped earth, little of which has as a result survived.[20] The Qin wall, with forts and guarded gates, differed from the earlier long walls because it also encompassed the wide area of the northern Ordos Desert bordering the East Asian steppe to provide security against raiding by the nomadic pastoralists that lived beyond it.

The move triggered the first serious response from people the Chinese called *hu* or *ti* (barbarian/outsider), and it illustrated how the search for security, this time by the new Chinese Empire, could instead prompt a renewed insecurity. In the period after 209 BCE, the nomad tribes united in a loose federation generally referred to by the Chinese term Xiong-nu, ruled at first by the chieftain Modu Chanyu. The federation soon dominated the area of present-day Mongolia and Manchuria. To protect the empire, ruled from 206 BCE by the Han dynasty, the emperor Kai-ti attacked beyond the long wall, but in 200 he suffered a humiliating defeat. The Chinese were forced to supply goods to the nomads across the frontier, but when the Xiongnu considered the quantities of silk, wine, grain, and weapons insufficient, the tribes continued raiding. Uncertain about nomad ambitions and increasingly resentful at the payment of what amounted to tribute, emperor Wu-ti (141–81 BCE) launched a major campaign against the Xiongnu. The federation's defeat in 133 BCE removed the threat, but conflict continued along the frontier zone until a final decisive defeat in 48 CE. The Xiongnu federation broke up: some tribes were driven farther into Inner Asia, while others accepted Han rule in areas annexed by the Chinese.[21] The pattern established by the Chinese Empire of alternating its frontier strategy between appeasement towards nomadic federations and regular campaigns to restore the security of the north continued down to the thirteenth-century Mongol invasion and then resumed when the Mongol Yüan dynasty was replaced by the indigenous Ming a century later.[22]

The Ming long wall, origin of the modern conception of the 'Great Wall', arose from a fresh crisis of security prompted by the unstable frontier with the Mongols, whose leaders had returned to the steppe and the Ordos Desert after the collapse of the Mongol Empire to prey again on the margins of the renewed Chinese Empire. In 1449, the Ming emperor

Cheng-t'ung was defeated and captured by the Mongols at the battle of T'u-mu, as he tried to bring to heel the new Mongol leader, Esen. Only regular conflict between the different Mongol chieftains eased the threat of a further major invasion, but raiding for food and resources intensified from nomads now grazing their animals in the Ordos region. Warfare once again involved nomad demands for trade goods and frequent violent incursions to secure them. The security dilemma was resolved not by further costly campaigns across the boundary between the two sides but by the decision taken in the 1470s by the emperor and his military advisers to approve the start of what became eventually the 'Great Wall', a system of major fortifications south of the Ordos Desert. The first two stretches of what the Chinese called the *ta-pien*, or great border, 1,100 kilometres in length, were completed by 1474 and had more than 800 guard posts, signal towers, and fortlets along their length; more sections were added so that by the middle of the sixteenth century, there were two extensive lines of defence possessing innumerable watchtowers, signal posts, and garrisons.[23]

This defensive frontier could not stop regular nomad warfare when the Chinese court decided to withhold the goods the nomads needed, not least because it did not yet stretch along the whole northern region. Over the following century, as it became clear that existing walls would not suffice to secure the boundary, more walls, towers, and forts were added, making short-term raiding more difficult. Nevertheless, relations with the nomadic communities along the frontier remained a regular source of friction, until in 1571 the imperial court decided that appeasement made more sense than perpetual conflict. Agreement was reached with the Mongol chief, Altan Khan, to resume regular trade; the name of the city that the khan had founded near the Ordos Desert was changed four years later to 'city returning to civilization'. But Chinese prejudice against the nomads, expressed in derogatory terms – wormlike, goatlike, 'human-faced but bestial-hearted' – continued to undermine trust, while the Mongol nomads described Chinese merchants with words derived from *khudal*, meaning 'to lie'.[24] Along the wall, markets could be manipulated by unscrupulous officials and merchants, who tried to cheat the nomads. Sometimes the frontier centres were used to trap unsuspecting envoys or traders, where they could be murdered; on other occasions, the nomads retaliated by seizing the goods and looting the locality. The imperial policy of banishing criminals to the frontier zone and installing poverty-stricken peasants on land around the long wall contributed to an unstable and combustible mix, common to many isolated frontier zones.[25] The security dilemma was finally resolved in dramatic fashion when the Manchus, becoming the dominant power to the north of the wall, broke into northern China after years of failed incursions and in 1644 founded the new Qing dynasty. The old frontier vanished, along with the Ming.

Security in the Roman Empire had something in common with the Chinese example. In both cases expansion had created a long frontier, distant from the centre of political power in the capital and hard to defend against external threats, leading to periodic crises of security and resort to warfare. The major difference was geographic: China was faced with the problem of securing one major border between Chinese territory and the nomadic societies to the north and north-west, whereas Rome at the fullest extent of the empire had a frontier that embraced west, north, and central Europe, the Balkans, Anatolia, the Near East, and North Africa. Serious academic interest in the Roman frontier is a recent phenomenon, inspired partly by the publication in 1977 of Edward Luttwak's study of Roman imperial grand strategy, in which he used the frontier and its conflicts as a key element in defining what that strategy was in terms drawn from more modern strategic theory.[26] Though the idea that Roman leaders had a consistent long-term 'grand strategy' has been forcefully challenged, Luttwak's concern with how the frontiers of the empire were made secure has become a central issue in Roman historiography.

The frontier as a zone delimiting the empire was largely absent for republican Rome in the period of constant expansion featured in the past chapter. The frontiers of the empire were finally consolidated under the first emperor, Augustus, in approximately the form they were to take for the next 400 years. Two further provinces were added in the first century of the principate: most of Britain after the invasion by the emperor Claudius in 43 CE, and last of all the Danubian province of Dacia conquered by the emperor Trajan in 106 CE, the latter designed to protect the empire from regular incursions across its Danubian frontier. The whole imperial structure had at its greatest extent an estimated perimeter of between 8,000 and 9,000 kilometres.[27] Dangers to the security of the frontier varied widely through time and region, and as a result there was no standard frontier but rather zones that reflected the nature of the current perceived threat. There were four terms used by the Romans to define the frontiers, reflecting these differences: *clausura* for the defensive line of ditches, palisades, and watchtowers in Tripolitania; *fossatum* for the network of ditches in the province of Africa Proconsularis, farther to the west; *fines* for the frontier zones where Roman culture mixed with the indigenous cultures beyond the provincial boundary; and *limes*, which came to define a more fixed frontier of forts, walls, and roads, common from the last centuries of Roman rule.[28] There were even internal frontiers, made necessary by the difficulty of permanently pacifying the mountain tribes of Dalmatia, the Alps, the Pyrenees, and Mauritania.[29] The boundary of all these different frontiers was often merely notional, never marked, and was best indicated by the extent of Roman administration and commerce.

The openness of most frontiers made them an inviting target for tribes or chiefdoms beyond the boundary of the Roman provinces either for raiding in search of booty or slaves or to protect tribal security in response to the Roman threat. To cope with small-scale incursions – as most of them were until the crisis of large-scale invasion in the fourth and fifth centuries – there were networks of forts, fortlets, watchtowers, garrisons, and, where necessary, the stationing of larger legionary forces. Small outposts (*praesidia*) were widely established to control the provincial population, to regulate trade and the movement of people, and to pursue and punish raiders and bandits, who hovered around the limits of imperial rule.[30] Although there is much argument about the precise function of the Roman frontier, the different roles of surveillance, control of commercial routes, combat against bandits or pirates, and maintenance of the security of the hinterland were not mutually exclusive to the defensive functions allocated to frontier zones. Extending overall was the imperial ambition to maintain security against external threat, the imperative, expressed by the emperor Hadrian on his accession in 117 CE, 'to keep intact the empire'.

There were several ways in which that security could be maintained. Like the approach of the Chinese emperors, Rome's strategy alternated between aggressive and defensive responses to threat. The decision to cross the frontier to pacify a hostile population carried the risk that security would be further compromised rather than enhanced if pacification failed. A well-known example illustrates the dangers involved. The Rhine frontier was notoriously unstable as the Romans began to push across the river into regions occupied by different Germanic tribes. In 9 CE, the commander of the Rhineland army, Publius Quinctilius Varus, and three legions of between 15,000 and 20,000 men were stationed across the river and beyond the frontier in order to secure Roman influence over the local Ceruschi tribes. One of their leaders, Arminius, had served in the Roman army as an auxiliary and was attached to Varus's escort. He seems to have resented deeply the ambition of the Romans to extend the empire into his people's territory and secretly prepared a coup against Varus with the cooperation of neighbouring tribesmen. As Varus led his legions and a long train of civilian families, who serviced the military units, back to safer winter quarters on the Roman side of the Rhine, the Ceruschi and their allies launched a fatal ambush. The site of the subsequent battle has traditionally been located in the Teutoburg Forest, near the modern city of Osnabrück, but recent archaeology has located the true site farther to the north of the city, a narrow pass flanked by swamp on one side and woods on the other, where the long line of unsuspecting Roman soldiers and civilians was attacked repeatedly by warriors concealed in the trees behind wooden barriers. The topography made it impossible for the legions to form up as a coherent force. After two days of fighting, the column was slaughtered almost to the last man, woman, and child by the very enemy, as the contemporary Roman historian Velleius put it, 'whom it had always slaughtered as cattle'. The defeat so shocked Augustus that he declared an end to the effort to expand into the Germanic regions, and the Rhine became, for all intents and purposes, the permanent frontier in the north.[31]

Not every campaign beyond the frontier went so badly wrong. In Britain, the persistent threat posed by the tribes on the far side of the Roman frontier in the north led the Roman general, Gnaeus Agricola, to march north into Scotland to destroy the tribal federation formed by the Caledonian leader Calgacus. According to the account by the Roman historian Tacitus, much or perhaps most of which is imagined, Calgacus famously roused his tribesmen with a speech defying the Roman Empire, entreating his people to sustain their independence and warning of the consequences of defeat: 'To robbery, slaughter and plunder they give the lying name of empire: they make a desolation [literally "solitude" in Latin] and call it peace.'[32] The appeal proved fruitless. In 83 CE, at the battle of Mons Graupius (whose site in eastern Scotland has never been confirmed), the Caledonians were defeated, the men probably killed and the women and children taken into slavery. The northern frontier in Britain, however, proved like the Rhine, to be the limit of expansion. Forty years later, Hadrian built the Vallum Aelium – better known as Hadrian's Wall – to protect the Roman province; his successor, Antoninus Pius, built a second wall farther to the north, but that was soon abandoned. The emperor Septimus Severus in 209 CE campaigned in person in Scotland to suppress the insurgent Caledonians and Maeatae but then left, and Hadrian's Wall remained the frontier against the Celtic north. Only the absence of a major military threat made it possible to maintain the security of Rome's most distant boundary.[33]

There were many other ways of establishing enough security to ensure the protection of Rome's provincial frontiers. Local tribes or chiefdoms could be incorporated into the frontier zone, providing auxiliary troops for Roman garrisons and cohorts; alliances with kingdoms or tribal federations across the boundary line was another, though this relied on sufficient trust. When that trust was broken, Roman retribution was almost always savage, a reminder to other frontier peoples of the risks attached if they threatened Roman security. Like the Chinese Empire, Roman leaders recognized the utility of bribes and subsidies to buy peace at the frontier, as did Virius Lupus, governor of Britain, who gave a substantial sum to the Maeatae in 197 CE to buy their compliance. Even Attila, leader of the Hunnic federation that devastated Europe in the fifth century, was said to have received gifts of gold from Rome.[34] When diplomacy failed, Rome was willing to resort to abduction or assassination of tribal leaders or kings who proved a security threat. When the leader of the Quadi, Gabinius, complained of Roman encroachments on his Danubian territory, the local frontier commander, Marcellianus, invited him to dinner, there to have him assassinated. The plot quickly backfired as the Quadi invaded and plundered the Roman province of Pannonia in revenge. On another occasion, King Pap of Armenia, regarded as a doubtful ally by the fourth-century Roman emperor Valens, was invited to another murderous banquet. At least nine probable cases of strategic assassination can be identified between approximately 360 to 450 CE, an early example of 'realism' in practice.[35]

In the end, security of the long boundary over time depended on military force and fortification. Most of the 400,000 soldiers serving the Roman Empire were spread out along or near the frontiers, the *limitanei* as the men were known by the fourth century CE. As the threats to the empire grew from the second century onwards, so the strategy of frontier protection expanded. On some frontiers the threat was never a significant menace to security but enough to warrant protection. In the wide North African provinces, shielded to the south by the desert, there was a modest level of military commitment. Up to the mid-third century, raiding from tribes living beyond or within the notional provincial boundaries of the region seems to have been irregular and small scale, as it was rarely reported. Forts and signal stations were sufficient to ensure the peace; they were more densely concentrated near the mountains in Mauretania Tingitana, present-day Morocco, where peace was more fragile. Only by the fourth century did the African part of the empire face more severe threats. The rebellions of Firmus in 372–3 and

Gildo in 397–398 both required military campaigns to suppress them. In the Near East, the frontier was fluid and ill
defined, marked by garrisoned cities rather than fortresses
or walls. In the face of powerful rival empires in the Middle
East, and particularly the Sasanian Persian Empire from the
third century, Roman fortification was intensified. Neither
side proved strong enough to destroy the other, leaving a
more stable, if occasionally violent, frontier in the east. The
greatest threats were to be found in the European part of the
empire, along the Rhine, Danube, and the northern British
frontier.

One way to counter the threats was to fortify more thoroughly. Building walls as the Chinese did was scarcely an
option across the whole of central Europe, but extensive
monumental fortification was undertaken along frontier
zones and in defence of cities within reach of enemy incursions. Hadrian's Wall was an exception, as the distance
across the narrow neck of northern England, 117 kilometres,
made a fixed line feasible. Walls were not solely defensive
but could act as a springboard and protection for punitive
raids beyond the frontier in pursuit of an intruder. They
were also frontiers designed to intimidate potential aggressors and to control their movements.[36] Hadrian's Wall was
connected by roads to a network of forts and garrisons farther south to speed up reinforcement if needed; some outposts were based on the far side of the wall. Although there
were regular raids from the Celtic tribes (at least eleven recorded by Rome between 160 and 400 CE), the security network prevented any major invasion and protected the rest
of the British province.[37] The Rhine and Danube frontiers

were more difficult to make secure. A line of forts, ditches, embankments, and towers was constructed along them both; on the Rhine, frontier forts were spaced every five kilometres to make it easy for neighbouring garrisons to support one another or to pass on warnings. In the late third century, under emperor Diocletian, a former cavalry officer, the forts were strengthened with taller and more robust walls. Securing the frontier became the prime strategy in the last centuries of the Roman Empire in the west; emperors were routinely drawn from the military leadership and commanded large field armies held in readiness for a breakdown of security both within and beyond the frontiers.[38] But as the tribes along the frontier began to amalgamate into larger federations, they posed a threat distinct from that of earlier centuries. Despite the greater emphasis on security, the long and permeable frontiers proved inadequate to prevent major invasions by tribes whose own frontiers in the east were under constant pressure from nomads moving westward. Although the empire, now divided between east and west, sought to accommodate the invaders into the Roman system, by the fifth century the pressure proved irresistible: Vandals, Goths, Franks, and Huns between them overturned the European and African provinces of the empire as they swept aside the old frontiers.[39] As in China, a determined invasion by a united enemy undid centuries of effort to maintain security.

Much the same story could be told of many other territorial empires whose security depended on being able to establish a solid enough frontier, backed up by the use of force when needed.[40] Such was also the case for the expansion of European empires overseas, where the security of distant territory was compromised not only by the reaction of indigenous peoples made insecure by colonial seizure of land and challenges to established cultures but also by competition from other states engaged in the struggle for empire. The long colonization of North America is an obvious example, where colonists engaged from the seventeenth century in what one historian of the frontier has described as 'extirpative war' along the insecure boundary between Native Americans and European colonists.[41] Frontiers in this history were constant sites of warfare and security often a strategic chimera.

The centuries of overseas imperialism coincided with a general move towards the establishment of fixed and recognized national borders in Europe and beyond, the violation of which constituted an evident challenge to security. The past 200 years have witnessed numerous conflicts over contested frontiers or frontier territory, not least from the desire to establish nations with a shared ethnic or cultural identity: Greece, Italy, and Germany in the nineteenth century and a host of new nations in the aftermath of the collapse of the Habsburg, Russian, German, and Ottoman Empires in 1917–18. Although the American president Woodrow Wilson wanted a clause inserted in the covenant of the League of Nations that would allow for ethnic and cultural 'homogenization' as a key to security, his Allies disagreed on practical grounds, and the final postwar settlement left a situation where frontiers were bound to be contested by ethnic fractions on the wrong side of the new boundaries.[42] Conflict between Greece and Turkey in 1919–22, between the infant

Soviet Union and Poland in 1920, and the eventual ambition of Hitler's Germany to redraw the ethnic boundaries of central and eastern Europe in the late 1930s were all contests over frontier zones.

Only after 1945 were European frontiers settled, largely as a result of major movements of population or direct annexation. Of the twentieth-century changes in border territory globally, 112 have involved military conflict, although not all could be judged issues of security. There have been fewer in former colonial territories after the independence of states in Africa and Asia because the original frontiers, drawn arbitrarily by the European powers across ethnic and cultural boundaries, have encouraged a commitment to existing territorial integrity.[43] The principle in this case was the ancient Roman legal concept of *uti possidetis, ita possideatis* ('who is in possession, so it is possessed'), which was used by Latin American colonies of Spain in the nineteenth century to assert their territorial sovereignty and prevent recolonization and then adopted in Africa in the 1960s during decolonization under the aegis of the Organization of African Unity. After a decision by the International Court of Justice in 1986 on the dispute between Burkina Faso and Mali, the concept is now widely regarded as a general principle to protect the frontiers of new states and so avoid conflict, and it was applied in the breakup of Yugoslavia and the Soviet Union, although the principle did not protect Ukraine from later encroachment by Russia.[44]

In the post-1945 world, frontiers have lost some of their salience in explaining the relationship between security and warfare, not least because aircraft and missiles pay them no attention. Fighting over frontier territory has generally been small scale, but there remain a number of what have been called 'frozen conflicts' that have serious security implications. They include the long and troubled history of Israel's relationship with Arab neighbours, where warfare over frontiers reflected Israeli insecurity in a perennially hostile environment; the Northern Ireland civil war that challenged British security and still poses challenges after the difficulty of negotiating the status of the frontier with Ireland during the British withdrawal from the European Union; and perhaps the most dangerous of all, the long arguments over the frontier between China, India, and Pakistan that have remained 'frozen' since the first decades immediately after the end of the Second World War but now in the first decades of the twenty-first century involve three of the world's nine nuclear powers. The confrontations among them have involved intermittent warfare, small-scale incursions, an insurgency, and terrorist violence. Although all three states see the issues as fundamental to their territorial security, it is difficult to understand why remote, mountainous, thinly populated, and literally 'frozen' territory should have provoked so long a conflict. Frontier security in this case has a symbolic significance, more related to wider political issues than to the nature of the territory.

The conflict over Kashmir dates from the partition of India in 1947; the conflict between China and India dates from the unification of China under Communist rule in 1949. The northern Indian state of Jammu and Kashmir had a Hindu monarch but a majority Muslim population. On partition, Pakistan and India fought briefly over control of the state, and Pakistan seized one-third, while India kept the rest. Neither side was content to leave the frontier uncontested, and regular small wars and military confrontations have resulted. Indian politicians see Jammu and Kashmir as part of India, as the British intended when they left; Pakistan sees the area as one where fellow Muslims should have been integrated with the Muslim state when it was created. Although the wars have been followed by ceasefires under international pressure, neither side has been willing to trust the other. The Lahore Agreement signed in 1999 to respect Pakistani sovereignty in one-third of the state was followed almost at once by the Kargil War, disputing the so-called Line of Control, the military boundary separating the two states.[45] With the emergence of a Kashmiri insurgency against continued Indian rule, fuelled by regular Islamic terrorist attacks against Indian targets, the gap between the two sides has widened. Hindu nationalism under prime minister Narendra Modi has made any reconciliation in the near future unlikely. India imposed a strict security clampdown on Kashmir and in 2019 abolished the constitutional status of the region, placing it under direct rule from New Delhi. For Pakistan, the status of Kashmir is now defined as 'illegally occupied' by India. A close political and economic alignment between Pakistan and China, developed over the past decade, has only encouraged Indian uncertainty and a sense of insecurity. Occasional military clashes highlight that instability.[46]

The British departure from India also left an ill-defined frontier between India and China that has been a cause of dispute ever since. On the long common frontier from the Kashmiri Ladakh Range in the west, past Chinese-occupied

Tibet, to the Chinese province of Xinjiang in the east, there has been no agreement on the precise boundary lines. India has relied on two rough lines imposed by the British: the 'Johnson Line' drawn by William Johnson in 1865 on the northwest frontier; and the 'McMahon Line' on the eastern frontier, agreed by Henry McMahon with Tibet in 1914 but never agreed to by the Chinese authorities.[47] In the 1950s, both sides made brief incursions across the informal frontier that separated them, until in 1961, after the Chinese annexation of Tibet in 1959, China occupied and claimed a major area of the mountains on the Kashmir frontier, the Aksai Chin. India objected and in October 1962, Prime Minister Jawaharlal Nehru ordered the Indian army to drive out the Chinese, 'otherwise they'll march on'.[48] Indian defeat in the brief war left China in occupation, but no agreement, even though China has managed to resolve at least seventeen other territorial disputes without conflict.[49]

Although efforts have been made by both sides to create a defined frontier, the search for military advantage by occupying higher mountain ridges or building outposts and bunkers has led to persistent incursions from one side or the other.[50] Both states seek a completely secure frontier, but as in the confrontation over Kashmir, the frontier issue has become the lightning rod for a more profound alienation between the two states over their geopolitical position in southern Asia, not least as a result of the growing rapprochement between India and the United States. In 2017, a military stand-off avoided open conflict, but in 2019, after reform of the Kashmiri constitutional status, India claimed that the enlarged Ladakh Union Territory now included Aksai Chin, still occupied by Chinese forces. When Indian troops crossed the line separating the two sides in 2020 into the Galwan River valley, Chinese soldiers retaliated violently with improvised clubs and sticks (to respect the agreement made in the 1960s not to fire weapons). The result was the first major fight with fatalities between the two sides since 1962.[51] The three-way conflict between India, China, and Pakistan has become a source of potential instability in Asia on a larger scale, as all three possess nuclear weapons, and there are no institutional checks on their use. The 'trust deficit' between them, evident in the regular breakdown of talks on resolving the disputes, exemplifies the long history of frontier insecurity as a potential trigger for major conflict, even, so it has been argued, for regional nuclear war.[52]

The remit of security studies is to study these modern conflicts, including the vexed issue of territoriality. The purpose of the discipline, established and defined in the years after 1945, is the study of the causes of war and ways in which war might be prevented. Although historical examples such as early China or Rome can help to explain what is termed the 'security dilemma' – how to be secure while avoiding conflict – the discipline has focused on the Cold War and the post-Cold War world in order to construct a theoretical basis for understanding why war might or might not break out. The central explanation remains security, either enough of it or too little.

The field of security studies has its roots in the breakdown of the international system after the economic Crash of 1929 and the violent empire-building of Japan, Italy, and

Germany from 1931 onwards. Although Europeans tried to understand and interpret the challenge to security that these changes represented, it was in the United States that a more formal effort was made not just to explain the crisis but also to see how American security might be guaranteed in a system collapsing into global warfare. One contributor was Quincy Wright, whose seminal volume *Study of War*, published in 1942 just after American entry to the Second World War, was based on a long research project going back to the 1920s on what caused warfare. He viewed war as a malady for which a cure had to be found, but his work posed the question how the prevalence of war, waged from a wide variety of motives, might be challenged and a more secure world created.[53] Another contributor was the historian Edward Mead Earle, who joined the newly founded Institute for Advanced Study in Princeton, New Jersey, in 1933, where he ran a high-level seminar on 'the study of the place of war in history' as a contribution to understanding what strategy the United States should pursue to ensure national security, a term already in use before the onset of world war. The key for Earle, as for other academics and advisers in Franklin D. Roosevelt's orbit, was the pursuit of power as the only key to ensuring 'the ability of the nation-state to secure its territory, rights, political independence, and national interests'. Although Earle was unimpressed by Spykman's realist argument that national security could be brought about only 'by a constant devotion to power politics', his view that the United States had to become a 'Great Power' to survive had in fact a solid realist core.[54]

In the aftermath of the Second World War and the new nuclear threat to security, the discipline expanded rapidly.

'Security studies' became a recognized field with centres at New York's Columbia University, at Yale, and at Princeton. The American Social Science Research Council in 1952 set up a dedicated Committee on National Security Research. A generation of young scholars, among them a junior Henry Kissinger, began to embrace security as a subject that needed a firm theoretical foundation and an avenue to policymakers, whose decisions might reduce or augment the ever-present threat of war.[55] They were united by attachment to 'realism' as a paradigm for state security, traced back through time to Machiavelli and Hobbes. The key was survival by any means, moral or otherwise; power was the key to security, and in the modern age that meant military power. Realism, it was assumed, ought to be the guiding principle in a state's foreign policy, even if the end result was war.

The field of security studies has always been most concerned with how states manage their own safety when faced with the perennial issue of war. The principal objective, regularly repeated as a definitional statement, was to understand 'the threat, use, and control of military force'. In the early decades after 1945 that meant in effect coping with the menace of nuclear weapons. This was now a problem that civilian theorists could engage with, not just the military leadership. The theory of deterrence produced by the security establishment dominated the security discourse until arms control and détente in the 1960s made deterrence less urgent. From the 1970s onwards, security studies have moved to analysing how states behave in a broader international security order rather than maintaining the initial narrow focus on national security. This was an approach already pioneered in Europe,

where 'realism' in its crude Hobbesian form was widely criti-
cized. In Britain, a group of historians and scholars of international relations founded in 1959 the British Committee on
the Theory of International Politics, which was led by the
Cambridge historian Herbert Butterfield and which until the
mid-1980s debated regularly on issues of international order
and how to sustain it. The group included Hedley Bull, whose
later book, *The Anarchical Society*, judged that international order had always been determined by war and its consequences. 'It is war and the threat of war', he wrote, 'that help
to determine whether particular states survive or are eliminated, whether they rise or decline, whether their frontiers
remain the same or are changed.'[56] He and his colleagues,
collectively known as the 'English school', nevertheless
sought to explain how war might be avoided given the anarchic character of relations between states, and they found
a solution in the recent history of international relations in
which, despite the two World Wars, order seemed the more
common condition than disorder. In their view, war was one
consequence of the international structure, but it was more
important to understand how to secure peace. Harry Hinsley,
Butterfield's contemporary at Cambridge, wrote *Power and
the Pursuit of Peace* in 1963 as a further contribution to better
understanding how to evolve a modern international order
as an 'antidote to international unsettlement'.[57]

The emphasis on explaining war or its absence through
understanding the international system rather than the behaviour of individual states came to be described among
American strategic theorists as 'neorealism' (not to be confused with 'neoclassical realism', which deals with the foreign

policy of individual states). It is generally assumed that the founding text of neorealism was the book by Kenneth Waltz, a professor at the University of California, Berkeley, on the *Theory of International Politics*, published in 1979. Although allegedly distinct from the theory of national security that had dominated the bipolar Cold War since the 1940s, Waltz defined the international system as an aggregate of states, all hoping to use power to protect their security. His conclusions differed radically from those of Bull and Hinsley. He assumed that conflict and competition defined the system itself. 'States in an anarchic order', wrote Waltz, 'must provide for their own security, and threats, or seeming threats to their security abound.' The recurrence of war, he continued, is explained by the structure of the international system. 'In an anarchic realm', argued Waltz, 'peace is fragile.'[58]

To complicate the theoretical picture further still, neorealists have bifurcated into two distinct schools of thought, the 'offensive realists' and the 'defensive realists'. The former are hardline realists who argue that states should never relax in relations with others but should always be prepared for the possibility of aggression by adopting a military profile that is deliberately geared to offence when needed. States under this form of neorealism should always strive after more power to ensure their security, rather as Rome during the republic. Power in this sense is not pursued for its own sake but so as to become more secure.[59] To achieve order, there has to be at any one point a balance of power, like the balance in the Cold War between two heavily armed superpowers. Defensive realists, on the other hand, argue like the English school that security can better be managed by adopting a more moderate stance with a military profile more suited to defence. In addition, states can solve security dilemmas by cooperation, alliances, conventions, even by disarmament. The constraints that a more conciliatory and collaborative structure imposes will make war less likely and indeed is characteristic of modern international relations. These 'structural modifiers', as they have been called, reduce the state of anarchy and allow the international system to function at all.[60]

What neither school really addresses directly is when realism of either kind fails and war results. The answer is something of a paradox. Rather than enhancing security, offensive realism can undermine it. A military buildup can encourage a competitive arms race and increase the risk of war; an offensive stance may encourage other states to combine, in the Hobbesian model, to obstruct militarily states seeking to increase their power.[61] Defensive realism suffers the same problem. If states indicate that they have renounced an offensive military posture, or begin to disarm unilaterally, or make clear their foreign policy aims, security is once again compromised. An aggressive state in these circumstances might be tempted to expand power at the expense of states that have chosen defensive moderation as the path to security.[62] The most likely form of war in these circumstances is a result of misperception of other states' intentions, a feature of the outbreak of both the World Wars, in which German leaders misinterpreted the British government's reaction to crisis. The uncertainty generated by the effort to double-guess what other states will do can quickly spiral into a crisis to produce an inadvertent war among powers, none of whom may initially have intended to wage a major war. The opaque nature of strategic intentions, which most modern states deliberately obscure, can also encourage preemptive or preventive war, to strike before a potential enemy can do so.[63] Since the end of the Cold War, multipolarity has increased the risk of war, so it is claimed, because it multiplies the chances of miscalculation where every major state is anxious about threats to security. The bipolar world of the Cold War, in which 'mutually assured destruction' kept the long peace, is now regarded ironically as a more secure structure for avoiding major war than the fragmented structure that has followed.

It is easy to criticize the theoretical foundation of security studies as an explanation for the causes of war. History is made to fit the theory, rather than the other way round. The degree of abstraction in neorealist accounts of the security dilemma is deliberate, because they are not intended as a guide to how individual states will actually perform but only to describe the system in which they have to act, which at any one time may enhance security or throw it into jeopardy. There are numerous examples in the modern age of leaders who have failed the test of realism – Hitler's declaration of war on the United States is an obvious example – and as a result created conditions in which security is sacrificed to strategic fantasy. Nor does neorealism address aspects of security other than the military – environmental security, economic security, human security – that have come to play a major role in security studies since the 1990s.[64] Neorealism is most persuasive in explaining the risk of war when it comes to the problem of evaluating the intentions of other states, as the margin for error in overestimating or under-estimating threat can have important implications for a willingness to risk war or to arm heavily to avert it. Even in cases where the security risks from neighbouring states are now almost nonexistent, military spending and preparation are maintained for the unexpected threat in other parts of the world either from predatory states, or from violent non-state movements, or from the unpredictable ambitions of hubristic leaders. The neorealist insistence that security is always relative in a dynamic international order is used to explain why states cannot relax their vigilance or rely on trust. 'The security dilemma', wrote the American neoclassical realist Jeffrey Taliaferro a decade after the end of the Cold War, 'is an intractable feature of anarchy.'[65]

That dilemma still exists with the threat to security posed by nuclear weapons, the condition that first prompted the emergence of security studies in the 1940s. Deterrence worked just enough in a bipolar system between the United States and the Soviet Union, though it did not prevent both superpowers from engaging in conventional warfare. It was possible for Waltz to argue in 1990 that the probability of major war among states that have a nuclear arsenal 'approaches zero'.[66] At that point there were five nuclear powers: the United States, the Soviet Union, Britain, France, and China. They have been joined since by Pakistan, India, and North Korea; Israel is assumed to be a nuclear power but has not made its nuclear status public. Nonproliferation of nuclear weapons, governed by a treaty first negotiated in 1968, has been agreed to by all states except the four new nuclear powers, although in the 1960s and 1970s the United

States put pressure on the German Federal Republic, South Korea, and Taiwan to abandon the idea of developing their own nuclear weapons.[67] More than 90 percent of the existing nuclear warheads are still held by the United States and Russia, successor to the Soviet Union, so that the original Cold War security standoff has not disappeared. The conventional assumption among politicians, military leaders, and the wider public – even in a world with nine nuclear powers – is that the weapons will not be used in anger because of the strong probability of mutual mass destruction. That assumption begs the question of why India, Pakistan, Israel, and North Korea need nuclear weapons in the first place if they are a resource that can never be used. In all four cases, there are regional issues of security in which the nuclear option might indeed be used deliberately or preemptively or as a measure of last resort.

The question of what circumstances might trigger a nuclear conflict has recently been explored through examination of American nuclear war gaming in records that are now declassified. In 1961, the US Joint Chiefs of Staff established a Joint War Games Control Group (later the Joint War Games Agency) to conduct regular games five or six times a year, one series pitting the United States against nuclear powers, another series against nonnuclear powers. In the nuclear games, two teams, one blue, one red, would work out their game moves in separate rooms, monitored by a controller. In all but two of the games in the 1960s and early 1970s, the teams did not invoke the use of nuclear weapons. But in one case where the nuclear option was accepted, the choice closely replicated what might happen in a situation where crisis management fails. The BETA I game in 1967 involved ninety-six people from the military, politics, and strategy think-tanks. The scenario was Soviet seizure of West Berlin and American efforts to respond. The difficulties involved inspired the blue team (the United States) to use tactical nuclear weapons; the red team (Soviet Union) then retaliated, taking out six American divisions with a nuclear strike. Blue escalated at once to use of out-of-theater missiles, and red decided that blue was moving to full nuclear strike strategy. A first strike against the United States was ordered, and blue retaliated with a second strike. In the post-game analysis, the blue team complained that it had not been given enough time to reflect on its options and, faced with a sudden crisis, opted for the first tactical nuclear attack. The red team confirmed that it had not been deterred from nuclear war, which would not be much worse than the fate of the Soviet Union in the Second World War.[68] The game was a model example of how escalation could result from poor crisis management – misperception, temporary panic, a sudden narrowing of strategic options – which still remains a twenty-first-century possibility.

The risks to security involved in a nuclear showdown were suddenly exposed in a real conflict when the Russian president, Vladimir Putin, ordered invasion of Ukraine in February 2022. Western support for Ukraine immediately raised the stakes, as three of the states providing aid via NATO were nuclear states, confronting a nuclear-armed Russia and a Chinese regime generally hostile to Western involvement. Intermittent threats from Putin that he would not shirk from deploying nuclear weapons if Russia's security were seriously threatened were difficult to interpret but could not be ignored. Security studies for decades assumed that deterrence worked, but rogue states are more difficult to integrate into a structure of agreed restraint. The invasion of Ukraine is yet a further example of the potential instability of frontiers. Russian warfare in Chechnya in 1994–6 and again from 1999, against Georgia in 2008, and in irredentist defence of Russians living in southern Ukraine from 2014 onwards is the product of a desire for a frontier that secures Russian territorial integrity and ethnic solidarity, even if that means invading neighbours. Security as a function of territoriality, evident in Kashmir as well as Ukraine, echoes the centuries in which boundaries marked a particular site of persistent warfare. But as in the past, the search for security can instead prompt greater insecurity, and it is under such conditions that resort to the absolute weapon can never be ruled out.

The perennial search for security as an explanation for the persistence of war can hardly be denied. Hobbes's 'posture of war' is characteristic of almost all known historic societies and widely evident among peoples without a written history, both archaic and modern. Security is not an abstraction but describes practical efforts to defend clan, tribe, chiefdom, state, or empire from external or internal threat. Pursuit of security need not necessarily involve warlike violence if there are other avenues to achieve it; if security means warfare, it can be either defensive or aggressive. War for security can also involve other motives that can be difficult to separate from the effort to resolve the 'security dilemma' – seizing resources and territory, enhancing political power, extending a belief system – but security is the principal priority, after which other priorities can be secured. There are evidently many periods and regions throughout history where stability is achieved, however temporarily, otherwise Hobbes's war of all against all would have made human existence intolerable.

Nevertheless, there remains the sober fact that the creation of the League of Nations in 1919 amid hopes for perpetual peace was followed in two decades by the largest and bloodiest conflict in world history. The governing factor is trust or its absence. Uncertainty or distrust of the motives or behaviour of neighbours has prompted warfare even where there are no grounds for the decision; hence the importance of frontiers, either notional or fixed, when explaining security as a root of war. The historical evidence confirms that security has always been an elusive condition, conditional and temporary, dependent in the modern age on the prevailing military technology and the robustness of international agreements or institutions, but evident millennia ago in the long defence of the Roman and Chinese Empires. In the twenty-first century, new frontiers have emerged in the possibilities of warfare in space and cyber-warfare. Both prospects compromise current concerns with security, even nuclear security. These new frontiers are open frontiers with all that such a status implies.

Conclusion

Theorists explain what historians know: War is normal.
— Kenneth Waltz, 1989[1]

Theories abound on the causes of war. This reality has tempted the view that warfare cannot be satisfactorily explained because the many theories produce a messy cocktail of ideas rather than the single, coherent answer that Einstein hoped to get from Freud. There is certainly no consensus among those from all the major human sciences who have tried to explain the cause of war over the past century, as the previous chapters have demonstrated. The obvious conclusion is that there is no single or straightforward cause to explain the persistence of warfare throughout the human past: the effort to construct a monocausal explanation for war is futile. That does not mean warfare cannot be explained, simply that there are multiple explanations, dependent on time and place, just as collective violence defined as warfare has varied widely through time, from lethal early skirmishes and ambushes in the Paleolithic to the threat of thermonuclear obliteration in the present century.

The absence of consensus is clear in the attempt by scholars across the disciplines to demonstrate that warfare is an evolutionary aberration, largely absent for pre-state humans and in the historic period no more than an interruption of peace. Such approaches are driven by the need to prove that peace is 'normal', not war. Margaret Mead's assertion that war is a cultural invention that can be 'uninvented' if humans will it enough is reflected in the pacifist argument that over the past hundred years or so, institutions and norms have been developed to make war less acceptable or likely, even in an age that witnessed the two largest and costliest wars in world history. This is an argument that can be taken to extremes. The political scientist Michael Mousseau has suggested that the evolution over five centuries of a world of market-oriented states committed to liberal market norms and values is 'likely to culminate in permanent world peace' by reducing to zero the propensity for war.[2] Few of those who argue for peace as the normal element in human evolution would go so far. The anthropologist Douglas Fry, the leading advocate of the concept of the (relatively) peaceful human past, has echoed Mead in arguing that 'war, like slavery before it, *can* be abolished.' He has advocated the further development of legal and institutional governance of international affairs to control conflict before it escalates: 'We are faced with the challenge of bringing the sheriff and the judge to the global Wild West.'[3] This is a challenge that has eluded humankind so far. The problem with many of the arguments for peace as the human destination lies in the search for the causes of war. The assumption that properly understanding why warfare occurs will make it possible to eliminate it, like finding the final cure for all cancers, is open to the obvious objection that warfare is too diverse and historically widespread to be cured by any single prevailing remedy or remedies. Even the sheriff and the judge had to tame the Wild West at the point of a gun.

War, as Kenneth Waltz claimed, is normal, for historians no more than for students of the other human sciences. 'Normal' in the sense that it is not an aberration, but an integral part of the long human story. Moreover, whatever the circumstances that dictate an act of collective violence, small or large, warfare has been practised in every region of the world and through manifold changes in social and political organization, suggesting that there are fundamental explanations for the cause of war in general. Otherwise, human communities would have chosen to behave differently. Human beings, principally the males, are the only animal species that over long evolutionary time have killed their own kind in large numbers, often inflicting violence with calculated cruelty, irrespective of sex or age. This is true for human beings thousands of years ago and is true in the savage conflicts that have already marked the first quarter of the twenty-first century. For the argument that men, modern men in particular, have an aversion to killing others, there is the counterevidence that in the Second World War, it was possible to take 100 million men, a cross section of their societies, and, after often brief spells of training, to get them to bomb, shell, shoot, and bayonet millions of their fellow species.

There are several levels of explanation for the exceptional violence displayed by humans. The first level comprises the general causes, internal and external, that have affected human evolution. That humans have adapted biologically to engage in violence when necessary to preserve the gene pool and secure reproductive success now seems likely to be the first building block in explaining intraspecific conflict. Warfare is on this reading not *in* our genes but *for* our genes. Because humans act consciously rather than from raw instinct, the biological imperative to fight when needed was reinforced by an evolved psychology that divided the human world into 'them' and 'us', justifying intraspecific killing while creating a psychological predisposition to accept collective violence as a normative social responsibility, particularly for men. As archaic human communities developed language and symbolic culture, so it was possible to invest warfare with more meaning, as a manifestation of cosmological belief or of cultures in which warfare was viewed as both necessary and valued. The coevolution of culture and biology for most of the long human past created conditions within which nature and nurture together, not either one or the other, reinforced the resort to violence when regarded as necessary or advantageous. In addition, the natural environment in which humans evolved supplied external imperatives to act violently when ecological resources were depleted and human competition for them intensified. These general causes can be traced through time and space and can be found to operate even in the recent past or, in the case of climate change or militarized culture, in the present. The evolution of warfare may possibly have emerged independently in different parts of the globe as humans spread out of Africa, but the result was a common one, that warfare from internal and external imperatives was one way, though not by any means the only way, in which human beings coped with survival.

The second level of explanation moves from the general

context for warfare to specific motives to act. Human beings acted and act within the broad parameters already outlined, but they do so from conscious motives. These can be broadly defined under the four headings explored in the four chapters of part II: resources, belief, power, and security. These are not mutually exclusive, because it is likely, for example, that pursuit of power will also enhance security, just as it is likely to bring additional resources. A war for belief may also bring resource advantages, as it did briefly for the crusaders, and at the same time increase the security of the faith. In most cases, however, it is possible with wars ancient and modern to isolate the principal motive behind any given conflict. It is also possible for a single ambitious individual, an Alexander or a Napoleon, to supply the driving force for warfare – a unique and unpredictable cause difficult to integrate with the broader parameters of warfare or with the common range of motives. These motives are, like the level of general factors, universal rather than historically contingent. The search for security, the pursuit of power, the greed for others' resources, wars for faith or ideology are built into the human condition. These ends can of course be found by means other than warfare, but when they are obstructed or intractable or culturally dictated, there remains the option of violence to secure them, whether nomads raiding the frontiers of imperial China or the Russian army in Ukraine today.

Warfare viewed through the two levels of explanation, the general context framing the specific motives, can be understood as a mixture of imperatives that have remained remarkably constant over human history, though the mix can vary from case to case. The complex ways in which warfare has been shaped by natural imperatives and human agency operating in tandem means abandoning the idea that explaining warfare can be simple. There remains what Azar Gat has called 'the causal array that leads to war'.[4] This still leaves work for the historian, as every war will have its own narrative and actors, but at the level of a general answer to the question 'Why war?', the causal nexus has a universal applicability.

All discussion of the causes of war begs the question of whether war is likely to remain on the human agenda. There has been much discussion of the obsolescence of war or of war in decline. The idea that there will never again be war between great powers has been common to strategic argument since the collapse of the Soviet bloc in 1990–91, though much the same argument existed before 1914 and the onset of the second 'Thirty Years' War'.[5] Predictions of the future of warfare suffer from all the obvious drawbacks of prediction, not least because the uncertainty generated by the rise of China and American insecurity has prompted a wave of Cassandras warning of impending conflict. One statistical project on predicting warfare by region and country up to the year 2050, published in 2013, demonstrated that conflict within states rather than between them was set to decline by around 50 percent by mid-century. Tanzania was predicted very precisely to have a 21 percent probability of conflict in 2030, and so on. As the measures used to infer the decline of conflict are levels of infant mortality and advances in education, it might well be better to rely on Nostradamus.[6] A more recent study has suggested that the element of surprise will be a critical factor in great-power war in the current century, which is certainly more convincing historically even if it poses the conundrum of trying to predict the unpredictable.[7]

Aside from the divided opinion of whether a power clash between China and the United States is inevitable, there are other forms of 'future warfare' that have attracted a good deal of popular attention. The first is cyberwar, the deliberate and aggressive effort to disrupt the computer network operations of a rival or enemy. This has so far been attempted only by Russia, against Estonia in 2007, Georgia in 2008, and Ukraine in 2022–3. Cyberattacks can be directed at military and civilian networks, undermining daily life as well as military communications and capability. So seriously has the US government taken the threat that President Barack Obama in 2009 declared the digital infrastructure to be a 'strategic national asset'. A year later, the US Strategic Command created USCYBERCOM as a subdivision charged with developing computer network defences and attacks. The American Stuxnet computer worm was used since then to damage Iran's nuclear programme.[8] Cyberwar, it is evident, has indirect effects as no one will be killed by it, but it is expected that over the coming century it will become an increasingly significant part of any major state's warfare armoury. The same might be said of the threat of war in space. General agreement since the 1970s that space ought to be a weaponless sanctuary has been progressively challenged as more states put satellites into orbit and develop the technology capable of knocking out or blinding a rival satellite, as China has shown with antisatellite exercises over the past decade. Because satellite communication has a vital military dimension, there has been growing concern about how to defend against war fighting in space. In 2017, the United States set up US Space Command and the US Space Force with a brief like the one for the cyberwar command, to develop anti-satellite capability and forms of satellite defense, which includes the Geosynchronous Space Situational Awareness Program, a title that would flatter H. G. Wells or the cast of *Star Trek*.[9]

Warfare will evidently change during the coming century but between whom and from what motives is unpredictable. The wars so far this century confirm the causal nexus. The idea that war is programmed to die out is impossible to reconcile with the crop of conflicts since 2000 or with the anticipated ecological crisis, resource stress, and religious conflict in the coming decades that could result in the kinds of war for which there is a long historical pedigree. There are scant grounds for thinking that a warless world is about to emerge from the current or future international order. The causes of war have been persistent for millennia. As this book is being written, the major powers are posturing for potential conflict over Russian aggression in Ukraine; no one observing the heavily armed adversaries on the ground, or the proxy war waged by the West, or the regular threats of nuclear escalation could be persuaded that warfare in all its many iterations will become a thing of the past. If war has a very long human history, it also has a future.

Abbreviations

BCE: Before the Common Era (also BC = before Christ)
CAN: Center for Naval Analyses
CE: Common Era (also AD = anno Domini)
CINC: Composite Indicator of National Capability
DNA: Deoxyribonucleic acid
GAM: Gerakan Aceh Merdeka (Free Aceh Movement)
GDP: Gross domestic product
IPCC: Intergovernmental Panel on Climate Change
ISIS: Islamic State of Iraq and Syria
MPLA: Movimento Popular de Libertação de Angola
NATO: North Atlantic Treaty Organization
PTT: Power transition theory
RUF: Revolutionary United Front (Sierra Leone)
SS: Schutzstaffel (Security Squadron)
UNITA: União Nacional par a Independêcia Total de Angola
USCYBERCOM: US Cyber Command

Notes

PROLOGUE: WHY WAR?

1. Einstein to Freud, July 30, 1932, in *Why War? 'Open Letters' Between Einstein and Freud* (London: New Commonwealth, 1934), 5.
2. Freud to Einstein, September 1932, in *Why War? 'Open Letters' Between Einstein and Freud*, 10, 15.
3. Most recently Christopher Coker, *Why War?* (London: Hurst & Co., 2021). See also the Penguin Special by Cyril Joad, *Why War?* (London: Penguin, 1939); Edward Conze and Ellen Wilkinson, *Why War? A Handbook for Those Who Will Take Part in the Second World War* (London: National Council of Labour Colleges, 1934); Jacqueline Rose, *Why War? Psychoanalysis, Politics, and the Return to Melanie Klein* (Oxford: Blackwell, 1993); and George Pitman, *Why War? An Inquiry into the Genetic and Social Sources of Human Warfare* (Indianapolis, IN: Dog Ear Publishing, 2015). Dean Inge chose 'Why War?' as the title of a talk subsequently published in H. J. Stenning, ed., *The Causes of War* (New York: Telegraph Press, 1935). Other books on the causes of war include Jack Levy and William Thompson, *Causes of War* (Oxford: Wiley-Blackwell, 2010); Keith Otterbein, *How War Began* (College Station: Texas A&M University Press, 2004); and Geoffrey Blainey, *The Causes of War* (New York: Free Press, 1973). On war in general, the best recent analysis is Beatrice Heuser, *War: A Genealogy of Western Ideas and Practices* (Oxford: Oxford University Press, 2022). See also Anthony Grayling, *War: An Enquiry* (New Haven, CT: Yale University Press, 2017). There are two classic studies: Quincy Wright, *A Study of War* (Chicago: University of Chicago Press, 1942); and Azar Gat, *War in Human Civilization* (Oxford: Oxford University Press, 2008).
4. Edward Durbin and John Bowlby, *Personal Aggressiveness and War* (London: Kegan Paul, Trench, Trubner & Co., 1939), vii, 12.

5. Azar Gat, 'Proving Communal Warfare Among Hunter-Gatherers: The Quasi-Rousseauan Error', *Evolutionary Anthropology* 24, no. 1 (2015): 123.

6. A good account of the dichotomy between deterministic and nondeterministic explanations for war can be found in Clayton Robarchek, 'Primitive Warfare and the Ratomorphic Image of Mankind', *American Anthropologist* 91, no. 4 (1989): 913–14.

7. Joseph Schneider, 'Primitive Warfare: A Methodological Note', *American Sociological Review* 15 (1950): 732–77; and Paul Roscoe, 'The Anthropology of War and Violence', in *Ethnology, Ethnography and Cultural Anthropology: Encyclopedia of Life Support Systems*, ed. Paul Barbaro (Oxford: EOLSS Publishers, 2017).

8. Bronisław Malinowski, 'Man's Primeval Pacifism and the Modern Militarist Argument', draft paper, 22/1; 'Disarmament', war lecture IX, February 17, 1933, 22/4, Malinowski Papers, London School of Economics.

9. See especially Douglas Fry, ed., *War, Peace and Human Nature: The Convergence of Evolutionary and Cultural Views* (Oxford: Oxford University Press, 2015); and Douglas Fry, *Beyond War: The Human Potential for Peace* (New York: Oxford University Press, 2007).

10. The principal protagonists are Steven LeBlanc, *Constant Battles: Why We Fight* (New York: St. Martin's Press, 2003); and Lawrence Keeley, *War Before Civilization* (New York: Oxford University Press, 1996).

11. Keith Otterbein, 'The Earliest Evidence of Warfare?', *Current Anthropology* 52, no. 3 (2011): 439; and the response by the archaeologists, 'A Reply to Otterbein', *Current Anthropology* 52, no. 3 (2011): 441.

12. Domenec Campillo, Oriol Mercadel, and Rosa-Maria Blanch, 'A Mortal Wound Caused by a Flint Arrowhead in Individual MF–18 of the Neolithic Period Exhumed at Sant Quirze del Valles', *International Journal of Osteoarchaeology* 3 (1993): 145–50.

13. Patricia Lambert, 'The Archaeology of War: A North American Perspective', *Journal of Archaeological Research* 10, no. 3 (2002): 209–30.

14. Mark Golitko and Lawrence Keeley, 'Beating Ploughshares Back into Swords; Warfare in the *Linearbandkeramik*', *Antiquity* 81 (2007): 333–35.

15. Gat, 'Proving Communal Warfare', 116–23; and Mark Allen, 'Hunter-Gatherer Violence and Warfare in Australia', in *Violence and Warfare Among Hunter-Gatherers*, ed. Mark Allen and Terry Jones (New York: Routledge, 2016), 97–107.

16. Barry Isaac, 'Aztec Warfare: Goals and Battlefield Comportment', *Ethnology* 22, no. 2 (1983): 124.

17. David Webster, 'Not So Peaceful Civilization: A Review of Maya War', *Journal of World Prehistory* 14, no. 1 (2000): 96–97.

18. Marc Kissel and Nam Kim, 'The Emergence of Human Warfare: Current Perspectives', *Yearbook of Physical Anthropology* 168, no. S67 (2018): 141–63.

19. John Archer, 'The Nature of Human Aggression', *International Journal of Law and Psychiatry* 32 (2009): 202–8.

20. Steven Pinker, *The Better Angels of Our Nature: The Decline of Violence in History and Its Causes* (London: Allen Lane, 2011). For a critical review of the thesis, see Philip Dwyer and Mark Micale, eds., *The Darker Angels of Our Nature: Refuting the Pinker Theory of History and Violence* (London: Bloomsbury, 2021).

21. See two review essays: Carl Keysen, 'Is War Obsolete?', *International Security* 14, no. 4 (1990): 42–64; and Azar Gat, 'Is War Declining and Why?', *Journal of Peace Research* 50, no. 2 (2013): 149–57. On the frequency of modern conflict, see Mark Harrison and Nikolaus Wolf, 'The Frequency of Wars', *Economic History Review* 65 (2012): 1055–76, who conclude that conflict 'has risen steadily over 131 years' to the present.

22. Einstein to Freud, July 30, 1932, in *Why War? 'Open Letters' Between Einstein and Freud*, 7.

CHAPTER 1: BIOLOGY

1. 'Progress and Prejudice', *Nature* 127, no. 3216 (June 20, 1931): 917.

2. 'Seville Statement on Violence, Spain, 1986', *Peace Research* 34, no. 2 (2002): 75–77.

3. Peter Bowler, 'Malthus, Darwin and the Concept of Struggle', *Journal of the History of Ideas* 37, no. 4 (1976): 631–33.

4. Charles Darwin, *The Descent of Man* (1871; repr. London: Gibson Square Books, 2003), 182, 191–92.

5. Christopher Hutton, *Race and the Third Reich* (Cambridge: Polity, 2005), 17–18.

6. Friedrich von Bernhardi, *Germany and the Next War* (London: Edward Arnold, 1912), 18–19; and Richard Weikart, *From Darwin to Hitler: Evolutionary Ethics, Eugenics, and Racism in Germany* (New York: Palgrave-Macmillan, 2004), 168–74.

7. Adolf Hitler, *Mein Kampf*, ed. Donald Watt (London: Weidenfeld & Nicolson, 1969), 262; and Weikart, *From Darwin to Hitler*, 209–15.

8. Michel Prum, 'Perception of War in Darwinist Perspective', *Revue Lisa* 20 (2022): 13.

9. Arthur Keith, *Essays on Human Evolution* (London: Watts & Co., 1946), 130, 134, 144–46.

10. Foreword to Alfred Machin, *Darwin's Theory Applied to Mankind* (London: Longman, 1937), v–vi; Arthur Keith, 'What Is Wrong with the World?', 13–15, Keith Papers, MS 0018/1/9–10, Royal College of Surgeons.

11. Paul Crook, *Darwinism, War and History* (Cambridge: Cambridge University Press, 2009), 7–8, 20–21; and Doyne Dawson, 'The Origins of War: Biological and Anthropological Theories', *History and Theory* 35, no. 1 (1996): 11.

12. UNESCO, *The Race Concept* (Paris: UNESCO, 1952); and Ullica Segerstråle, *Defenders of the Truth: The Battle for Science in the Sociobiology Debate and Beyond* (Oxford: Oxford University Press, 2000), 30–31.

13. Keith, *Essays on Human Evolution*, 149–52.

14. Solly Zuckerman, *The Social Life of Monkeys and Apes* (London: Kegan Paul, Trench & Co., 1932), 217–21; and John Bowlby and Edward Durbin, *Personal Aggressiveness and War* (London: Routledge, Kegan Paul, 1939), 8–11, 25–29.

15. Konrad Lorenz, *On Aggression* (London: Methuen, 1966).

16. Lorenz, *On Aggression*, 29, 231–32.

17. Theodora Kalikow, 'Konrad Lorenz's Ethological Theory: Explanation and Ideology 1938–1943', *Journal of the History of Biology* 16, no. 1 (1983): 54–56.

18. Lionel Tiger and Robin Fox, 'The Human Biogram', in *The Sociobiology Debate: Readings on the Ethical and Scientific Issue Concerning Sociobiology*, ed. Arthur Caplan (New York: Harper & Row, 1978), 57–61.

19. Niko Tinbergen, 'On War and Peace in Animals and Man', in *The Sociobiology Debate: Readings on the Ethical and Scientific Issue Concerning Sociobiology*, ed. Arthur Caplan (New York: Harper & Row, 1978), 85–93; Jürgen Heinze, 'Aggression in Humans and Other Primates – A Biological Prelude', in *Aggression in Humans and Other Primates: Biology, Psychology, Sociology*, ed. Hans-Henning Kortüm and Jürgen Heinze (Berlin: De Gruyter, 2013), 1–3; and Irenäus Eibl-Eibesfeldt, *The Biology of Peace and War: Men, Animals and Aggression* (New York: Viking, 1979), 9–10.

20. Sociobiology Study Group, 'Sociobiology – Another Biological Determinism', in *The Sociobiology Debate: Readings on the Ethical and*

Scientific Issue Concerning Sociobiology, ed. Arthur Caplan (New York: Harper & Row, 1978), 281–86; Johan van der Dennen, 'Studies of Conflict', in *The Sociobiological Imagination*, ed. Mary Maxwell (Albany: State University of New York Press, 1991), 230–31.

21. Edward Wilson, *On Human Nature* (Cambridge, MA: Harvard University Press, 1978), 99–120.

22. Segerstråle, *Defenders of the Truth*, 14–16, 23; and John Alcock, *The Triumph of Sociobiology* (Oxford: Oxford University Press, 2001), 3–4.

23. On the arguments over disciplinary boundaries, see Cora Stuhrmann, '"It Felt More Like a Revolution": How Behavioural Ecology Succeeded Ethology, 1970–90', *Berichte zur Wissenschaftsgeschichte* 45, no. 1–2 (2022): 136, 145–55.

24. Jane Morris-Goodall, *Through a Window: Thirty Years with the Chimpanzees of Gombe* (London: Weidenfeld & Nicolson, 1990), 12–13. Goodall succeeded in getting the ruling on gender overturned.

25. Morris-Goodall, *Through a Window*, 83–94.

26. Richard Wrangham and Dale Petersen, *Demonic Males: Apes and the Origins of Human Violence* (London: Bloomsbury, 1996), 20–21; and Richard Wrangham, 'Evolution of Coalitionary Killing', *Yearbook of Physical Anthropology* 42 (1999): 6–11.

27. Richard Wrangham and Luke Glowacki, 'Intergroup Aggression in Chimpanzees and War in Nomadic Hunter-Gatherers', *Human Nature* 23 (2012): 8–10.

28. Sagar Pandit, Gauri Pradhan, Hennadii Balashov, and Carel Van Schaik, 'The Conditions Favoring Between-Community Raiding in Chimpanzees, Bonobos, and Human Foragers', *Human Nature* 27 (2016): 141–45; and Frank Marlowe, 'Hunter-Gatherers and Human Evolution', *Evolutionary Anthropology* 14 (2005): 55–58.

29. Michelle Scalisi Sugiyama, 'Fitness Costs of Warfare for Women', *Human Nature* 25 (2014): 480–81.

30. James Neel, 'The Population Structure of an Amerindian Tribe, the Yanomama', *Annual Review of Genetics* 12 (1978): 370–71, 404–7.

31. José Gómez et al., 'The Phylogenetic Roots of Human Lethal Violence', *Nature* 538 (2016): 233–35; and Mark Pagel, 'Lethal Violence Deep in the Human Lineage', *Nature* 538 (2016): 180–81.

32. Daniel Barreiros, 'Warfare, Ethics, Ethology: Evolutionary Fundamentals for Conflict and Co-operation in the Lineage of Man', *Journal of Big History* 2, no. 2 (2018): 23–27.

33. Agustin Fuentes, 'Searching for the "Roots" of Masculinity in Primates and the Human Evolutionary Past', *Current Anthropology* 62, no. S23

(2021): S15–S18; and Nam Kim and Marc Kissel, *Emergent Warfare in Our Evolutionary Past* (New York: Routledge, 2018), 20–21, 27–39.

34. Allan Siegel and Jeff Victoroff, 'Understanding Human Aggression: New Insights from Neuroscience', *International Journal of Law and Psychiatry* 32, no. 1 (2009): 209–10; Roger Pitt, 'Warfare and Human Brain Evolution', *Journal of Theoretical Biology* 72, no. 3 (1978): 553–54, 558–64; and R. Paul Shaw and Yuwa Wong, *Genetic Seeds of Warfare: Evolution, Nationalism and Patriotism* (Boston: Unwin Hyman, 1989), 57–58.

35. William Hamilton, 'The Genetic Evolution of Social Behaviour: Parts I and II', *Journal of Theoretical Biology* 7 (1964): 1–56.

36. Richard Alexander, *Darwinism and Human Affairs* (London: Pitman, 1980), 36–47; Shaw and Wong, *Genetic Seeds of Warfare*, 26–27, 47–49; and Donald Symons, 'Adaptiveness and Adaptation', *Ethology and Sociobiology* 11 (1990): 428–30.

37. Eibl-Eibesfeldt, *The Biology of Peace and War*, 25.

38. Shaw and Wong, *Genetic Seeds of Warfare*, 49–51.

39. Christian Mesquida and Neil Wiener, 'Human Collective Aggression: A Behavioural Ecology Perspective', *Ethology and Sociobiology* 17, no. 4 (1996): 248–49.

40. Bonaventura Majolo, 'Warfare in Evolutionary Perspective', *Evolutionary Anthropology* 28 (2019): 323–26; Toshio Yamagishi and Nobuhiro Mifune, 'Parochial Altruism: Does It Explain Modern Human Group Psychology?', *Current Opinion in Psychology* 7 (2016): 39–40; and Laura Betzig, 'Rethinking Human Ethology: A Response to Some Recent Critiques', *Ethology and Sociobiology* 10, no. 5 (1989): 317–19.

41. Luke Colquhoun, Lance Workman, and Jo Fowler, 'The Problem of Altruism and Future Directions', in *The Cambridge Handbook of Evolutionary Perspectives on Human Behaviour*, ed. Lance Workman, Will Reader, and Jerome Barkow (Cambridge: Cambridge University Press, 2020), 127–30.

42. Bradley A. Thayer, *Darwin and International Relations: On the Evolutionary Origins of War and Ethnic Conflict* (Lexington: University Press of Kentucky, 2009), 113–14; and Jung-Kyoo Choi and Samuel Bowles, 'The Coevolution of Parochial Altruism and War', *Science* 318 (2007): 636–37.

43. Laurent Lehmann and Marcus Feldman, 'War and the Evolution of Belligerence and Bravery', *Proceedings of the Royal Society B: Biological Sciences* 275 (2008): 2877–83.

44. Melissa McDonald, Carlos Navarrete, and Mark Van Vugt, 'Evolution and the Psychology of Intergroup Conflict: The Male Warrior Hypothesis', *Philosophical Transactions of the Royal Society B: Biological Sciences* 367 (2012): 671–74.

45. Sugiyama, 'Fitness Costs of Warfare for Women', 483–91.

46. J. Bengtson and J. O'Gorman, 'Women's Participation in Prehistoric Warfare: A Central Illinois River Valley Case Study', *International Journal of Osteoarchaeology* 27, no. 2 (2017): 230–35; and Brian Ferguson, 'Masculinity and War', *Current Anthropology* 62, no. S23 (2021): S118–S119.

47. John Morgan, *The Life and Adventures of William Buckley* (Firle, UK: Caliban Books, 1979), 49–50. Text based on the original 1852 edition.

48. Susan Kelly and R. Dunbar, 'Who Dares, Wins', *Human Nature* 12, no. 2 (2001): 89–100.

49. Wilson, *On Human Nature*, 115.

50. Neel, 'Population Structure', 377.

51. Bruce Knauft, 'Violence and Sociality in Human Evolution', *Current Anthropology* 32, no. 4 (1991): 391–94; Hannes Ruoch, 'Two Sides of Warfare: An Extended Model of Altruistic Behaviour in Ancestral Human Intergroup Conflict', *Human Nature* 25, no. 1 (2014): 373–74.

52. Alex Mesoudi, 'The Study of Culture and Evolution Across Disciplines', in *The Cambridge Handbook of Evolutionary Perspectives on Human Behaviour*, ed. Lance Workman, Will Reader, and Jerome Barkow (Cambridge: Cambridge University Press, 2020), 68.

53. Maciej Chudek and Joseph Henrich, 'Culture-Gene Coevolution, Norm-Psychology and the Emergence of Human Pro-sociality', *Trends in Cognitive Science* 15, no. 5 (2016): 218–24; and William Durham, 'Resource Competition and Human Aggression. Part I: A Review of Primitive Warfare', *Quarterly Review of Biology* 51 (1976): 385–87.

54. Azar Gat, 'Is War in Our Nature?', *Human Nature* 30 (2019): 149–50.

55. Danilyn Rutherford, 'Toward an Anthropological Understanding of Masculinities, Maleness, and Violence', *Current Anthropology* 62, no. S23 (2021): S1.

56. Alcock, *The Triumph of Sociobiology*, 130.

57. Hans-Henning Kortüm and Jürgen Heinze, eds., *Aggression in Humans and Other Primates: Biology, Psychology, Sociology* (Berlin: De Gruyter, 2013), 4.

CHAPTER 2: PSYCHOLOGY

1.   Edward Glover, *War, Sadism and Pacifism: Further Essays on Group Psychology and War* (London: George Allen & Unwin, 1947), 12–13.

2.   Daniel Edward Phillips, 'The Psychology of War', *Scientific Monthly* 3, no. 6 (1916): 569–71.

3.   Sigmund Freud, 'Thoughts for the Times on War and Death', in *Collected Works*, vol. 4 (London: Hogarth Press, 1956), 295–96.

4.   Angel Garma, 'Within the Realm of the Death Instinct', *International Journal of Psychoanalysis* 52 (1971): 145–46.

5.   Alexander Mitscherlich, 'Psychoanalysis and the Aggression of Large Groups', *International Journal of Psychoanalysis* 52 (1971): 164–65; and H. Goldhammer, 'The Psychological Analysis of War', *Sociological Review* 26 (1934): 255.

6.   Edward Glover and Morris Ginsberg, 'A Symposium on the Psychology of Peace and War', *British Journal of Medical Psychology* 14 (1934): 275.

7.   Edward Glover, *The Dangers of Being Human* (London: George Allen & Unwin, 1936), 92–94; and Glover, *War, Sadism and Pacifism*, 14–21.

8.   Joseph Schwartz, *Cassandra's Daughter: A History of Psychoanalysis* (London: Allen Lane, 1999), 197–98.

9.   Schwartz, *Cassandra's Daughter*, 197.

10. Joseph Aguayo, 'Historicising the Origins of Kleinian Psychoanalysis', *International Journal of Psychoanalysis* 78 (1997): 1175–76.

11. E. Sánchez-Pardo, *Cultures of the Death Drive: Melanie Klein and Modernist Melancholia* (Durham, NC: Duke University Press, 2003), 139–47; D. Harding, *The Impulse to Dominate* (London: George Allen & Unwin, 1941), 96–99; and Roger Money-Kyrle, 'The Development of War: A Psychological Approach', *British Journal of Medical Psychology* 16 (1937): 222–23.

12. Alix Strachey, *The Unconscious Motives of War: A Psycho-Analytical Contribution* (London: George Allen & Unwin, 1957), 204.

13. Marie Bonaparte, *Myths of War* (London: Imago, 1947), 80–81.

14. Franco Fornari, *The Psychoanalysis of War* (New York: Doubleday, 1974), ix.

15. Fornari, *The Psychoanalysis of War*, xvii–xx, 30–32, 50–51, 101.

16. Michelle Scalisi Sugiyama, 'Fitness Losses of Warfare for Women', *Human Nature* 25 (2014): 481. This happened in a raid by the Koyukon tribe on an Inupiat village.

17. R. Givens et al., eds., *Discussions on War and Human Aggression* (The Hague: Mouton, 1976), 89–91.

18. Givens et al., *Discussions on War and Human Aggression*, 92, 98, 110–12.

19. Diana Birkett, 'Psychoanalysis and War', *British Journal of Psychotherapy* 8, no. 3 (1992): 300–304.

20. Paul Griffiths, 'Evolutionary Psychology: History and Current Status', in *The Philosophy of Science: An Encyclopedia*, ed. Sahotra Sarkar and Jessica Pfeifer (New York: Taylor & Francis, 2006), 5–8.

21. Anthony Lopez, 'The Evolution of War: Theory and Controversy', *International Theory* 8, no. 1 (2016): 98–99, 109–11.

22. Melissa McDonald, Carlos Navarrete, and Mark Van Vugt, 'Evolution and the Psychology of Intergroup Conflict: The Male Warrior Hypothesis', *Philosophical Transactions of the Royal Society B: Biological Sciences* 367 (2012): 671–74.

23. Jo Groebel and Robert Hinde, 'A Multi-level Approach to the Problems of Aggression and War', in *Aggression and War: Their Biological and Social Bases*, ed. Jo Groebel and Robert Hinde (Cambridge: Cambridge University Press, 1989), 224–26; and Matthew Zefferman and Sarah Mathew, 'An Evolutionary Theory of Large-Scale Human Warfare: Group-Structural Cultural Selection', *Evolutionary Anthropology* 24, no. 2 (2015): 50–51.

24. For this paragraph, see Andrew Bayliss, *The Spartans* (Oxford: Oxford University Press, 2020), 13–14, 26–27, 32, 76–77.

25. Ben Raffield, 'Playing Vikings: Militarism, Hegemonic Masculinities, and Childhood Enculteration in Viking Age Scandinavia', *Current Anthropology* 60, no. 6 (2019): 813–88, 821–23.

26. Ben Raffield, Claire Greenlow, Neil Price, and Mark Collard, 'Ingroup Identification, Identity Fusion, and the Formation of Viking War Bands', *World Archaeology* 48, no. 1 (2016): 36–39.

27. Godfrey Maringira, 'Soldiers, Masculinities, and Violence', *Current Anthropology* 62, no. S23 (2021): S103–S105.

28. Ramon Hinojosa, 'Doing Hegemony: Military, Men, and Constructing a Hegemonic Masculinity', *Journal of Men's Studies* 18, no. 2 (2010): 179–80.

29. Anthony Lopez, 'The Evolutionary Psychology of War: Offense and Defense in the Adapted Mind', *Evolutionary Psychology* 15, no. 4 (2017): 2–5; and Anthony Lopez, 'Evolutionary Psychology and Warfare', in *The SAGE Handbook of Evolutionary Psychology: Applications of Evolutionary Psychology*, ed. T. K. Shackelford (Thousand Oaks, CA: Sage, 2021), 316–30.

30. Lopez, 'The Evolutionary Psychology of War', 10–27.

31. Joyce Benenson with Henry Markovits, *Warriors and Worriers: The Survival of the Sexes* (Oxford: Oxford University Press, 2014), 24–25, 26–30, 59–62.

32. Wendy Varney, 'Playing with "War Fare"', *Peace Review* 12, no. 3 (2000): 385–90.

33. Andrew Bacevich, *The New American Militarism: How Americans Are Seduced by War* (Oxford: Oxford University Press, 2013), 2–9; Carl Boggs and Tom Pollard, *The Hollywood War Machine: U.S. Militarism and Popular Culture* (Boulder, CO: Paradigm, 2007), 10–16, 21–24; and Hugh Gusterson and Catherine Besteman, 'Cultures of Militarism', *Current Anthropology* 60, no. S19 (2019): S4–S10.

34. See, for example, the special issue edited by Elizabeth Cashdan and Stephen Downes, 'Evolutionary Perspectives on Human Aggression', *Human Nature* 23 (2012): 1–4. The objections to biological theories of aggression also apply to evolutionary psychology. See Brian Ferguson, 'Masculinity and War', *Current Anthropology* 62, no. S23 (2021): S112–S115; and Agostin Fuentes, 'Searching for the "Roots" of Masculinity in Primates and the Human Evolutionary Past', *Current Anthropology* 62, no. S23 (2021): S16–S22.

35. Lopez, 'The Evolution of War', 101–2, 117–19.

36. Howard Worgan, 'What Does Schmitt Mean when He Argues That the Friend/Enemy Relation Is the Key Defining Feature of the Political?', *Political Theory Since 1918*, Essay 1. https://www.researchgate.net/profile/Howard_Worgan/publication/294088554_Carl_Schmitt's_FriendEnemy_Distinction/links/56bded6108ae44da37f8831e; and Andreas Koenen, *Der Fall Carl Schmitt: sein Aufstieg zum 'Kronjuristen des Dritten Reiches'* (Darmstadt: Wissenschaftliche Buchgesellschaft, 1995), 608–9.

37. Marilyn Brewer, 'The Psychology of Prejudice: Ingroup Love and Outgroup Hate?', *Journal of Social Issues* 55, no. 3 (1999): 430–35; Jeroen Vaes, Jacques-Philippe Leyens, Maria Paladino, and Mariana Miranda, '"We Are Human, They Are Not": Driving Forces Behind Outgroup Dehumanization and the Humanization of the Ingroup', *European Review of Social Psychology* 23, no. 1 (2012): 66–69; and Alexander Haslam, Stephen Reicher, and Rakshi Rath, 'Making a Virtue of Evil: A Five-Step Social Identity Model of the Development of Collective Hate', *Social and Personality Psychology Compass* 2, no. 3 (2008): 1326–31.

38. Vaes et al., '"We Are Human, They Are Not"', 74–77. On the theoretical approaches, see in particular Robert Böhm, Hannes Rusch, and Jonathan Baron, 'The Psychology of Intergroup Conflict: A Review of the Theories

and Measures', *Journal of Economic Behaviour and Organization* 178 (2020): 951–57; on the idea of 'otherization', see Kathleen Taylor, *Cruelty: Human Evil and the Human Brain* (Oxford: Oxford University Press, 2009), 6–13.

39. Edmund Russell, '"Speaking of Annihilation": Mobilizing for War Against Human and Insect Enemies', *Journal of American History* 82 (1996): 1520–21.

40. Peter Schrijvers, *The GI War Against Japan: American Soldiers in Asia and the Pacific During World War II* (New York: New York University Press, 2002), 218.

41. John Dower, *War Without Mercy: Race & Power in the Pacific War* (New York: Pantheon, 1996), 84–92, 240–48.

42. Emanuele Castano and Roger Giner-Sorolla, 'Not Quite Human: Infrahumanization in Response to Collective Responsibility for Intergroup Killing', *Journal of Personality and Social Psychology* 90, no. 5 (2006): 804–5. For a general survey of language and dehumanization, see Nick Haslam, Steve Loughnan, and Pamela Sun, 'Beastly: What Makes Animal Metaphors Offensive?', *Journal of Language and Social Psychology* 30, no. 3 (2011): 312, 318–22.

43. Colin Pardoe, 'Conflict and Territoriality in Aboriginal Australia', in *Violence and Warfare Among Hunter-Gatherers*, ed. Mark Allen and Terry Jones (London: Routledge, 2014), 115–16.

44. Clayton Robarchek, 'Primitive Warfare and the Ratomorphic Image of Mankind', *American Anthropologist* 91, no. 4 (1989): 911–13.

45. Nils-Christian Bormann, Lars-Erik Cederman, and Manuel Vogt, 'Language, Religion, and Ethnic Civil War', *Journal of Conflict Resolution* 61, no. 4 (2017): 744–46.

46. Stuart Kaufman, *Modern Hatreds: The Symbolic Politics of Ethnic War* (Ithaca, NY: Cornell University Press, 2001), 1–12.

47. On Roman sacking of cities and murder or enslavement of the population, see Robin Waterfield, *Taken at the Flood: The Roman Conquest of Greece* (Oxford: Oxford University Press, 2014), 73–74, 202.

48. Brewer, 'The Psychology of Prejudice', 435–38; Haslam, Reicher, and Rath, 'Making a Virtue of Evil', 1336–37; and Albert Bandura, 'Moral Disengagement in the Perpetration of Inhumanities', *Personality and Social Psychology Review* 3, no. 3 (1999): 193–96.

49. Azar Gat, 'Proving Communal Warfare Among Hunter-Gatherers: The Quasi-Rousseauan Error', *Evolutionary Anthropology* 24, no. 1 (2015): 116–19.

50. Victor Nell, 'Cruelty's Rewards: The Gratifications of Perpetrators and Spectators', *Behavioral and Brain Sciences* 29, no. 3 (2006): 225–26.

51. Valerie Andrushko, Al Schwitalla, and Philip Walker, 'Trophy-Taking and Dismemberment as Warfare Strategies in Prehistoric Central California', *American Journal of Physical Anthropology* 141, no. 1 (2010): 85–88.

52. Elsa Redmond, *Tribal and Chiefly Warfare in South America* (Ann Arbor: University of Michigan Museum of Anthropology, 1994), 3–7, 25–27.

53. James Weingartner, 'Trophies of War: U.S. Troops and the Mutilation of Japanese War Dead', *Pacific Historical Review* 61 (1992): 56–62.

54. David Cesarani, *Eichmann: His Life and Crimes* (London: Heinemann, 2004), 219.

55. Gilbert Murray to M. I. David, October 28, 1936, file 364, Murray Papers, Bodleian Library, Oxford.

CHAPTER 3: ANTHROPOLOGY

1. Margaret Mead, 'Warfare Is Only an Invention – Not a Biological Necessity', *Asia*, 40 (1940): 405.

2. Elsa Redmond, *Tribal and Chiefly Warfare in South America* (Ann Arbor: Michigan Museum of Anthropology, 1994), 57.

3. Thomas Beyer and Erik Trinkman, 'Patterns of Trauma Among the Neanderthals', *Journal of Archaeological Science* 22, no. 6 (1995): 845–49.

4. Virginia Estabrook and David Frayer, 'Trauma in the Krapina Neanderthals', in *The Routledge Handbook of the Bioarchaeology of Human Conflict*, ed. Christopher Knüsel and Martin Smith (New York: Routledge, 2014), 67–69, 84–86; and T. Douglas Price, *Europe Before Rome: A Site-by-Site Tour of the Stone, Bronze and Iron Ages* (Oxford: Oxford University Press, 2013), 35–36.

5. Samuel Bowles, 'Did Warfare Among Ancestral Hunter-Gatherers Affect the Evolution of Human Social Behaviours?', *Science* 324 (2009): 1296.

6. William Parkinson and Paul Duffy, 'Fortifications and Enclosures in European Prehistory: A Cross-Cultural Perspective', *Journal of Archaeological Research* 15, no. 2 (2007): 105–13.

7. Kristian Kristiansen, 'The Tale of the Sword – Swords and Swordfighters in Bronze Age Europe', *Oxford Journal of Archaeology* 21, no. 4 (2002): 319–26.

8. Raymond Kelly, *Warless Societies and the Origin of War* (Ann Arbor: University of Michigan Press, 2000), 6–7, 37.

9. Debra Martin, 'Violence and Masculinity in Small-Scale Societies', *Current Anthropology* 62, no. S23 (2021): S175–S178.

10. Paul Roscoe, 'Margaret Mead, Reo Fortune, and Mountain Arapesh Warfare', *American Anthropologist* 105, no. 3 (2003): 581.

11. Polly Schaarfsma, 'Documenting Conflict in the Prehistoric Pueblo', in *North American Indigenous Warfare and Ritual Violence*, ed. Richard Chacon and Rubén Mendoza (Tucson: University of Arizona Press, 2013), 114–15; and Keith Otterbein, 'A History of Research on Warfare in Anthropology', *American Anthropologist* 101, no. 4 (2000): 796.

12. Richard Overy, *The Morbid Age: Britain Between the Wars* (London: Allen Lane, 2009), 201–2.

13. Otterbein, 'A History of Research on Warfare in Anthropology', 796–7; and Keith Otterbein, *How War Began* (College Station: Texas A&M University Press, 2004), 34–38.

14. Otterbein, 'A History of Research on Warfare in Anthropology', 797–801.

15. Leonard Hobhouse, Morris Ginsberg, and Gerald Wheeler, *The Material Culture and Social Institutions of the Simpler Peoples* (London: Chapman & Hall, 1915), 228–33.

16. Roscoe, 'Margaret Mead, Reo Fortune, and Mountain Arapesh Warfare', 581–82.

17. Martin, 'Violence and Masculinity', S176–S77; Patricia Lambert, 'The Archaeology of War: A North American Perspective', *Journal of Archaeological Research* 10, no. 3 (2002): 220–21; and Ventura Pérez, 'The Politicization of the Dead: Violence as Performance, Politics as Usual', in *The Bioarchaeology of Violence*, ed. Debra Martin, Ryan Harrod, and Ventura Pérez (Gainesville: University Press of Florida, 2012), 19–22.

18. Philip Walker, 'A Bioarchaeological Perspective on the History of Violence', *Annual Review of Anthropology* 30 (2001): 584–86; and Nam Kim and Marc Kissel, *Emergent Warfare in Our Evolutionary Past* (New York: Routledge, 2018), 21–23.

19. Werner Soloch et al., 'New Insights on the Wooden Weapons from the Paleolithic Site at Schöningen', *Journal of Human Evolution* 89 (2015): 214–23.

20. E. Carbonell et al., 'Reply to Otterbein', *Current Anthropology* 52, no. 3 (2011): 441; and Kim and Kissel, *Emergent Warfare*, 98.

21. Virginia Estabrook, 'Violence and Warfare in the European Mesolithic and Paleolithic', in *Violence and Warfare Among Hunter-Gatherers*, ed. Mark Allen and Terry Jones (London: Routledge, 2014),53–59, 66; and Alain Bayneix, 'Neolithic Violence in France', in *Sticks, Stones, & Broken Bones:*

Neolithic Violence in European Perspective, ed. Rick Schulting and Linda Fibiger (Oxford: Oxford University Press, 2012), 208–9.

22. Redmond, *Tribal and Chiefly Warfare*, 3–12.

23. Colin Pardoe, 'Conflict and Territoriality in Aboriginal Australia', in *Violence and Warfare Among Hunter-Gatherers*, ed. Mark Allen and Terry Jones (London: Routledge, 2014), 121–28; and Mark Allen, 'Hunter-Gatherer Violence and Warfare in Australia', in *Violence and Warfare Among Hunter-Gatherers*, ed. Mark Allen and Terry Jones (London: Routledge, 2014), 101–6.

24. Patrick Nolan, 'Toward an Ecological-Evolutionary Theory of the Incidence of Warfare in Preindustrial Societies', *Sociological Theory* 21, no. 1 (2003): 23.

25. Pierre Clastres, *Archéologie de la violence: La guerre dans les sociétés primitives* (Paris: Éditions de l'Aube, 1999), 78, 82–83.

26. Bonnie Glencross and Başak Boz, 'Representing Violence in Anatolia and the Near East During the Transition to Agriculture', in *The Routledge Handbook of the Bioarchaeology of Human Conflict*, ed. Christopher Knüsel and Martin Smith (London: Routledge, 2014), 90–104.

27. Parkinson and Duffy, 'Fortifications and Enclosures', 105–15.

28. Sarah Monks, 'Conflict and Competition in Spanish Prehistory: The Role of Warfare in Societal Development from the Late Fourth to the Third Millennium BC', *Journal of Mediterranean Archaeology* 10, no. 1 (1997): 14–18; and Richard Osgood, Sarah Monks, and Judith Toms, *Bronze Age Warfare* (Stroud, UK: History Press, 2010), 37–39.

29. Jonas Christensen, 'Warfare in the European Neolithic', *Acta Archaeologica* 75 (2004): 146–48.

30. Price, *Europe Before Rome*, 318–19.

31. Mark Golitko and Lawrence Keeley, 'Beating Ploughshares Back into Swords: Warfare in the *Linearbandkeramik*', *Antiquity* 81 (2007): 336–39; Christensen, 'Warfare in the European Neolithic', 150–51; Osgood, Monks, and Toms, *Bronze Age Warfare*, 67.

32. David Anthony, *The Horse, the Wheel, and Language: How Bronze-Age Riders of the Eurasian Steppes Shaped the Modern World* (Princeton, NJ: Princeton University Press, 2007), 390–95; and Robin Yates, 'Early China', in *War and Society in the Ancient and Medieval Worlds*, ed. Kurt Raaflaub and Nathan Rosenstein (Cambridge, MA: Harvard University Press, 1999), 9–10.

33. Thomas Emerson, 'Cahokia and the Evidence for late Pre-Columbian War in the North American Mid-Continent', in *North American Indigenous*

Warfare and Ritual Violence, ed. Richard Chacon and Rubén Mendoza (Tucson: University of Arizona Press, 2013), 130–37.

34. David Dye, 'The Transformation of Mississippian Warfare: Four Case Studies from the Mid-South', in *The Archaeology of Warfare: Prehistories of Raiding and Conquest*, ed. Elizabeth Arkush and Mark Allen (Gainesville: University of Florida Press, 2006), 102–11.

35. Golitko and Keeley, 'Beating Ploughshares Back into Swords', 333–35; Bruno Boulestin et al., 'Mass Cannibalism in the Linear Pottery Culture at Herxheim (Palatinate, Germany)', *Antiquity* 83 (2009): 969–75; and Dirk Husemann, *Als der Mensch den Krieg erfand* (Ostfildern, Germany: Jan Thorbecke Verlag, 2005), 36–38, 43–45.

36. Redmond, *Tribal and Chiefly Warfare*, 69.

37. Dye, 'The Transformation of Mississippian Warfare', 105, 119–21.

38. Lambert, 'The Archaeology of War', 214–15.

39. Teresa Fernández-Crespo et al., 'Make a Desert and Call It Peace: Massacre at the Iberian Iron Age Village of La Hoya', *Antiquity* 94, no. 377 (2020): 1245–51.

40. Monks, 'Conflict and Competition', 23–24; Wiesław Lorkiewicz, 'Skeletal Trauma and Violence Among the Early Farmers of the North European Plain', in *Sticks, Stones, and Broken Bones: Neolithic Violence in European Perspective*, ed. Rick Schulting and Linda Fibiger (Oxford: Oxford University Press, 2012), 73–74.

41. Fanny Chenal, Bertrand Perrin, Hélène Barrand-Emam, and Bruno Boulestin, 'A Farewell to Arms: A Deposit of Human Limbs and Bodies at Bergheim, France, c.4,000 BC', *Antiquity* 89, no. 348 (2015): 1315–24.

42. John Blitz, 'Adoption of the Bow in Prehistoric North America', *North American Archaeologist* 9, no. 2 (1988): 126–36; and Christensen, 'Warfare in the European Neolithic', 139–41.

43. Redmond, *Tribal and Chiefly Warfare*, 32–33; Anne Underhill, 'Warfare and the Development of States in China', in *The Archaeology of Warfare: Prehistories of Raiding and Conquest*, ed. Elizabeth Arkush and Mark Allen (Gainesville: University of Florida Press, 2006), 270–71; Mark Allen, 'Transformations in Maori Warfare', in *The Archaeology of Warfare: Prehistories of Raiding and Conquest*, ed. Elizabeth Arkush and Mark Allen (Gainesville: University of Florida Press, 2006), 188–90; and David Webster, 'Not So Peaceful Civilization: A Review of Maya War', *Journal of World Prehistory* 14, no. 1 (2000): 66.

44. Christian Horn, 'Trouble in Paradise? Violent Conflict in Funnel-Beaker Societies', *Oxford Journal of Archaeology* 40, no. 1 (2021): 43–48.

45. Lorkiewicz, "Skeletal Trauma and Violence', 54.

46. Timothy Earle, *How Chiefs Come to Power: The Political Economy in Prehistory* (Stanford, CA: Stanford University Press, 1997), 122–27.

47. Paul Taçon and Christopher Chippendale, 'Australia's Ancient Warriors: Changing Depiction of Fighting in the Rock Art of Arnhem Land, N. T.', *Cambridge Archaeological Journal* 4, no. 2 (1994): 214–24.

48. Redmond, *Tribal and Chiefly Warfare*, 118–19.

49. Clayton Robarchek, 'Primitive Warfare and the Ratomorphic Image of Mankind', *American Anthropologist* 91, no. 4 (1989): 908–9.

50. Redmond, *Tribal and Chiefly Warfare*, 27–31, 74–75.

51. Martin, 'Violence and Masculinity', S173–S174.

52. Rebecca Redfern, 'Iron Age "Predatory Landscapes": A Bioarchaeological and Funerary Explanation of Captivity and Enslavement in Britain', *Cambridge Archaeological Journal* 30, no. 4 (2020): 532–39.

53. Adrian Goldsworthy, *Roman Warfare* (London: Cassell, 2000), 32–33.

54. Jonathan Roth, *Roman Warfare* (Cambridge: Cambridge University Press, 2009), 8–13; and Goldsworthy, *Roman Warfare*, 33–34.

55. Wolfgang Spickermann, 'The Roman Empire', in *The Limits of Universal Rule: Eurasian Empires Compared*, ed. Yuri Pines, Michal Biran, and Jörg Rüpke (Cambridge: Cambridge University Press, 2021), 113–16.

56. A. D. Lee, *Warfare in the Roman World* (Cambridge: Cambridge University Press, 2020), 31–33.

57. Lee, *Warfare in the Roman World*, 37–42.

58. Kazuo Aoyama, 'Classic Maya Warfare and Weapons: Spear, Dart and Arrow Points of Aguateca and Copan', *Ancient Mesoamerica* 16, no. 2 (2005): 291.

59. George Bey and Tomas Gallareto Negrón, 'Reexamining the Role of Conflict in the Development of Puuc Maya Society', in *Seeking Conflict in Mesoamerica: Operational, Cognitive, and Experiential Approaches*, ed. Meaghan Peuramaki-Brown and Shawn Morton (Denver: University Press of Colorado, 2019), 131–33.

60. Webster, 'Not So Peaceful Civilization', 78–81; and Jason Barrett and Andrew Scherer, 'Stones, Bones and Crowded Plazas: Evidence for Terminal Classic Maya Warfare at Colha, Belize', *Ancient Mesoamerica* 16, no. 1 (2005): 112.

61. Bey and Negrón, 'Reexamining the Role of Conflict', 127–28.

62. Webster, 'Not So Peaceful Civilization', 92–96; and Charles Suhler and David Friedel, 'Life and Death in a Maya War Zone', *Archaeology* 51, no. 3 (1998): 33. It should be noted that there is still much debate

about how to interpret the glyphs thought to relate to war events. See, for example, Gerardo Aldana, 'Agency and the "Star War" Glyph: A Historical Reassessment of Classic Maya Astrology and Warfare', *Ancient Mesoamerica* 16, no. 2 (2005): 305–20.

63. Christopher Hernandez and Joel Palka, 'Maya Warfare, Symbols and Ritual Landscape', in *Seeking Conflict in Mesoamerica: Operational, Cognitive, and Experiential Approaches*, ed. Meaghan Peuramaki-Brown and Shawn Morton (Denver: University Press of Colorado, 2019), 32–36.

64. Suhler and Friedel, 'Life and Death in a Maya War Zone', 33–34.

65. Barrett and Scherer, 'Stones, Bones and Crowded Plazas', 104–12.

66. Mead, 'Warfare Is Only an Invention', 405.

CHAPTER 4: ECOLOGY

1. CNA Corporation, *National Security and the Threat of Climate Change* (Alexandria, VA: CNA, 2007).

2. Ragnhild Nordås and Nils Gleditsch, 'Climate Change and Conflict', *Political Geography* 26 (2007): 627–30; and Jon Barnett and W. Neil Adger, 'Climate Change, Human Security and Violent Conflict', *Political Geography* 26 (2007): 639–42.

3. Quotations from Philip Appleman, ed., *An Essay on the Principle of Population: Thomas Robert Malthus* (New York: Norton, 1976), 28–31.

4. Friedrich Ratzel, *Der Lebensraum* (Tübingen: Laupp'schen Buchhandlung, 1901), 51–52. See also Mark Bassin, 'Imperialism and the Nation State in Friedrich Ratzel's Political Geography', *Progress in Human Geography* 11 (1987): 475–77.

5. Benjamin Lieberman and Elizabeth Gordon, *Climate Change in Human History* (London: Bloomsbury, 2022), 149–50; and Philip Jenkins, *Climate, Catastrophe, and Faith: How Changes in Climate Drive Religious Upheaval* (Oxford: Oxford University Press, 2021), 6.

6. David Yesner et al., 'Maritime Hunter-Gatherers: Ecology and Prehistory', *Current Anthropology* 21 (1980): 727–32.

7. For this conclusion, see Gregory Dow, Leanna Mitchell, and Clyde Reed, 'The Economics of Early Warfare over Land', *Journal of Development Economics* 127 (2017): 303–4. On territorial defence, see Elizabeth Cashdan, 'Territoriality Among Human Foragers: Ecological Models and an Application to Four Bushmen Groups', *Current Anthropology* 24 (1983): 47–50.

8. Patrick Nolan, 'Toward an Ecological-Evolutionary Theory of the Incidence of Warfare in Preindustrial Societies', *Sociological Theory* 21, no. 1 (2003): 23–26.

9. Melvin Ember, 'Statistical Evidence for an Ecological Explanation of Warfare', *American Anthropologist* 84, no. 3 (1982): 646–47.

10. M. Mirazón Lahr et al., 'Inter-group Violence Among Early Holocene Hunter-Gatherers of West Turkana, Kenya', *Nature* 529 (2016): 394–98. For a strongly critical rejection of the idea of a massacre, see Christopher Stojanowski et al., 'Contesting the Massacre at Nataruk', *Nature* 539 (2016): E8–E9, and Lahr's response rejecting the criticisms (E10–E11).

11. David Anthony, *The Horse, the Wheel, and Language: How Bronze-Age Riders from the Eurasian Steppes Shaped the Modern World* (Princeton, NJ: Princeton University Press, 2007), 221–22, 227–29; and G. D. Medden et al., 'Violence at Verteba Cave, Ukraine: New Insights into the Late Neolithic Intergroup Violence', *International Journal of Osteoarchaeology* 28 (2018): 44–53.

12. Douglas Bamforth, 'Indigenous People, Indigenous Violence: Precontact Warfare on the North American Great Plains', *Man* 29 (1994): 104–12; and Patricia Lambert, 'The Archaeology of War: A North American Perspective', *Journal of Archaeological Research* 10, no. 3 (2002): 224–26.

13. Brian Billman, Patricia Lambert, and Banks Leonard, 'Cannibalism, Warfare, and Drought in the Mesa Verde Region During the Twelfth Century AD', *American Anthropologist* 65, no. 1 (2000): 145–56; and Polly Schaafsma, 'Documenting Conflict in the Prehistoric Pueblo', in *North American Indigenous Warfare and Ritual Violence*, ed. Richard Chacon and Rubén Mendoza (Tucson: University of Arizona Press, 2013), 116–17, 123.

14. Mark Allen, 'Transformation in Maori Warfare: Toa, Pa and Pu', in *The Archaeology of Warfare: Prehistories of Raiding and Conquest*, ed. Elizabeth Arkush and Mark Allen (Gainesville: University Press of Florida, 2006), 187–200.

15. S. Jones, H. Walsh-Haney, and R. Quinn, '*Kana Tamata* or Feasts of Men: An Interdisciplinary Approach for Identifying Cannibalism in Prehistoric Fiji', *International Journal of Osteoarchaeology* 25, no. 2 (2015): 127–28.

16. Lawrence Barham and Peter Mitchell, *The First Africans: African Archaeology from the Earliest Toolmakers to Recent Foragers* (Cambridge: Cambridge University Press, 2008), 218, 249–50.

17. Bruno Boulestin et al., 'Mass Cannibalism in the Linear Pottery Culture at Herxheim (Palatinate, Germany)', *Antiquity* 83 (2009): 969–79.

18. Isabel Cáceres, Marina Lozano, and Palmira Saladié, 'Evidence for Bronze Age Cannibalism in El Mirador Cave', *American Journal of Physical Anthropology* 133, no. 3 (2007): 899–913.

19. Paolo Villa, 'Cannibalism in Prehistoric Europe', *Evolutionary Anthropology* 1, no. 3 (1992): 93–98.

20. Billman, Lambert, and Leonard, 'Cannibalism, Warfare and Drought', 145–46, 166–69.

21. Christy Turner and Jacqueline Turner, *Man Corn: Cannibalism and Violence in the Prehistoric American Southwest* (Salt Lake City: University of Utah Press, 1999), 2–4.

22. Ernest Burch, 'Traditional Native Warfare in Western Alaska', in *North American Indigenous Warfare and Ritual Violence*, ed. Richard Chacon and Rubén Mendoza (Tucson: University of Arizona Press, 2013), 12–22; and Charles Bishop and Victor Lytwyn, '"Barbarism and Ardor of War from the Tenderest Years": Cree–Inuit Violence in the Hudson Bay Region', in *North American Indigenous Warfare and Ritual Violence*, ed. Richard Chacon and Rubén Mendoza (Tucson: University of Arizona Press, 2013), 32–37.

23. Bishop and Lytwyn, '"Barbarism and Ardor of War"', 40–45; Dean Snow, 'Iroquois–Huron Warfare', in *North American Indigenous Warfare and Ritual Violence*, ed. Richard Chacon and Rubén Mendoza (Tucson: University of Arizona Press, 2013), 151–59; and Dean Snow, *The Iroquois* (Oxford: Blackwell, 1996), 94–96, 110–17.

24. William Durham, 'Resource Competition and Human Aggression: Part I: A Review of Primitive War', *Quarterly Review of Biology* 51 (1976): 403–5.

25. Rada Dyson-Hudson and Eric Smith, 'Human Territoriality: An Ecological Reassessment', *American Anthropologist* 80, no. 1 (1978): 36.

26. Cashdan, 'Territoriality Among Human Foragers', 49–50.

27. Gerhard Weinberg, ed., *Hitler's Second Book: The Unpublished Sequel to Mein Kampf* (New York: Enigma Books, 2003), 16–18.

28. Gerry Kearns, *Geopolitics and Empire: The Legacy of Halford Mackinder* (Oxford: Oxford University Press, 2009), 14; and Trevor Barnes and Christian Abrahamson, 'Tangled Complicities and Moral Struggles: The Haushofers, Father and Son, and the Spaces of Nazi Geopolitics', *Journal of Historical Geography* 47 (2015): 67.

29. See Christian Ingrao, *The Promise of the East: Nazi Hopes and Genocide 1939–1943* (Cambridge: Polity Press, 2019), prologue and chap. 1 and 4. For the figure of 600 million Germans, see p. 101.

30. Patrick Bernhard, 'Borrowing from Mussolini: Nazi Germany's Colonial Aspirations in the Shadow of Italian Expansionism', *Journal of Imperial*

and Commonwealth History 41 (2013): 617–18; and Ray Moseley, *Mussolini's Shadow: The Double Life of Count Galeazzo Ciano* (New Haven, CT: Yale University Press, 1999), 52.

31. Ben Kiernan, *Blood and Soil: A World History of Genocide and Extermination from Sparta to Darfur* (New Haven, CT: Yale University Press, 2007), 463–67, 477–79.

32. Colleen Devlin and Cullen Hendrix, 'Trends and Triggers Redux: Climate Change, Rainfall, and Interstate Conflict', *Political Geography* 43 (2014): 27–28; Thomas Homer-Dixon, *Environment, Scarcity and Violence* (Princeton, NJ: Princeton University Press, 1999), 139–41.

33. See, for example, Thomas Bernauer and Tobias Siegfried, 'Climate Change and International Water Conflict in Central Asia', *Journal of Peace Research* 499, no. 1 (2012): 227–37.

34. Thomas Bernauer and Tobias Böhmelt, 'International Conflict and Cooperation over Freshwater Resources', *Nature Sustainability* 3 (2020): 350–55.

35. Stefan Döhring, 'Come Rain, Come Wells: How Access to Groundwater Affects Communal Violence', *Political Geography* 76 (2020): 1–4, 12.

36. Wenche Hauge and Tanja Ellingsen, 'Beyond Environmental Scarcity: Causal Pathways to Conflict', *Journal of Peace Research* 35, no. 3 (1998): 301–10; and Vally Koubi et al., 'Do Natural Resources Matter for Interstate and Intrastate Armed Conflict?', *Journal of Peace Research* 51, no. 2 (2014): 229–32; and Henrik Urdal, 'People Versus Malthus: Population Pressure, Environmental Degradation, and Armed Conflict Revisited', *Journal of Peace Research* 42, no. 4 (2005): 425–30.

37. Lieberman and Gordon, *Climate Change in Human History*, 11–20, 28–45.

38. See Hubert Lamb, *Climate History and the Modern World* (London: Methuen, 1982), 67–92 on reconstructing past climate.

39. Anthony, *The Horse, the Wheel, and Language*, 227–29, 389–97.

40. Qiang Chen, 'Climate Shocks, Dynastic Cycles, and Nomadic Conquests: Evidence from Historic China', *Oxford Economic Papers* 67, no. 2 (2015): 185–88.

41. David Zhang et al., 'Climatic Change, Wars, and Dynastic Cycles in China over the Last Millennium', *Climatic Change* 76, no. 3 (2006): 464–69; and Ying Bai and James Kai-sing Kung, 'Climate Shocks and Sino-Nomadic Conflict', *Review of Economics and Statistics* 93, no. 3 (2011): 9970–72, 9978.

42. David Zhang et al., 'Climate Change and War Frequency in Eastern China over the Last Millennium', *Human Ecology* 35, no. 4 (2007): 403–7;

and Weiwen Yin, 'Climate Shocks, Political Institutions, and Nomadic Invasions in Early Modern East Asia', *Journal of Conflict Resolution* 64, no. 6 (2020): 1049–60.

43. Terry Jones et al., 'Environmental Imperatives Reconsidered: Demographic Crisis in Western North America During the Medieval Climate Anomaly', *American Journal of Physical Anthropology* 40, no. 2 (1999): 137–50.

44. Richard Tol and Sebastian Wagner, 'Climate Change and Violent Conflict in Europe over the Past Millennium', *Climatic Change* 99 (2010): 65–77; Jenkins, *Climate, Catastrophe, and Faith*, 7–11; and Brian Fagan, *The Little Ice Age: How Climate Made History 1300–1850* (New York: Basic Books, 2019), 80–83.

45. Lamb, *Climate History*, 274–77.

46. Kendra Sakaguchi, Anil Varughese, and Graeme Auld, 'Climate Wars? A Systematic Review of Empirical Analyses on the Links Between Climate Change and Violent Conflict', *International Studies Review* 19 (2017): 638–41.

47. Secretary-General's Remarks to the Security Council: Climate and Security, September 23, 2021. https://www.un.org/sg/en/content/sg/statement/2021-09-23/secretary-general%E2%80%99s-remarks-the-security-council-high-level-open-debate-the-maintenance-of-international-peace-and-security-climate-and-security.

48. Nils Gleditsch and Ragnhild Nordås, 'Conflicting Messages? The IPCC on Conflict and Human Security', *Political Geography* 43 (2014): 82–86.

49. Marianne Young and Rik Leemans, 'Group Report: Future Scenarios of Human-Environment Systems', in *Sustainability or Collapse? An Integral History and Future of People on Earth*, ed. Robert Costanza and Lisa Graumlich (Cambridge, MA: MIT Press for the IGBP, 2006), 454; and Gleditsch and Nordås, 'Conflicting Messages?', 629.

50. Sakaguchi, Varughese, and Auld, 'Climate Wars?', 624.

51. Carol Ember, Ian Skoggard, Teferi Abate Adem, and A. J. Faas, 'Rain and Raids Revisited: Disaggregating Ethnic Group Livestock Raiding in the Ethiopian-Kenyan Border Region', *Civil Wars* 16, no. 3 (2014): 330–32, 308–13.

52. Jean-François Maystadt, Margherita Calderone, and Liangzhi You, 'Local Warming and Violent Conflict in North and South Sudan', *Journal of Economic Geography* 15, no. 3 (2015): 650–58.

53. Stija van Weezel, 'Local Warming and Violent Conflict in Africa', *World Review* 126 (2020): 1–5.

54. Joshua Eastin, 'Hell and High Water: Precipitation Shocks and Conflict Violence in the Philippines', *Political Geography* 63 (2018): 116–27.

55. Marshall Burke, Solomon Hsiang, and Edward Miguel, 'Climate and Conflict', *Annual Review of Economics* 7 (2015): 609–10.

56. Cullen Hendrix and Idean Salehyan, 'Climate Change, Rainfall, and Social Conflict in Africa', *Journal of Peace Research* 49, no. 1 (2012): 45–46.

57. Sechin Jagchid and Van Symons, *Peace, War, and Trade Along the Great Wall* (Bloomington: Indiana University Press, 1989), 13–16, 52–57.

CHAPTER 5: RESOURCES

1. As with so many Hitler quotations, this was passed on as reported speech. In this case, Hitler's head of supreme headquarters, General (later Field Marshal) Wilhelm Keitel, sent Hitler's assertion to General Georg Thomas, head of the Armed Forces Defense Economy Office on June 20, 1941. See Steven Fritz, *The First Soldier: Hitler as Military Leader* (New Haven, CT: Yale University Press, 2018), 152.

2. Michael Bloch, *Ribbentrop* (London: Bantam Press, 1992), 317.

3. Gerhard Weinberg, ed., *Hitler's Second Book* (New York: Enigma Books, 2003), 158.

4. Carol and Melvin Ember, 'Resource Unpredictability, Mistrust and War: A Cross-Cultural Study', *Journal of Conflict Resolution* 36 (1992): 246–51.

5. Josef Stalin, *Problems of Leninism* (Moscow: Foreign Languages Publishing House, 1947), 456, 462, 'Report to the Seventeenth Congress of the CPSU, January 26, 1934'.

6. Dona Torr, *Marxism, Nationality and War; Part One* (London: Lawrence & Wishart, 1941), 111.

7. Ercole Ercoli [Palmiro Togliatti], *The Fight Against War and Fascism: Report No. 5, Seventh World Congress of the Communist International* (London: Modern Books, 1935), 3, 6, 26–32.

8. Ellen Wilkinson and Edward Conze, *Why War? A Handbook for Those Who Will Take Part in the Second World War* (London: National Council of Labour Colleges, 1934), 44, 54.

9. Dona Torr, *Marxism and War* (London: Marx Memorial Library, 1942), 3.

10. Peter Brunt, 'A Marxist View of Roman History', *Journal of Roman Studies* 72 (1982): 155–63; and Elizabeth Brumfiel, 'Aztec Religion and Warfare:

Past and Present Perspectives', *Latin American Research Review* 25, no. 2 (1990): 255–58.

11. Torr, *Marxism and War*, 9.

12. *Marxism-Leninism on War and Army* (Moscow: Progress Publishers, 1972), 51–52.

13. Shimshon Bichler and Jonathan Nitzan, 'Arms and Oil in the Middle East: A Biography of Research', *Rethinking Marxism* 30, no. 3 (2018): 420–23, 437; and Shimshon Bichler and Jonathan Nitzan, 'Dominant Capital and the New Wars', *Journal of World-Systems* 10, no. 2 (2004): 258–60, 301–9.

14. Peter Taaffe, *Marxism in Today's World* (London: Committee for a Workers' International, 2006), 16.

15. *Marxism-Leninism on War*, 140–42.

16. David Anthony, *The Horse, the Wheel and Language: How Bronze-Age Riders from the Eurasian Steppes Shaped the Modern World* (Princeton, NJ: Princeton University Press, 2007), 222–23, 239; and Bruce Lincoln, 'The Indo-European Cattle-Raiding Myth', *History of Religions* 16, no. 1 (1976): 43–44, 62–64.

17. Jonas Christensen, 'Warfare in the European Neolithic', *Acta Archaeologica* 75 (2004): 131–32, 152–53; and Andreas Hårde, 'The Emergence of Warfare in the Early Bronze Age: The Nitra Group in Slovakia and Moravia, 2200–1800 BC', in *Warfare, Violence, and Slavery in Prehistory*, ed. Mike Pearson and I. Thorpe (Oxford: BAR Publishing, 2016), 88–91, 101–3.

18. Richard Osgood, Sarah Monks, and Judith Toms, *Bronze Age Warfare* (Stroud: History Press, 2010), 10–14, 42–45, 78–83, 89–91, 95–99.

19. Anne Underhill, 'Warfare and the Development of States in China', in *The Archaeology of Warfare: Prehistories of Raiding and Conquest*, ed. Elizabeth Arkush and Mark Allen (Gainesville: University of Florida Press, 2006), 267–68.

20. Elsa Redmond and Charles Spencer, 'From Raiding to Conquest: Warfare Strategies and Early State Development in Oaxaca, Mexico', in *The Archaeology of Warfare: Prehistories of Raiding and Conquest*, ed. Elizabeth Arkush and Mark Allen (Gainesville: University of Florida Press, 2006), 338–40, 351–57.

21. David Webster, 'Not So Peaceful Civilization: A Review of Maya War', *Journal of World Prehistory* 14, no. 1 (2000): 81–92.

22. Elsa Redmond, *Tribal and Chiefly Warfare in South America* (Ann Arbor: University of Michigan Museum of Anthropology, 1994), 25–30, 32–37, 39–47.

23. Brian Ferguson, 'Materialist, Cultural and Biological Theories on Why Yanomami Make War', *Anthropological Theory* 1, no. 1 (2001): 100–103; and Daniel Steel, 'Trade Goods and Jívaro Warfare: The Shuar 1850–1957, and the Achuar, 1940–1978', *Ethnohistory* 41, no. 4 (1999): 754–56.

24. Robin Waterfield, *Taken at the Flood: The Roman Conquest of Greece* (Oxford: Oxford University Press, 2014), 17, 26–31, 199–205.

25. Peter Wilson, *Iron and Blood: A Military History of the German-Speaking Peoples Since 1500* (London: Allen Lane, 2022), 18.

26. Roger Crowley, *Constantinople: The Last Great Siege, 1453* (London: Faber & Faber, 2005).

27. James Hevia, *English Lessons: The Pedagogy of Imperialism in Nineteenth-Century China* (Durham, NC: Duke University Press, 2003), 199–212.

28. See, for example, the discussion in Gwyn Campbell, 'Introduction: Slavery and Other Forms of Unfree Labour in the Indian Ocean World', *Slavery & Abolition* 24, no. 2 (2003): x–xviii; and Hans Hägerdal, 'Introduction: Enslavement and Slave Trade in Asia', *Slavery & Abolition* 43, no. 3 (2022): 446–49.

29. Herbert Klein, *The Atlantic Slave Trade* (Cambridge: Cambridge University Press, 2012), xviii; Hägerdal, 'Introduction', 449–52.

30. Timothy Taylor, 'The Arrogation of Slavery: Pre-history, Archaeology, and the Pre-Theoretical Commitments Concerning People as Property', in *The Archaeology of Slavery in Mediaeval Northern Europe: An Invisible Commodity?*, ed. Felix Biermann and Marek Jankowiak (Berlin: Springer Verlag, 2021), 10–11.

31. Daniel Snell, 'Slavery in the Ancient Near East', in *The Cambridge World History of Slavery: Volume 1*, ed. Keith Bradley and Paul Cartledge (Cambridge: Cambridge University Press, 2011), 4–16.

32. David Braund, 'The Slave Supply in Classical Greece', in *The Cambridge World History of Slavery: Volume 1*, ed. Keith Bradley and Paul Cartledge (Cambridge: Cambridge University Press, 2011), 112–20.

33. Walter Scheidel, 'The Roman Slave Supply', in *The Cambridge World History of Slavery: Volume 1*, ed. Keith Bradley and Paul Cartledge (Cambridge: Cambridge University Press, 2011), 287–96.

34. Rebecca Redfern, 'Iron Age "Predatory Landscapes": A Bioarchaeological and Funerary Exploration of Captivity and Enslavement', *Cambridge Archaeological Journal* 30, no. 4 (2020): 533–35.

35. Klein, *The Atlantic Slave Trade*, 53–73.

36. Hans Hägerdal, 'Warfare, Bestowal, Purchase: Dutch Acquisition of Slaves in the World of Eastern Indonesia, 1650–1800', *Slavery & Abolition* 43, no. 3 (2022): 553–65.

37. Andrew Thornton, 'Violent Capture of People for Exchange on the Karen-Tai Border in the 1830s', *Slavery & Abolition* 24, no. 2 (2003): 70–76.

38. Iain Smith, *The Origins of the South African War, 1899–1902* (London: Longman, 1996), 394, 408.

39. Stephen Cote, 'A War for Oil in the Chaco, 1932–1935', *Environmental History* 18, no. 4 (2013): 750–51.

40. Iain Smith, 'A Century of Controversy Over Origins', in *The South African War Reappraised*, ed. Donal Lowry (Manchester, UK: Manchester University Press, 2000), 25.

41. John Darwin, *The Empire Project: The Rise and Fall of the British World System 1830–1970* (Cambridge: Cambridge University Press, 2009), 239–42.

42. Mira Kohl, 'Between Louisiana and Latin America: Oil Imperialism and Bolivia's 1937 Nationalization', *Diplomatic History* 44, no. 2 (2020): 214–15.

43. Robert Niebuhr, 'The Road to the Chaco War: Bolivia's Modernization in the 1920s', *War & Society* 37, no. 2 (2018): 94–103; and Stephen Cote, *Oil and Nation: A History of Bolivia's Petroleum Sector* (Morgantown: West Virginia University Press, 2016), 62–68.

44. Kohl, 'Between Louisiana and Latin America', 210–11, 225–27; and Cote, 'A War for Oil', 743–50.

45. Michael Klare, *Resource Wars: The New Landscape of Global Conflict* (New York: Henry Holt, 2001), 13, 213.

46. John Maxwell and Rafael Reuveny, 'Resource Scarcity and Conflict in Developing Countries', *Journal of Peace Research* 37, no. 3 (2000): 301–2.

47. Humphrey Jasper, 'Resource Wars: Searching for a New Definition', *International Affairs* 88, no. 5 (2012): 1065–66, 1069–70; and Philippe Le Billon, 'The Political Ecology of War: Natural Resources and Armed Conflicts', *Political Geography* 20 (2001): 564–65, 569–70.

48. See generally Philippe Le Billon, *Wars of Plunder: Conflicts and Profits and the Politics of Resources* (London: Hurst & Co., 2012), 13–37; and Klare, *Resource Wars*, chap. 8.

49. Päiri Lujala, 'Deadly Combat over Natural Resources: Gems, Petroleum, Drugs, and the Severity of Armed Civil Conflict', *Journal of Conflict Resolution* 53, no. 1 (2009): 51, 68.

50. Klare, *Resource Wars*, 196–97.

51. Kirsten Schulze, 'The Conflict in Aceh: Struggle over Oil?', in *Oil Wars*, ed. Mary Kaldor, Terry Karl, and Yahia Said (London: Pluto Press, 2007), 183–219.

52. Susanne Peters, 'Coercive Western Energy Security Strategies – "Resource Wars" as a New Threat to Global Security', *Geopolitics* 5, no. 1 (2004): 192–95.

53. Andrew Bacevich, *The New American Militarism: How Americans Are Seduced by War* (Oxford: Oxford University Press, 2013), 181–82.

54. Klare, *Resource Wars*, 11, 33–34.

55. Okey Ibeanu and Robin Luckham, 'Nigeria: Political Violence, Governance and Corporate Responsibility in a Petro-State', in *Oil Wars*, ed. Mary Kaldor, Terry Karl, and Yahia Said (London: Pluto Press, 2007), 41.

56. Ibeanu and Luckham, 'Nigeria', 58–59, 63–68.

57. Ben Raffield, 'The Slave Markets of the Viking World: Comparative Perspectives on an "Invisible Archaeology"', *Slavery & Abolition* 40, no. 4 (2019): 682–92.

CHAPTER 6: BELIEF

1. Ghazi bin Muhammad, Ibrahim Kalin, and Mohammad Hadin Karrali, eds., *War and Peace in Islam: The Uses and Abuses of Jihad* (Amman, Jordan: Royal Islamic Strategic Studies Centre, 2013), 13.

2. Version according to Fulcher of Chartres (there are at least four others) in Oliver Thatcher and Edgar McNeal, eds., *A Source Book for Medieval History* (New York: Scribners, 1905), 517.

3. Bin Muhammad, Kalin, and Karrali, *War and Peace in Islam*, 18–20.

4. On this attitude, see Stefan Costalli and Andrea Ruggeri, 'Emotions, Ideologies, and Violent Political Mobilization', *PS: Political Science and Politics* 50, no. 4 (2017): 923–26.

5. Charles Prior and Glenn Burgess, eds., *England's War of Religion Revisited* (Farnham, UK: Ashgate, 2011), 15–16.

6. On Sudan, see Monica Toft, 'Getting Religion? The Puzzling Case of Islam and Civil War', *International Security* 31, no. 4 (2007): 117–28.

7. Elizabeth Brumfiel, 'Aztec Religion and Warfare: Past and Present Perspectives', *Latin American Research Review* 25, no. 2 (1990): 255–58.

8. For a spirited defence of this position, see Philippe Buc, *Holy War, Martyrdom and Terror* (Philadelphia: University of Pennsylvania Press, 2015), 10–11.

9. See, for example, Michael Horowitz, 'Long Time Going: Religion and the Duration of Crusading', *International Security* 34, no. 2 (2009): 162–65, 180–89.

10. Christopher Tyerman, *God's War: A New History of the Crusades* (London: Allen Lane, 2006), 33–34.

11. Thomas Sizgorich, *Violence and Belief in Late Antiquity: Militant Devotion in Christianity and Islam* (Philadelphia: University of Pennsylvania Press, 2009), 3, 9.

12. Sizgorich, *Violence and Belief in Late Antiquity*, 112–25.

13. Sizgorich, *Violence and Belief in Late Antiquity*, 38.

14. Jonathan Phillips, *Holy Warriors: A Modern History of the Crusades* (London: The Bodley Head, 2009), 3–5.

15. Jay Rubinstein, *Nebuchadnezzar's Dream: The Crusades, Apocalyptic Prophecy and the End of History* (Oxford: Oxford University Press, 2019), 33–34, 45.

16. Christopher Maier, 'Crisis, Liturgy, and the Crusade in the Twelfth and Thirteenth Centuries', *Journal of Ecclesiastical History* 48, no. 4 (1997): 628–30.

17. Amin Maalouf, *The Crusades Through Arab Eyes* (London: Al Saqi Books, 1984), 49–50; Buc, *Holy War*, 99–101; and Phillips, *Holy Warriors*, 25–27.

18. Rubinstein, *Nebuchadnezzar's Dream*, 9–11.

19. Adnan Zulfiqar, 'Jurisdiction over *Jihād*: Islamic Law and the Duty to Fight', *West Virginia Law Review* 120, no. 2 (2017): 428, 436; and S. M. Farid Mirbagheri, *War and Peace in Islam: A Critique of Islamic/ist Political Discourses* (New York: Palgrave Macmillan, 2012), 129–34.

20. Carole Hillenbrand, *Crusades: Islamic Perspectives* (Edinburgh: Edinburgh University Press, 1999), 90; and Fatemah Albadar, 'Islamic Law and the Right to Armed Jihad', *Indonesian Journal of International and Comparative Law* 5, no. 4 (2018): 582–89.

21. Carole Hillenbrand, *Islam and the Crusades: Collected Essays* (Edinburgh: Edinburgh University Press, 2022), 269–74; and Zulfiqar, 'Jurisdiction over *Jihād*', 440–42.

22. Hillenbrand, *Crusades*, 101–4; and Maalouf, *The Crusades Through Arab Eyes*, 3–4.

23. Hillenbrand, *Islam and the Crusades*, 44–47.

24. Hillenbrand, *Crusades*, 20–23, 141–48, 164; and Maalouf, *The Crusades Through Arab Eyes*, 180–81, 198–200.

25. Richard Bonney, *From Qur'an to Bin Laden* (Basingstoke, UK: Palgrave Macmillan, 2004), 114.

26. Wayne Brake, *Religious War and Religious Peace in Early Modern Europe* (Cambridge: Cambridge University Press, 2017), 2–5.

27. Natalie Davis, 'The Rites of Violence: Religious Riot in Sixteenth-Century France', *Past & Present* 59 (1973): 56–68; and Judith Pollman, 'Countering the Reformation in France and the Netherlands: Clerical Leadership and Catholic Violence 1560–1585', *Past & Present* 190 (2006): 85–87.

28. See Mack Holt, 'Putting Religion Back into the Wars of Religion', *French Historical Studies* 18, no. 2 (1993): 534–35.

29. Holt, 'Putting Religion Back', 539–41.

30. Puc, *Holy War*, 8, 34.

31. Philip Benedict, 'The Saint Bartholomew's Massacres in the Provinces', *Historical Journal* 21, no. 2 (1978): 205–6, 210–19.

32. Brake, *Religious War*, 117–18.

33. Puc, *Holy War*, 210.

34. Prior and Burgess, *England's Wars of Religion*, 19–20.

35. Edward Vallance, 'Preaching to the Converted: Religious Justifications for the English Civil War', *Huntington Library Quarterly* 65 (2002): 396–98; and Charles Prior, 'Religion, Political Thought and the English Civil War', *History Compass* 11, no. 1 (2013): 28–31.

36. Jordan Downs, 'The Curse of Meroz and the English Civil War', *Historical Journal* 57, no. 2 (2014): 343–52; Puc, *Holy War*, 11.

37. Glen Burgess, 'Was the English Civil War a War of Religion? The Evidence of Political Propaganda', *Huntington Library Quarterly* 61, no. 2 (2000): 173–74.

38. Vallance, 'Preaching to the Converted', 415–16; and David Cressy, *England on Edge: Crisis and Revolution 1640–1642* (Oxford: Oxford University Press, 2006), 169–74.

39. Vallance, 'Preaching to the Converted', 407.

40. Barbara Donegan, 'Did Ministers Matter? War and Religion in England, 1642–1649', *Journal of British Studies* 33, no. 2 (1994): 121–30.

41. Downs, 'The Curse of Meroz', 355–58.

42. Puc, *Holy War*, 255.

43. Colin Renfrew, '"The Unanswered Question": Investigating Early Conceptualisations of Death', in *Death Rituals, Social Order and the Archaeology of Immortality in the Ancient World*, ed. Colin Renfrew, Michael Boyd, and Iain Morley (Cambridge: Cambridge University Press, 2016), 1–8.

44. Robin Yates, 'Early China', in *War and Society in the Ancient and Medieval Worlds*, ed. Kurt Raaflaub and Nathan Rosenstein (Cambridge, MA: Harvard University Press, 1999), 8–9, 14, 19–20.

45. Bruce Lincoln, *Death, War, and Sacrifice: Studies in Ideology and Practice* (Chicago: University of Chicago Press, 1991), 10–13; and Bruce Lincoln, 'The Indo-European Cattle-Raiding Myth', *History of Religions* 16, no. 1 (1976): 43–44, 62–64.

46. Edward Swenson, 'Dramas of the Dialectic: Sacrifice and Power in Ancient Polities', in *Violence and Civilization: Studies of Social Violence in History and Prehistory*, ed. Roderick Campbell (Oxford: Oxbow Books, 2014), 42–44; and Jeffrey Quilter, 'Moche Politics, Religion and Warfare', *Journal of World Prehistory* 16, no. 2 (2002): 163–69.

47. By far the most convincing analysis of this relationship is Inga Clendinnen, *Aztecs: An Interpretation* (Cambridge: Cambridge University Press, 1991).

48. Herbert Burhenn, 'Understanding Aztec Cannibalism', *Archiv für Religionspsychologie* 26 (2004): 2–3; and Clendinnen, *Aztecs*, 90–91.

49. Caroline Pennock, 'Mass Murder or Religious Homicide? Rethinking Human Sacrifice and Interpersonal Violence in Aztec Society', *Historische Sozialforschung* 37, no. 3 (2012): 280–82, 286.

50. Guilhem Olivier, 'Humans and Gods in the Mexica Universe', in *The Oxford Handbook of the Aztecs*, ed. Deborah Nichols and Enrique Rodríguez-Alegría (Oxford: Oxford University Press, 2016), 571–76; and Guilhem Olivier, '"Why Give Birth to Enemies?": The Warrior Aspects of the Aztec Goddess Tlazolteotl-Ixcuina', *Anthropology and Aesthetics* 65, no. 6 (2014/2015): 56–60.

51. Clendinnen, *Aztecs*, 97.

52. Clendinnen, *Aztecs*, 2, 111–14.

53. Nicholas Saunders, 'Predators of Culture: Jaguar Symbolism and Mesoamerican Elites', *World Archaeology* 26, no. 1 (1994): 104–9.

54. Clendinnen, *Aztecs*, 91–97.

55. Marco Obregón, 'Mexica War: New Perspectives', in *The Oxford Handbook of the Aztecs*, ed. Deborah Nichols and Enrique Rodríguez-Alegría (Oxford: Oxford University Press, 2016), 454–55.

56. James Maffie, *Aztec Philosophy: Understanding a World in Motion* (Colorado Springs: University Press of Colorado, 2013), 523–26.

57. For the most developed theory of 'political religion', see Emilio Gentile, *Politics and Religion* (Princeton, NJ: Princeton University Press, 2006), particularly chap. 4.

58. Werner Maser, ed., *Hitler's Letters and Notes* (London: Bantam Press, 1973), 227, 307, notes for speeches 1919–1920.

59. On the idea of conspiracy, see Richard Evans, *The Hitler Conspiracies: The Third Reich and the Paranoid Imagination* (London: Allen Lane, 2020), 29–45.

60. Alon Confino, *A World Without Jews: The Nazi Imagination from Persecution to Genocide* (New Haven, CT: Yale University Press, 2014), 7.

61. Gentile, *Politics and Religion*, 69.

62. Melvin Rader, *No Compromise: Conflict Between Two Worlds* (New York: Macmillan, 1939), 1.

63. Gentile, *Politics and Religion*, 88–89.

64. Keith Feiling, *The Life of Neville Chamberlain* (London: Macmillan, 1946), 416.

65. Milan Babik, 'The Christian Historical Consciousness: Understanding War in Twentieth-Century Europe', *Totalitarian Movements and Political Religions* 5, no. 1 (2004): 59–60, 80–82.

66. Carl Boggs and Tom Pollard, *The Hollywood War Machine: U.S. Militarism and Popular Culture* (Boulder, CO: Paradigm, 2007), 6–9, 19–21.

67. Jon Abbink, 'Religion and Violence in the Horn of Africa: Trajectories of Mimetic Rivalry and Escalation Between "Political Islam" and the State', *Politics, Religion and Ideology* 21, no. 2 (2020): 195–96, 200; and Masood Ashraf, *ISIS: Ideology, Symbolics and Counter Narratives* (New York: Routledge, 2019), 62–67.

68. Hillenbrand, *Crusades*, 600–602; Anna Krŭglova, '"I Will Tell You a Story About Jihad": ISIS's Propaganda and Narrative Advertising', *Studies in Conflict and Terrorism* 44, no. 2 (2021): 122–3; and Ashraf, *ISIS*, p. 73.

69. Zulfiqar, 'Jurisdiction over *Jihād*', 429–30; and David Cook, 'Islamism and Jihadism: The Transformation of Classical Notions of *Jihad* into an Ideology of Terrorism', *Totalitarian Movements and Political Religions* 10, no. 2 (2009): 180–82.

70. Abdulbasit Kassim, 'Defining and Understanding the Religious Philosophy of *Jihadi-Salafism* and the Ideology of Boko Haram', *Politics, Religion and Ideology*, 16, no. 2–3 (2015): 175–83; and Mona Sheikh, 'Sacred Pillars of Violence: Findings from a Study of the Pakistani Taliban', *Politics, Religion and Ideology* 13, no. 4 (2012): 442–45.

71. Kassim, 'Defining and Understanding', 186–88; Sheikh, 'Sacred Pillars of Violence', 439–40; and Abbink, 'Religion and Violence', 201–3.

72. Thomas Hegghammer, 'The Rise of Muslim Foreign Fighters: Islam and the Globalization of Jihad', *International Security* 35, no. 3 (2010/2011): 72–73, 80–84.

73. See, for example, Shmuel Bar, 'Religion in War in the 21st Century', *Comparative Strategy* 39, no. 5 (2020): 455–62.

74. Kassim, 'Defining and Understanding', 173–75, 187–88.

75. Scott Segrest, 'ISIS's Will to Apocalypse', *Politics, Religion and Ideology* 17, no. 4 (2016): 352–60; and Omar Anchassi, 'The Logic of the Conquest Society: ISIS, Apocalyptic Violence and the "Reinstatement" of Slave Concubinage', in *Violence in Islamic Thought from European Imperialism to the Post-Colonial Era*, ed. Mustafa Baig and Robert Gleave (Edinburgh: Edinburgh University Press, 2021), 228–37.

76. Cook, 'Islamism and Jihadism', 185.

77. Ashraf, *ISIS*, 73; and Sheikh, 'Sacred Pillars of Violence', 447–50.

78. Bar, 'Religion in War', 443–46.

79. David Leeming, *Myth: A Biography of Belief* (Oxford: Oxford University Press, 2002), 8, 12.

CHAPTER 7: POWER

1. Polybius, *The Rise of the Roman Empire*, trans. Ian Scott-Kilvert (London: Penguin, 1979), 473, book XV. This was probably written some half-century after Zama by using a mix of documentary and oral evidence.

2. Polybius, *The Rise of the Roman Empire*, 44, introduction to book I.

3. Robert Dahl, 'The Concept of Power', *Behavioral Science* 2, no. 3 (1957): 201.

4. Dahl, 'The Concept of Power', 203. For a critical view on Dahl's definition, see David Winter, *Roots of War: Wanting Power, Seeing Threat, Justifying Force* (Oxford: Oxford University Press, 2018), 94–95.

5. Michael Barnett and Raymond Duvall, 'Power in International Politics', *International Organization* 59, no. 1 (2005): 46–51.

6. Robert Carneiro, 'A Theory of the Origins of the State', *Science* 169 (1970): 734–37.

7. Timothy Earle, *How Chiefs Come to Power: The Political Economy in Prehistory* (Stanford, CA: Stanford University Press, 1997), 6–10, 105–9.

8. Guy Halsall, *Warfare and Society in the Barbarian West, 450–900* (London: Routledge, 2003), 27–30.

9. Susan Mattern, *Rome and the Enemy: Imperial Strategy in the Principate* (Berkeley: University of California Press, 1999), 168; and Sarah Davies, *Rome, Global Dreams, and the International Origins of Empire* (Leiden: Brill, 2019), 2–3.

10. Andrew Erskine, *Roman Imperialism* (Edinburgh: Edinburgh University Press, 2010), 5–6, 27–29, 40–43.

11. Mattern, *Rome and the Enemy*, 165–66.

12. David Potter, 'The Roman Army and Navy', in *The Cambridge Companion to the Roman Republic*, ed. Harriet Flower (Cambridge: Cambridge University Press, 2014), 68–71.

13. J. C. Mann, 'Power, Force and the Frontiers of the Empire', *Journal of Roman Studies* 69 (1979): 176–78; Mattern, *Rome and the Enemy*, 162–63, 168; and Erskine, *Roman Imperialism*, 40–43.

14. Davies, *Rome, Global Dreams*, 3, 11.

15. Yuri Pines, 'Limits of All-Under-Heaven: Ideology and Praxis of "Great Unity" in Early Chinese Empire', in *The Limits of Universal Rule: Eurasian Empires Compared*, ed. Yuri Pines, Michal Biran, and Jörg Rüpke (Cambridge: Cambridge University Press, 2021), 82–83, 93–94.

16. Michal Biran, 'The Mongol Imperial Space: From Universalism to Glocalization', in *The Limits of Universal Rule: Eurasian Empires Compared*, ed. Yuri Pines, Michal Biran, and Jörg Rüpke (Cambridge: Cambridge University Press, 2021), 222–28.

17. For an example of this usage, see Alistair Horne, *Hubris: The Tragedy of War in the Twentieth Century* (London: Weidenfeld & Nicolson, 2015), 1, 283–85.

18. Waldemar Heckel, *In the Path of Conquest: Resistance to Alexander the Great* (Oxford: Oxford University Press, 2020), 9–14; and Edward Anson, *Alexander the Great: Themes and Issues* (London: Bloomsbury, 2013), 46–50.

19. Edmund Bloedow, 'Why Did Philip and Alexander Launch a War Against the Persian Empire?', *L'Antiquité Classique* 72 (2003): 262–73; and Ian Worthington, *By the Spear: Philip II, Alexander the Great, and the Rise and Fall of the Macedonian Empire* (Oxford: Oxford University Press, 2014), 141.

20. Details in Waldemar Heckel, *The Conquests of Alexander the Great* (Cambridge: Cambridge University Press, 2008), 67–74; and Hugh Bowden, *Alexander the Great: A Very Short Introduction* (Oxford: Oxford University Press, 2014), 32–37.

21. Arrian, *The Anabasis*, trans. Martin Hammond (Oxford: Oxford University Press, 2013), 223; and Anson, *Alexander the Great*, 83–85.

22. Heckel, *The Conquests of Alexander the Great*, 54–55; and Worthington, *By the Spear*, 159.

23. Bowden, *Alexander the Great*, 62–65; Anson, *Alexander the Great*, 105–9; and Worthington, *By the Spear*, 182–83.

24. Anson, *Alexander the Great*, 121; F. S. Naiden, *Soldier, Priest, and God: A Life of Alexander the Great* (New York: Oxford University Press, 2019).

25. Heckel, *The Conquests of Alexander the Great*, 112–33; and Heckel, *In the Path of Conquest*, 253–69.

26. Naiden, *Soldier, Priest, and God*, 201.

27. Andrew Collins, 'The Persian Royal Tent and the Ceremonial of Alexander the Great', *Classical Quarterly* 67, no. 1 (2017): 71–76; and Heckel, *The Conquests of Alexander the Great*, 100–108.

28. On his early life, see Charles Esdaile, *Napoleon's Wars: An International History, 1803–15* (London: Allen Lane, 2007), 18–21, 28–32.

29. On the wars of the 1790s as a backdrop to Napoleon, see Gunther Rothenberg, 'The Origins, Causes and Extension of the Wars of the French Revolution and Napoleon', *Journal of Interdisciplinary History* 18, no. 4 (1988): 785–89.

30. Philip Dwyer, 'Napoleon Bonaparte as Hero and Saviour: Image, Rhetoric and Behaviour in the Construction of a Legend', *French History* 18, no. 4 (2004): 381–82.

31. Patrice Gueniffey, *Bonaparte* (Cambridge, MA: Harvard University Press, 2015), 803.

32. *The Table Talk and Opinions of Napoleon Bonaparte* (London: Sampson Lowe & Marston, 1870), 15–16.

33. Bruno Colson, ed., *Napoleon on War* (Oxford: Oxford University Press, 2015), 40.

34. Dwyer, 'Napoleon Bonaparte', 385–89; and Esdaile, *Napoleon's Wars*, 51–55.

35. Alexander Mikaberidze, *The Napoleonic Wars: A Global History* (Oxford: Oxford University Press, 2020), 193–94.

36. Alan Forrest, 'Propaganda and Legitimation of Power in Napoleonic France', *French History* 18, no. 4 (2004): 435–37.

37. Maximilien Novak, 'Napoléon et l'Empire de l'opinion: acteurs et enjeux du contrôle de l'opinion publique sous le Premier Empire', *French Cultural Studies* 32, no. 2 (2021): 70–73.

38. Philp Dwyer, *Citizen Emperor: Napoleon in Power 1799–1815* (London: Bloomsbury, 2013), 212–15; and Forrest, 'Propaganda and Legitimation of Power', 438–39.

39. Dwyer, *Citizen Emperor*, 345–48.

40. Alan Forrest, 'Napoleon's Vision of Empire and the Decision to Invade Russia', in *Russia and the Napoleonic Wars*, ed. Janet Hartley, Paul Keenan, and Dominic Lieven (Basingstoke, UK: Palgrave Macmillan, 2015), 44–47; and Dwyer, *Citizen Emperor*, 355–61.

41. On the flawed campaign in Germany, see Michael Leggiere, 'From Berlin to Leipzig: Napoleon's Gamble in North Germany', *Journal of Military History* 67, no. 1 (2003): 47–65.

42. *The Table Talk and Opinions of Napoleon Bonaparte*, 78–79.

43. On Hitler as narcissistic personality, see John Mankelwicz and Robert Kane, 'Hitler as a Narcissistic Leader', *Journal of Psychohistory* 50, no. 2 (2022): 137–44.

44. M. Rainer Lepsius, 'The Model of Charismatic Leadership and Its Applicability to the Rule of Adolf Hitler', *Totalitarian Movements and Political Religions* 7, no. 2 (2006): 175–79.

45. Jost Hermand, *Der alte Traum vom neuen Reich: völkische Utopien und Nationalsozialismus* (Weinheim: Beltz Athenäum, 1995), 359.

46. Richard Bessel, *Nazism and War* (London: Weidenfeld & Nicolson, 2004), 32–33; and Hermand, *Der alte Traum*, 315–16.

47. Lepsius, 'The Model of Charismatic Leadership', 185.

48. François Genoud, ed., *The Testament of Adolf Hitler: The Hitler-Bormann Documents* (London: Cassell, 1960), 101–2.

49. Volker Ullrich, *Hitler: Downfall 1939–45* (London: The Bodley Head, 2020), 615; and Mankelwicz and Kane, 'Hitler as a Narcissistic Leader', 149.

50. Angela Kurtz, 'God, Not Caesar: Revisiting National Socialism as "Political Religion"', *History of European Ideas* 35, no. 2 (2009): 246–49.

51. Hermand, *Der alte Traum*, 316; and Ralf Reuth, *Hitler's Tyranny* (London: Haus Publishing, 2022), 164.

52. Hugh Trevor-Roper, ed., *Hitler's Table Talk 1941–44* (London: Weidenfeld & Nicolson, 1973), 383, entry for March 31, 1942. These are stenographic records of what Hitler is supposed to have said and are used as reported speech not direct quotation.

53. Gavriel Rosenfeld, 'Who Was "Hitler" Before Hitler? Historical Analogies and the Struggle to Understand Nazism', *Central European History* 51 (2018): 251–55.

54. Despina Stratigakos, *Hitler's Northern Utopia: Building the New Order in Occupied Norway* (Princeton, NJ: Princeton University Press, 2020), 194–96, 209.

55. Art Padilla, Robert Hogan, and Robert Kaiser, 'The Toxic Triangle: Destructive Leaders, Susceptible Followers, and Conducive Environments', *Leadership Quarterly* 18, no. 3 (2007): 177–81.

56. Richard Breitman, 'Hitler and Genghis Khan', *Journal of Contemporary History* 25, no. 2–3 (1990): 348; and Hermand, *Der alte Traum*, 340.

57. Carl von Clausewitz, *On War* (1832; repr. Oxford: Oxford University Press, 2007), 28.

58. Clausewitz, *On War*, 29.

59. Robert Gilpin, 'The Theory of Hegemonic War', *Journal of Interdisciplinary History* 18, no. 4 (1988): 602–13.

60. Carsten Rauch, 'Challenging the Power Consensus: GDP, CINC, and Power Transition Theory', *Security Studies* 26, no. 4 (2017): 646–52; Michael Beckley, 'The Power of Nations: Measuring What Matters', *International Security* 43, no. 2 (2018–19): 7–11. See also J. David Singer, Stuart Bremer, and John Stuckey, 'Capability Distribution, Uncertainty, and Major Power War, 1820–1965', in *Peace, War, and Numbers*, ed. Bruce Russett (Beverly Hills, CA: Sage, 1972), 19–29.

61. Gilpin, 'The Theory of Hegemonic War', 591–96; and Alexander Debs and Nuno Monteiro, 'Known Unknowns: Power Shifts, Uncertainty and War', *International Organization* 68, no. 1 (2014): 1–2.

62. Stephen Brooks and William Wohlforth, 'The Rise and Fall of the Great Powers in the Twenty-First Century: China's Rise and the Fate of America's Global Position', *International Security* 40, no. 3 (2015): 28–30.

63. Rauch, 'Challenging the Power Consensus', 649–54.

64. Christopher Layne, 'The Unipolar Illusion: Why New Great Powers Will Rise', *International Security* 17, no. 4 (1993): 6–7, 32–37.

65. Peter Gries and Yiming Jing, 'Are the US and China Fated to Fight? How Narratives of "Power Transition" Shape Great Power War or Peace', *Cambridge Review of International Affairs* 32, no. 4 (2019): 456–57; and Steve Chan, *Rumbles of Thunder: Power Shifts and the Dangers of Sino-American War* (New York: Columbia University Press, 2023), 3, 29–30.

66. Beckley, 'The Power of Nations', 43–44; Christopher Layne, 'The US–Chinese Power Shift and the End of the Pax Americana', *International Affairs* 94, no. 1 (2018): 95–102; Brooks and Wohlforth, 'The Rise and Fall of the Great Powers', 8–11; and Joseph Nye, *The Future of Power* (New York: Public Affairs, 2011), 202–4.

67. Lawrence Freedman, 'The Rise and Fall of Great Power War', *International Affairs* 95, no. 1 (2019): 115–17.

CHAPTER 8: SECURITY

1. Thomas Hobbes, *Leviathan, or The Matter, Forme, & Power of a Common-Wealth Ecclesiasticall and Civil* (1651; repr. London: Penguin, 1985), 187–88.
2. Hobbes, *Leviathan*, 186, 190, 224–25.
3. John Mearsheimer, *The Tragedy of Great Power Politics* (New York: Norton, 2002), 36.
4. Stephen Van Evera, *Causes of War: Power and the Roots of Conflict* (Ithaca, NY: Cornell University Press, 1999), 11, 76–77; Benjamin Miller, 'Polarity, Nuclear Weapons, and Major War', *Security Studies* 3, no. 4 (1994): 602–4; and Jeffrey Taliaferro, 'Security Seeking Under Anarchy: Defensive Realism Revisited', *International Security* 25, no. 3 (2000–2001): 136–42.
5. Colin Gray, 'Nicholas John Spykman, the Balance-of-Power, and World Order', *Journal of Strategic Studies* 38, no. 6 (2015): 879–80.
6. Monika Toft, 'Territory and War', *Journal of Peace Research* 51, no. 2 (2014): 185–86; Monika Toft and Dominic Johnson, 'Grounds for War: The Evolution of Territorial Conflict', *International Security* 38, no. 3 (2013–14): 12; and Paul Hensel, 'Territory: Theory and Evidence on Geography and Conflict', in *What Do We Know About War?*, ed. John Vasquez (Lanham, MD: Rowman & Littlefield, 2000), 57–64.
7. John Vasquez and Marie Henehan, *Territory, War, and Peace* (New York: Routledge, 2011), 6–7, 11–14.
8. Lord George Curzon, *Frontiers: The Romanes Lecture* (London: Dodo Press, 2008), 4. Repr. from the original text.
9. Nicholas Spykman, 'Frontiers, Security, and International Organization', *Geographical Review* 32, no. 3 (1942): 437–38.
10. Barbara Walter, 'Explaining the Intractability of Armed Conflict', *International Studies Review* 5, no. 4 (2003): 137, 149–50; and Robert Mandel, 'The Roots of Modern Interstate Border Disputes', *Journal of Conflict Resolution* 24, no. 3 (1980): 427–30, 437–41.
11. David Dye, 'The Transformation of Mississippi Warfare: Four Case Studies from the Mid-South', in *The Archaeology of Warfare: Prehistories of Raiding and Conquest*, ed. Elizabeth Arkush and Mark Allen (Gainesville: University of Florida Press, 2006), 102–3; and Elsa Redmond and Charles Spencer, 'From Raiding to Conquest: Warfare Strategies and Early State Development in Oaxaca, Mexico', in *The Archaeology of Warfare: Prehistories of Raiding and Conquest*, ed. Elizabeth Arkush and Mark Allen (Gainesville: University of Florida Press, 2006), 342.

12. Timothy Earle, *How Chiefs Come to Power: The Political Economy of Prehistory* (Stanford, CA: Stanford University Press, 1997), 10.

13. Douglas Bamforth, 'Indigenous People, Indigenous Violence: Precontact Warfare on the North American Great Plains', *Man* 29 (1994): 102–5.

14. William Parkinson and Paul Duffy, 'Fortifications and Enclosures in European Prehistory: A Cross-Cultural Perspective', *Journal of Archaeological Research* 15, no. 2 (2007): 98–115; and Jonas Christensen, 'Warfare in the European Neolithic', *Acta Archaeologica* 75 (2004): 148–53.

15. Inés Sastre, 'Community, Identity, and Conflict: Iron Age Warfare in the Iberian North-West', *Current Anthropology* 49, no. 6 (2008): 1022–28.

16. Aribidesi Usman, 'On the Frontiers of Empire: Understanding the Enclosure Walls in Northern Yoruba, Nigeria', *Journal of Anthropological Archaeology* 23, no. 1 (2004): 120–30.

17. Bradley Parker, 'At the Edge of Empire: Conceptualizing Assyria's Anatolian Frontier ca. 700 BC', *Journal of Anthropological Archaeology* 21 (2002): 373–83.

18. Thomas Barfield, *The Perilous Frontier: Nomadic Empires and China 221 BC to AD 1757* (Oxford: Blackwell, 1989), 2–7, 16–18; and Nicola di Cosmo, 'Ancient Inner Asia Nomads: Their Economic Base and Its Significance in Chinese History', *Journal of Asian Studies* 53, no. 4 (1994): 1092–93, 1100.

19. Sechin Jagchid and Van Jay Symons, *Peace, War, and Trade Along the Great Wall* (Bloomington: Indiana University Press, 1999), 24.

20. Mark Lewis, 'Warring States Political History', in *The Cambridge History of Ancient China: From the Origins to 221 BC*, ed. Michael Loewe and Edward Shaughnessy (Cambridge: Cambridge University Press, 1999), 629–30; and Yuri Pines, 'The Earliest "Great Wall"? The Long Wall of Qi Revisited', *Journal of the American Oriental Society* 138, no. 4 (2018): 743–53.

21. Barry Cunliffe, *By Steppe, Desert and Ocean: The Birth of Eurasia* (Oxford: Oxford University Press, 2016), 247–48, 268–71; and Robin Yates, 'Early China', in *War and Society in the Ancient and Medieval Worlds*, ed. Kurt Raaflaub and Nathan Rosenstein (Cambridge, MA: Harvard University Press, 1999), 27–31.

22. Jagchid and Symons, *Peace, War, and Trade*, 32–35, 77.

23. Arthur Waldron, *The Great Wall of China: From History to Myth* (Cambridge: Cambridge University Press, 1990), 87–90, 102–7.

24. Jagchid and Symons, *Peace, War, and Trade*, 173–5; and Waldron, *The Great Wall*, 186.

25. Jagchid and Symons, *Peace, War, and Trade*, 177–83.

26. J. C. Mann, 'Review: Power, Force and the Frontiers of the Empire', *Journal of Roman Studies* 69 (1979): 175–76.

27. David Breeze, 'The Value of Studying the Roman Frontiers', *Theoretical Roman Archaeology Journal* 1, no. 1 (2018): 5–6; and Michael Fulford, 'Territorial Expansion and the Roman Empire', *World Archaeology* 23, no. 3 (1992): 294–96.

28. Conor Whately, 'Strategy, Diplomacy and Frontiers: A Bibliographic Essay', *Late Antique Archaeology* 8, no. 1 (2010–11): 240–46. I am grateful to Philip Parker for the figures on the length of the frontier. The often-cited figures of 5,000 or 7,000 kilometres are evidently too short.

29. Hugh Elton, *Frontiers of the Roman Empire* (Bloomington: Indiana University Press, 1996), 62–64.

30. Matthew Symonds, *Protecting the Roman Empire: Fortlets, Frontiers, and the Quest for Post-Conquest Security* (Cambridge: Cambridge University Press, 2018), 2–5.

31. Rose Mary Sheldon, 'Insurgency in Germany: The Slaughter of Varus in the Teutoburger Wald', *Small Wars and Insurgencies* 31, no. 5 (2020): 1010–23.

32. Tacitus, *The Agricola and the Germania*, trans. H. Mattingley (London: Penguin Books, 1970), 80–81.

33. Jorit Wintjes, '"On the Side of a Righteous Vengeance": Counterinsurgency Operations in Roman Britain', *Small Wars and Insurgencies* 31, no. 5 (2020): 1109–19.

34. David Breeze, *The Frontiers of Imperial Rome* (Barnsley, UK: Pen & Sword, 2021), 180–87.

35. A. D. Lee, 'Abduction and Assassination: The Clandestine Face of Roman Diplomacy in Late Antiquity', *International History Review* 31, no. 1 (2009): 3–10.

36. Alexander Sarantis, 'Waging War in Late Antiquity', *Late Antique Archaeology* 8, no. 1 (2010–11): 2–10, 14–18.

37. Breeze, 'The Value of Studying the Roman Frontiers', 6–8; and Mann, 'Review: Power, Force, and the Frontiers', 180–82.

38. Breeze, *The Frontiers of Imperial Rome*, 170–2; and Elton, *Frontiers of the Roman Empire*, 64–72, 111–12.

39. A. D. Lee, *Warfare in the Roman World* (Cambridge: Cambridge University Press, 2020), 10–13.

40. See, for example, Jakub Grygiel, *Return of the Barbarians: Confronting Non-State Actors from Ancient Rome to the Present* (Cambridge: Cambridge University Press, 2018), chap. 6.

41. John Grenier, *The First Way of War: American War Making on the Frontier* (Cambridge: Cambridge University Press, 2005), 21ff.

42. David Carter and H. E. Goemans, 'The Making of the Territorial Order: New Borders and the Emergence of Interstate Conflict', *International Organization* 65 (2011): 279–80.

43. Carter and Goemans, 'The Making of the Territorial Order', 294–301; and Paul Diehl and Gary Goertz, 'Interstate Conflict over Exchanges of Homeland Territory, 1816–1980', *Political Geography Quarterly* 10, no. 4 (1991): 343–49. Using a different definition, Diehl and Goertz find that 49 out of 160 cases of land exchange resulted in warfare.

44. Malcolm Shaw, 'Peoples, Territorialism, and Boundaries', *European Journal of International Law* 8, no. 23 (1997): 492–96, 499–500; and Mark Zacher, 'The Territorial Integrity Norm: International Boundaries and the Use of Force', *International Organizations* 55, no. 2 (2001): 222–23, 234–35.

45. Sumit Ganguly et al., 'India, Pakistan, and the Kashmir Dispute: Unpacking the Dynamics of a South Asian Frozen Conflict', *Asia Europe Journal* 17, no. 1 (2019): 131–38.

46. Victoria Schofield, *Kashmir in Conflict: India, Pakistan, and the Unending War* (London: Bloomsbury, 2020), 261–68; and Myra Macdonald, *White as the Shroud: Pakistan and War on the Frontiers of Kashmir* (Uttar Pradesh, India: Harper Collins, 2021), vii–ix.

47. Reed Chervin, '"Cartographic Aggression": Media Politics, Propaganda, and the Sino-Indian Border Dispute', *Journal of Cold War Studies* 22, no. 3 (2020): 205, 230–32; and Liu Zongyi, 'Boundary Standoff and China-India Relations', *Chinese Quarterly of International Strategic Studies* 6, no. 2 (2020): 227–28.

48. Klaus Pringsheim, 'China, India and Their Himalayan Border (1961–1963)', *Asian Survey* 3, no. 10 (1963): 486–88.

49. M. Taylor Fravel, *Strong Borders, Secure Nation: Cooperation and Conflict in China's Territorial Disputes* (Princeton, NJ: Princeton University Press, 2008), 309–14.

50. Kevin Greene et al., 'Understanding the Timing of Chinese Border Incursions into India', *Humanities and Social Sciences Communications* 8, no. 1 (2021): 2–6.

51. Liu, 'Boundary Standoff', 238–43.

52. Ramesh Thakur, Shatabhisha Shetty, and Waheguru Pal Singh Sidur, 'China-India-Pakistan Nuclear Trilemma and the Imperative of Risk Reduction Measures', *Journal for Peace and Nuclear Disarmament* 5, no. 2 (2022): 215–23; and Rebecca Gibbons and Matthew Kroenig,

'Reconceptualizing Nuclear Risks: Bringing Deliberate Nuclear Use Back In', *Comparative Strategy* 35, no. 5 (2016): 411–14.

53. David Baldwin, 'Security Studies and the End of the Cold War', *World Politics* 48, no. 1 (1995): 119–20.

54. David Ekbladh, 'Present at the Creation: Edward Mead Earle and the Depression-Era Origins of Security Studies', *International Security* 36, no. 3 (2011/12): 108, 115–23, 127–34; and Gray, 'Nicholas John Spykman', 873.

55. Baldwin, 'Security Studies', 119–22.

56. Hedley Bull, *The Anarchical Society: A Study of Order in World Politics*, 3rd edn (Basingstoke, UK: Palgrave Macmillan, 2002), 181.

57. F. H. Hinsley, *Power and the Pursuit of Peace: Theory and Practice in the History of Relations Between States* (Cambridge: Cambridge University Press, 1963), 5–6.

58. Kenneth Waltz, 'The Origins of War in Neorealist Theory', in *The Origin and Prevention of Major Wars*, ed. Robert Rotberg and Theodore Rabb (Cambridge: Cambridge University Press, 1990), 43–44.

59. Kenneth Waltz, 'Realist Thought and Neorealist Theory', *Journal of International Affairs* 44, no. 1 (1990): 30–31.

60. Taliaferro, 'Security Seeking Under Anarchy', 136–40; and Benjamin Frankel, 'Restating the Realist Case: An Introduction', *Security Studies* 5, no. 3 (1996): xii–xv.

61. Eric Hamilton and Brian Rathbun, 'Scarce Differences: Toward a Material and Systemic Foundation for Offensive and Defensive Realism', *Security Studies* 22, no. 3 (2013): 443–46.

62. See, for example, Evan Montgomery, 'Breaking Out of the Security Dilemma: Realism, Reassurance and the Problem of Uncertainty', *International Security* 31, no. 2 (2006): 159–62.

63. Sebastian Rosato, 'The Inscrutable Intentions of Great Powers', *International Security* 39, no. 3 (2014–15): 49, 60–64, 87; and Miller, 'Polarity, Nuclear Weapons', 600–604.

64. Barry Buzan and Lena Hansen, *The Evolution of International Security Studies* (Cambridge: Cambridge University Press, 2009), 1–2, 259–61.

65. Taliaferro, 'Security Seeking Under Anarchy', 129.

66. Waltz, 'The Origins of War', 51.

67. Jeffrey Taliaferro and Francis Gavin, 'Critical Dialogue', *Perspectives on Politics* 19, no. 1 (2021): 227–28, 231.

68. Reid Pauley, 'Would U.S. Leaders Push the Button?', *Security Studies* 43, no. 2 (2018): 151–55, 184–85.

CONCLUSION

1. Kenneth Waltz, 'The Origins of War in Neorealist Theory', in *The Origin and Prevention of Major Wars*, ed. Robert Rotberg and Theodore Rabb (Cambridge: Cambridge University Press, 1989), 41.
2. Michael Mousseau, 'The End of War: How a Robust Marketplace and Liberal Hegemony Are Leading to Perpetual World Peace', *International Security* 44, no. 1 (2019): 160–62.
3. Douglas Fry, *Beyond War: The Human Potential for Peace* (Oxford: Oxford University Press, 2007), 213–14.
4. Azar Gat, *The Causes of War & the Spread of Peace* (Oxford: Oxford University Press, 2017), 249.
5. Lawrence Freedman, *The Future of War: A History* (London: Allen Lane, 2017), 15–26.
6. Hårard Hegre et al., 'Predicting Armed Conflict, 2010–2050', *International Studies Quarterly* 57, no. 2 (2013): 250.
7. Mick Ryan, *War Transformed: The Future of Twenty-First Century Great Power Competition and Conflict* (Annapolis, MD: Naval Institute Press, 2022), 3.
8. Adam Liff, 'Cyberwar: Another "Absolute Weapon"? The Proliferation of Cyberwarfare Capabilities and Interstate War', *Journal of Strategic Studies* 35, no. 3 (2012): 401–8; Gregory Koblentz and Brian Mazanec, 'Viral Warfare: The Security Implications of Cyber and Biological Weapons', *Comparative Strategy* 32, no. 5 (2015): 418–20; and Freedman, *The Future of War*, 230–36.
9. Steve Lambakis, 'Space as a Warfighting Domain: Reshaping Policy to Execute 21st Century Spacepower', *Comparative Strategy* 41, no. 4 (2022): 331–47.

Selected Readings

The following list is a selection of the most important books and articles used in the preparation of this text. All sources consulted and details such as specific chapters or relevant page numbers of cited sources can be found in the notes.

Allen, Mark, and Terry Jones, eds. *Violence and Warfare Among Hunter-Gatherers*. London: Routledge, 2014.

Anson, Edward. *Alexander the Great: Themes and Issues*. London: Bloomsbury, 2013.

Anthony, David. *The Horse, the Wheel, and Language: How Bronze-Age Riders from the Eurasian Steppes Shaped the Modern World*. Princeton, NJ: Princeton University Press, 2007.

Arkush, Elizabeth, and Mark Allen, eds. *The Archaeology of Warfare: Prehistories of Raiding and Conquest*. Gainesville: University Press of Florida, 2006.

Ashraf, Masood. *ISIS: Ideology, Symbolics and Counter Narratives*. New York: Routledge, 2019.

Babik, Milan. 'The Christian Historical Consciousness: Understanding War in Twentieth-Century Europe'. *Totalitarian Movements and Political Religions* 5, no. 1 (2004).

Bacevich, Andrew. *The New American Militarism: How Americans Are Seduced by War*. Oxford: Oxford University Press, 2013.

Bar, Shmuel. 'Religion in War in the 21st Century'. *Comparative Strategy* 39, no. 5 (2020).

Barfield, Thomas. *The Perilous Frontier: Nomadic Empires and China 221 BC to AD 1757*. Oxford: Blackwell, 1989.

Barnett, Michael, and Raymond Duvall. 'Power in International Politics'. *International Organization* 59, no. 1 (2005).

Barreiros, Daniel. 'Warfare, Ethics, Ethology: Evolutionary Fundamentals for Conflict and Co-operation in the Lineage of Man'. *Journal of Big History* 2, no. 2 (2018).

Bayliss, Andrew. *The Spartans*. Oxford: Oxford University Press, 2020.

Beckley, Michael. 'The Power of Nations: Measuring What Matters'. *International Security* 43, no. 2 (2018–19).

Benenson, Joyce, and Henry Markovits. *Warriors and Worriers: The Survival of the Sexes*. Oxford: Oxford University Press, 2014.

Bichler, Shimshon, and Jonathan Nitzan. 'Arms and Oil in the Middle East: A Biography of Research'. *Rethinking Marxism* 30, no. 3 (2018).

Boggs, Carl, and Tom Pollard. *The Hollywood War Machine: U.S. Militarism and Popular Culture*. Boulder, CO: Paradigm, 2007.

Böhm, Robert, Hannes Rusch, and Jonathan Baron. 'The Psychology of Intergroup Conflict: A Review of the Theories and Measures'. *Journal of Economic Behaviour and Organization* 178 (2020).

Bouthoul, Gaston. *Les Guerres: Éléments de polémologie*. Paris: Payot, 1951.

Bowden, Hugh. *Alexander the Great: A Very Short Introduction*. Oxford: Oxford University Press, 2014.

Bowles, Samuel. 'Did Warfare Among Ancestral Hunter-Gatherers Affect the Evolution of Human Social Behaviours?'. *Science* 324 (2009).

Bradley, Keith, and Paul Cartledge, eds. *The Cambridge World History of Slavery: Volume 1*. Cambridge: Cambridge University Press, 2011.

Brake, Wayne. *Religious War and Religious Peace in Early Modern Europe*. Cambridge: Cambridge University Press, 2017.

Breeze, David. *The Frontiers of Imperial Rome*. Barnsley, UK: Pen & Sword, 2021.

Brumfiel, Elizabeth. 'Aztec Religion and Warfare: Past and Present Perspectives'. *Latin American Research Review* 25, no. 2 (1990).

Brunt, Peter. 'A Marxist View of Roman History'. *Journal of Roman Studies* 72 (1982).

Brzezinski, Zbigniew. *The Grand Chessboard: American Strategy and Its Geostrategic Imperatives*. New York: Basic Books, 2016.

Buc, Philippe. *Holy War, Martyrdom, and Terror*. Philadelphia: University of Pennsylvania Press, 2015.

Bull, Hedley. *The Anarchical Society: A Study of Order in World Politics*. Basingstoke, UK: Palgrave Macmillan, 2002.

Burke, Marshall, Solomon Hsiang, and Edward Miguel. 'Climate and Conflict'. *Annual Review of Economics* 7 (2015).

Caplan, Arthur, ed. *The Sociobiology Debate: Readings on the Ethical and Scientific Issues Concerning Sociobiology*. New York: Harper & Row, 1978.

Carneiro, Robert. 'A Theory of the Origins of the State'. *Science* 169 (1970).

Chacon, Richard, and Rubén Mendoza, eds. *North American Indigenous Warfare and Ritual Violence*. Tucson: University of Arizona Press, 2013.

Chan, Steve. *Rumbles of Thunder: Power Shifts and the Danger of Sino-American War*. New York: Columbia University Press, 2023.

Christensen, Jonas. 'Warfare in the European Neolithic'. *Acta Archaeologica* 75 (2004).

Clastres, Pierre. *Archéologie de la violence: La guerre dans les sociétés primitives*. Paris: Éditions de l'Aube, 1999.

Clendinnen, Inga. *Aztecs: An Interpretation*. Cambridge: Cambridge University Press, 1991.

Coker, Christopher. *Why War?* London: Hurst & Co., 2021.

Confino, Alon. *A World Without Jews: The Nazi Imagination from Persecution to Genocide*. New Haven, CT: Yale University Press, 2014.

Cook, David. 'Islamism and Jihadism: The Transformation of Classical Notions of *Jihad* into an Ideology of Terrorism'. *Totalitarian Movements and Political Religions* 10, no. 2 (2009).

Cote, Stephen. 'A War for Oil in the Chaco, 1932–1935'. *Environmental History* 18, no. 4 (2013).

Crook, Paul. *Darwinism, War, and History*. Cambridge: Cambridge University Press, 2009.

Cunliffe, Barry. *By Steppe, Desert and Ocean: The Birth of Eurasia*. Oxford: Oxford University Press, 2016.

Dahl, Robert. 'The Concept of Power'. *Behavioral Science* 2, no. 3 (1957).

Davies, Sarah. *Rome, Global Dreams, and the International Origins of the Empire*. Leiden: Brill, 2019.

Davis, Natalie. 'The Rites of Violence: Religious Riot in Sixteenth-Century France'. *Past & Present* 59 (1973).

Dawson, Doyne. 'The Origins of War: Biological and Anthropological Theories'. *History and Theory* 35, no. 1 (1996).

Donegan, Barbara. 'Did Ministers Matter? War and Religion in England, 1642–1649'. *Journal of British Studies* 33, no. 2 (1994).

Durbin, Edward, and John Bowlby. *Personal Aggressiveness and War*. London: Kegan Paul, Trench, Trubner & Co., 1939.

Durham, William. 'Resource Competition and Human Aggression: Part I: A Review of Primitive War'. *Quarterly Review of Biology* 51 (1976).

Dwyer, Philip. *Citizen Emperor: Napoleon in Power, 1799–1815*. London: Bloomsbury, 2013.

Dwyer, Philip, and Mark Micale, eds. *The Darker Angels of Our Nature: Refuting the Pinker Theory of History and Violence*. London: Bloomsbury, 2021.

Earle, Timothy. *How Chiefs Come to Power: The Political Economy in Prehistory*. Stanford, CA: Stanford University Press, 1997.

Eibl-Eibesfeldt, Irenäus. *The Biology of Peace and War: Men, Animals, and Aggression*. New York: Viking, 1979.

Elton, Hugh. *The Frontiers of the Roman Empire*. Bloomington: Indiana University Press, 1996.

Ember, Carol, and Melvin Ember. 'Resource Unpredictability, Mistrust and War: A Cross-Cultural Study'. *Journal of Conflict Resolution* 36 (1992).

Erskine, Andrew. *Roman Imperialism*. Edinburgh: Edinburgh University Press, 2010.

Esdaile, Charles. *Napoleon's Wars: An International History, 1803–15*. London: Allen Lane, 2007.

Evera, Stephen Van. *Causes of War: Power and the Roots of Conflict*. Ithaca, NY: Cornell University Press, 1999.

Fornari, Franco. *The Psychoanalysis of War*. New York: Doubleday, 1974.

Freedman, Lawrence. *The Future of War: A History*. London: Allen Lane, 2017.

—. 'The Rise and Fall of Great Power War'. *International Affairs* 95, no. 1 (2019).

Fry, Douglas. *Beyond War: The Human Potential for Peace*. Oxford: Oxford University Press, 2007.

—, ed. *War, Peace, and Human Nature: The Convergence of Evolutionary and Cultural Views*. Oxford: Oxford University Press, 2015.

Fuentes, Agustin. 'Searching for the "Roots" of Masculinity in Primates and the Human Evolutionary Past'. *Current Anthropology* 62, no. S23 (2021).

Gat, Azar. *The Causes of War & the Spread of Peace*. Oxford: Oxford University Press, 2017.

—. 'Is War in Our Nature?'. *Human Nature* 30 (2019).

—. 'Proving Communal Warfare Among Hunter-Gatherers: The Quasi-Rousseauan Error'. *Evolutionary Anthropology* 24, no. 1 (2015).

Gentile, Emilio. *Politics and Religion*. Princeton, NJ: Princeton University Press, 2006.

Gibbons, Rebecca, and Matthew Kroenig. 'Reconceptualizing Nuclear Risks: Bringing Deliberate Nuclear Use Back In'. *Comparative Strategy* 35, no. 5 (2016).

Gilpin, Robert. 'The Theory of Hegemonic War'. *Journal of Interdisciplinary History* 18, no. 4 (1988).

Glover, Edward. *War, Sadism, and Pacifism: Further Essays on Group Psychology and War*. London: George Allen & Unwin, 1947.

Goldsworthy, Adrian. *Roman Warfare*. London: Cassell, 2000.

Grayling, Anthony. *War: An Enquiry*. New Haven, CT: Yale University Press, 2017.

Grenier, John. *The First Way of War: American War Making on the Frontier*. Cambridge: Cambridge University Press, 2005.

Groebel, Jo, and Robert Hinde, eds. *Aggression and War: Their Biological and Social Basis*. Cambridge: Cambridge University Press, 1989.

Gueniffey, Patrice. *Bonaparte*. Cambridge, MA: Harvard University Press, 2015.

Gusterson, Hugh, and Catherine Bestemann. 'Cultures of Militarism'. *Current Anthropology* 60, no. S19 (2019).

Halsall, Guy. *Warfare and Society in the Barbarian West, 450–900*. London: Routledge, 2003.

Haslam, Alex, Stephen Reicher, and Rakshi Rath. 'Making a Virtue of Evil: A Five-Step Social Identity Model of the Development of Collective Hate'. *Social and Personality Psychology Compass* 2, no. 3 (2008).

Hauge, Wenche, and Tanja Ellingsen. 'Beyond Environmental Scarcity: Causal Pathways to Conflict'. *Journal of Peace Research* 35, no. 3 (1998).

Heckel, Waldemar. *In the Path of Conquest: Resistance to Alexander the Great*. Oxford: Oxford University Press, 2020.

Heuser, Beatrice. *War: A Genealogy of Western Ideas and Practices*. Oxford: Oxford University Press, 2022.

Hillenbrand, Carole. *Crusades: Islamic Perspectives*. Edinburgh: Edinburgh University Press, 1999.

Hinsley, F. H. *Power and the Pursuit of Peace: Theory and Practice in the History of Relations Between States*. Cambridge: Cambridge University Press, 1963.

Holt, Mack. 'Putting Religion Back into the Wars of Religion'. *French Historical Studies* 18, no. 2 (1993).

Homer-Dixon, Thomas. *Environment, Scarcity and Violence*. Princeton, NJ: Princeton University Press, 1999.

Horn, Christian. 'Trouble in Paradise? Violent Conflict in Funnel-Beaker Societies'. *Oxford Journal of Archaeology* 40, no. 1 (2021).

Horne, Alistair. *Hubris: The Tragedy of War in the Twentieth Century*. London: Weidenfeld & Nicolson, 2015.

Husemann, Dirk. *Als der Mensch den Krieg erfand*. Ostfildern: Jan Thorbecke Verlag, 2005.

Ingrao, Christian. *The Promise of the East: Nazi Hopes and Genocide, 1939–1943*. Cambridge: Polity Press, 2019.

Isaac, Barry. 'Aztec Warfare: Goals and Battlefield Comportment'. *Ethnology* 22, no. 2 (1983).

Jagchid, Sechin, and Van Symons. *Peace, War and Trade Along the Great Wall.* Bloomington: Indiana University Press, 1989.

Kaldor, Mary, Terry Karl, and Yahia Said, eds. *Oil Wars.* London: Pluto Press, 2007.

Keeley, Lawrence. *War Before Civilization.* New York: Oxford University Press, 1996.

Kelly, Raymond. *Warless Societies and the Origin of War.* Ann Arbor: University of Michigan Press, 2000.

Kennedy, Paul. *The Rise and Fall of the Great Powers: Economic Change and Military Conflict from 1500–2000.* London: Unwin Hyman, 1988.

Keysen, Carl. 'Is War Obsolete?'. *International Security* 14, no. 4 (1990).

Kim, Nam, and Marc Kissel. *Emergent Warfare in Our Evolutionary Past.* New York: Routledge, 2018.

Klare, Michael. *Resource Wars: The New Landscape of Global Conflict.* New York: Henry Holt, 2001.

Klein, Herbert. *The Atlantic Slave Trade.* Cambridge: Cambridge University Press, 2012.

Knauft, Bruce. 'Violence and Sociality in Human Evolution'. *Current Anthropology* 32, no. 4 (1991).

Kortüm, Hans-Henning, and Jürgen Heinze, eds. *Aggression in Humans and Other Primates: Biology, Psychology, Sociology.* Berlin: De Gruyter, 2013.

Kurtz, Angela. 'God, Not Caesar: Revisiting National Socialism as "Political Religion"'. *History of European Ideas* 35, no. 2 (2009).

Lal, Deepak. *War or Peace: The Struggle for World Power.* Oxford: Oxford University Press, 2018.

Lamb, Hubert. *Climate History and the Modern World.* London: Methuen, 1982.

Lambakis, Steve. 'Space as a Warfighting Domain: Reshaping Policy to Execute 21st Century Spacepower'. *Comparative Strategy* 41, no. 4 (2022).

Lambert, Patricia. 'The Archaeology of War: A North American Perspective'. *Journal of Archaeological Research* 10, no. 3 (2002).

Layne, Christopher. 'The Unipolar Illusion: Why New Great Powers Will Emerge'. *International Security* 17, no. 4 (1993).

Le Billon, Philippe. *Wars of Plunder: Conflicts and Profits and the Politics of Resources.* London: Hurst & Co., 2012.

Leblanc, Steven. *Constant Battles: Why We Fight.* New York: St. Martin's Press, 2003.

Lee, A. D. *Warfare in the Roman World.* Cambridge: Cambridge University Press, 2020.

Lehmann, Laurent, and Marcus Feldman. 'War and the Evolution of Belligerence and Bravery'. *Proceedings of the Royal Society B: Biological Sciences* 275 (2008).

Lepsius, M. Rainer. 'The Model of Charismatic Leadership and Its Applicability to the Rule of Adolf Hitler'. *Totalitarian Movements and Political Religions* 7, no. 2 (2006).

Levy, Jack, and William Thompson. *The Causes of War*. Malden, MA: Wiley-Blackwell, 2010.

Liebermann, Benjamin, and Elizabeth Gordon. *Climate Change in Human History*. London: Bloomsbury, 2022.

Liff, Adam. 'Cyberwar: Another "Absolute Weapon"? The Proliferation of Cyberwarfare Capabilities and Interstate War'. *Journal of Strategic Studies* 35, no. 3 (2012).

Lincoln, Bruce. *Death, War, and Sacrifice: Studies in Ideology and Practice*. Chicago: University of Chicago Press, 1991.

Liu, Zongyi. 'Boundary Standoff and China-India Relations'. *Chinese Quarterly of International Strategic Studies* 6, no. 2 (2020).

Lopez, Anthony. 'The Evolutionary Psychology of War: Offense and Defense in the Adapted Mind'. *Evolutionary Psychology* 15, no. 4 (2017).

Lorenz, Konrad. *On Aggression*. London: Methuen, 1966.

Lujala, Päivi. 'Deadly Combat over Natural Resources: Gems, Petroleum, Drugs, and the Severity of Armed Civil Conflict'. *Journal of Conflict Resolution* 53, no. 1 (2009).

Maalouf, Amin. *The Crusades Through Arab Eyes*. London: Al Saqi Books, 1984.

MacMillan, Margaret. *War: How Conflict Shaped Us*. London: Profile Books, 2020.

Majolo, Bonaventura. 'Warfare in Evolutionary Perspective'. *Evolutionary Anthropology* 28 (2019).

Malešević, Siniša. *The Rise of Organised Brutality: A Historical Sociology of Violence*. Cambridge: Cambridge University Press, 2017.

Mankelwicz, John, and Robert Kane. 'Hitler as a Narcissistic Leader'. *Journal of Psychohistory* 67, no. 1 (2022).

Martin, Debra. 'Violence and Masculinity in Small-Scale Societies'. *Current Anthropology* 62, no. S23 (2021).

Martin, Debra, Ryan Harrod, and Ventura Pérez, eds. *The Bioarchaeology of Violence*. Gainesville: University Press of Florida, 2012.

Mattern, Susan. *Rome and the Enemy: Imperial Strategy in the Principate*. Berkeley: University of California Press, 1999.

Mead, Margaret. 'Warfare Is Only an Invention – Not a Biological Necessity'. *Asia* 40 (1940).

Mearsheimer, John. *The Tragedy of Great Power Politics*. New York: Norton, 2002.

Miller, Benjamin. 'Polarity, Nuclear Weapons, and Major War'. *Security Studies* 3, no. 4 (1994).

—. *States, Nations, and the Great Powers: The Sources of Regional War and Peace*. Cambridge: Cambridge University Press, 2007.

Miller, Manjari. *Why Nations Rise: Narratives and the Path to Great Power*. Oxford: Oxford University Press, 2021.

Mousseau, Michael. 'The End of War: How a Robust Marketplace and Liberal Hegemony Are Leading to Perpetual World Peace'. *International Security* 44, no. 1 (2019).

Nolan, Cathal. *The Allure of Battle: A History of How Wars Have Been Won or Lost*. New York: Oxford University Press, 2017.

Nolan, Patrick. 'Toward an Ecological-Evolutionary Theory of the Incidence of Warfare in Preindustrial Societies'. *Sociological Theory* 21, no. 1 (2003).

Nordås, Ragnhild, and Nils Gleditsch. 'Climate Change and Conflict'. *Political Geography* 26 (2007).

Nye, Joseph. *The Future of Power*. New York: Public Affairs, 2011.

Obregón, Marco. 'Mexica War: New Perspectives'. In *The Oxford Handbook of the Aztecs*, edited by Deborah Nichols and Enrique Rodríguez-Alegría. Oxford: Oxford University Press, 2016.

Osgood, Richard, Sarah Monks, and Judith Toms. *Bronze Age Warfare*. Stroud, UK: History Press, 2010.

Otterbein, Keith. 'The Earliest Evidence of Warfare?'. *Current Anthropology* 52, no. 3 (2011).

—. 'A History of Research on Warfare in Anthropology'. *American Anthropologist* 101, no. 4 (2000).

—. *How War Began*. College Station: Texas A&M University Press, 2004.

Padilla, Art, Robert Hogan, and Robert Kaiser. 'The Toxic Triangle: Destructive Leaders, Susceptible Followers, and Conducive Environments'. *Leadership Quarterly* 18, no. 3 (2007).

Pagel, Mark. 'Lethal Violence Deep in the Human Lineage'. *Nature* 538 (2016).

Parkinson, William, and Paul Duffy. 'Fortifications and Enclosures in European Prehistory: A Cross-Cultural Perspective'. *Journal of Archaeological Research* 15, no. 2 (2007).

Pauley, Reid. 'Would U.S. Leaders Push the Button'. *Security Studies* 43, no. 2 (2018).

Pearson, Mike, and I. Thorpe, eds. *Warfare, Violence and Slavery in Prehistory*. Oxford: BAR Publishing, 2016.

Pennock, Caroline. 'Mass Murder or Religious Homicide? Rethinking Human Sacrifice and Interpersonal Violence in Aztec Society'. *Historische Sozialforschung* 37, no. 3 (2012).

Peters, Susan. 'Coercive Western Energy Security Strategies – "Resource Wars" as a New Threat to Global Security'. *Geopolitics* 5, no. 1 (2004).

Pinker, Steven. *The Better Angels of Our Nature: The Decline of Violence in History and Its Causes*. London: Allen Lane, 2011.

Pitman, George. *Why War? An Inquiry into the Genetic and Social Sources of Human Warfare*. Indianapolis, IN: Dog Ear Publishing, 2015.

Prior, Charles, and Glenn Burgess, eds. *England's Wars of Religion Revisited*. Farnham, UK: Ashgate, 2011.

Prum, Michael. 'Perception of War in Darwinist Perspective'. *Revue Lisa* 20 (2022).

Raaflaub, Kurt, and Nathan Rosenstein, eds. *War and Society in the Ancient and Medieval Worlds*. Cambridge, MA: Harvard University Press, 1999.

Ratzel, Friedrich. *Der Lebensraum*. Tübingen: Laupp'schen Buchhandlung, 1901.

Rauch, Carsten. 'Challenging the Power Consensus: GDP, CINC, and Power Transition Theory'. *Security Studies* 26, no. 4 (2017).

Redfern, Rebecca. 'Iron Age "Predatory Landscapes": A Bioarchaeological and Funerary Exploration of Captivity and Enslavement'. *Cambridge Archaeological Journal* 30, no. 4 (2020).

Redmond, Elsa. *Tribal and Chiefly Warfare in South America*. Ann Arbor: University of Michigan Museum of Anthropology, 1994.

Robarchek, Clayton. 'Primitive Warfare and the Ratomorphic Image of Mankind'. *American Anthropologist* 91, no. 4 (1989).

Roscoe, Paul. 'The Anthropology of War and Violence'. In *Ethnology, Ethnogeography and Cultural Anthropology: Encyclopedia of Life Support Systems*, edited by Paolo Barbaro. Oxford: EOLSS Publishers, 2017.

—. 'Margaret Mead, Reo Fortune, and Mountain Arapesh Warfare'. *American Anthropologist* 105, no. 3 (2003).

Rosen, Stephen. *War and Human Nature*. Princeton, NJ: Princeton University Press, 2005.

Roth, Jonathan. *Roman Warfare*. Cambridge: Cambridge University Press, 2009.

Ryan, Mick. *War Transformed: The Future of Twenty-First Century Great Power Competition and Conflict*. Annapolis, MD: Naval Institute Press, 2022.

Sakaguchi, Kendra, Anil Varughese, and Graeme Auld. 'Climate Wars? A Systematic Review of Empirical Analyses on the Links Between Climate Change and Violent Conflict'. *International Studies Review* 19 (2017).

Sarantis, Alexander. 'Waging War in Late Antiquity'. *Late Antique Archaeology* 8, no. 1 (2010–11).

Schofield, Victoria. *Kashmir in Conflict: India, Pakistan, and the Unending War.* London: Bloomsbury, 2020.

Schubiger, Livia, and Matthew Zelina. 'Ideology in Armed Groups'. *PS: Political Science and Politics* 50, no. 4 (2017).

Schulting, Rick, and Linda Fibiger, eds. *Sticks, Stones, and Broken Bones: Neolithic Violence in European Perspective.* Oxford: Oxford University Press, 2012.

Segrest, Scott. 'ISIS's Will to Apocalypse'. *Politics, Religion and Ideology* 17, no. 4 (2016).

Sizgorich, Thomas. *Violence and Belief in Late Antiquity: Militant Devotion in Christianity and Islam.* Philadelphia: University of Pennsylvania Press, 2009.

Smith, David. *The Most Dangerous Animal: Human Nature and the Origins of War.* New York: St. Martin's Press, 2007.

Smith, Iain. *The Origins of the South African War.* London: Longman, 1996.

Snow, Dean. *The Iroquois.* Oxford: Blackwell, 1996.

Spykman, Nicholas. 'Frontiers, Security, and International Organization'. *Geographical Review* 32, no. 3 (1942).

Strachey, Alix. *The Unconscious Motives of War: A Psycho-Analytical Contribution.* London: George Allen & Unwin, 1957.

Suhler, Charles, and David Friedel. 'Life and Death in a Maya War Zone'. *Archaeology* 51, no. 3 (1998).

Swenson, Edward. 'Dramas of the Dialectic: Sacrifice and Power in Ancient Polities'. In *Violence and Civilization: Studies of Social Violence in History and Prehistory*, edited by Roderick Campbell. Oxford: Oxbow Books, 2014.

Symonds, Matthew. *Protecting the Roman Empire: Fortlets, Frontiers, and the Quest for Post-Conquest Security.* Cambridge: Cambridge University Press, 2018.

Taliaferro, Jeffrey. 'Security Seeking Under Anarchy: Defensive Realism Revisited'. *International Security* 25, no. 3 (2000–2001).

Taylor, Kathleen. *Cruelty: Human Evil and the Human Brain.* Oxford: Oxford University Press, 2009.

Toft, Monica. 'Territory and War'. *Journal of Peace Research* 51, no. 2 (2014).

Tol, Richard, and Sebastian Wagner. 'Climate Change and Violent Conflict in Europe over the Past Millennium'. *Climatic Change* 99 (2010).

Turner, Christy, and Jaqueline Turner. *Man Corn: Cannibalism and Violence in the Prehistoric American Southwest*. Salt Lake City: University of Utah Press, 1999.

Tyerman, Christopher. *God's War: A New History of the Crusades*. London: Allen Lane, 2006.

Vaes, Jeroen, Jacques-Philippe Leyens, Maria Paladino, and Mariana Miranda. '"We Are Human, They Are Not": Driving Forces Behind Outgroup Dehumanization and the Humanization of the Ingroup'. *European Review of Social Psychology* 23, no. 1 (2012).

Vallance, Edward. 'Preaching to the Converted: Religious Justifications for the English Civil War'. *Huntington Library Quarterly* 65 (2002).

Vasquez, John, ed. *What Do We Know About War?* Lanham, MD: Rowman & Littlefield, 2000.

Vasquez, John, and Marie Henehan. *Territory, War, and Peace*. New York: Routledge, 2011.

Walter, Barbara. 'Explaining the Intractability of Territorial Conflict'. *International Studies Review* 5, no 4 (2003).

Waltz, Kenneth. 'The Origins of War in Neorealist Theory'. In *The Origin and Prevention of Major Wars*, edited by Robert Rotberg and Theodore Rabb. Cambridge: Cambridge University Press, 1989.

—. 'Realist Thought and Neorealist Theory'. *Journal of International Affairs* 44, no. 1 (1990).

Waterfield, Robin. *Taken at the Flood: The Roman Conquest of Greece*. Oxford: Oxford University Press, 2014.

Webster, David. 'Not So Peaceful Civilization: A Review of Maya War'. *Journal of World Prehistory* 14, no. 1 (2000).

Weezel, Stijn van. 'Local Warming and Violent Conflict in Africa'. *World Development* 126 (2020).

Wilson, Edward. *On Human Nature*. Cambridge, MA: Harvard University Press, 1978.

Winter, David. *Roots of War: Wanting Power, Seeing Threat, Justifying Force*. Oxford: Oxford University Press, 2018.

Wrangham, Richard, and Luke Glowacki. 'Intergroup Aggression in Chimpanzees and War in Nomadic Hunter-Gatherers'. *Human Nature* 23 (2012).

Wrangham, Richard, and Dale Petersen. *Demonic Males: Apes and the Origins of Human Violence*. London: Bloomsbury, 1996.

Wright, Quincy. *A Study of War*. Chicago: University of Chicago Press, 1964.

Zefferman, Matthew, and Sarah Mathew. 'An Evolutionary Theory of Large-Scale Human Warfare: Group-Structural Cultural Selection'. *Evolutionary Anthropology* 24, no. 2 (2015).

Zhang, David, et al. 'Climate Change and War Frequency in Eastern China over the Last Millennium'. *Human Ecology* 35, no. 4 (2007).

Zulfiqar, Adnan. 'Jurisdiction over *Jihād*: Islamic Law and the Duty to Fight'. *West Virginia Law Review* 120, no. 2 (2017).

Index